MUST KNOW

HIGH SCHOOL BASIC FRENCH

Annie Heminway

Mc
Graw
Hill

New York Chicago San Francisco Athens London Madrid
Mexico City Milan New Delhi Singapore Sydney Toronto

2 3 4 5 6 7 8 9   LCR   25 24 23 22

ISBN   978-1-260-45303-4
MHID   1-260-45303-0

e-ISBN   978-1-260-45304-1
e-MHID   1-260-45304-9

Interior design by Steve Straus of Think Book Works.
Cover and letter art by Kate Rutter.

McGraw-Hill Education books are available at special quantity discounts to use as premiums and sales promotions or for use in corporate training programs. To contact a representative, please visit the Contact Us pages at www.mhprofessional.com.

Acknowledgments

The author would like to acknowledge Tylar Bloch, Ellen Sowchek, and Susan Barniker for their sharp eyes and deft touch. At last but foremost, I want to thank Garret Lemoi, my editor for so many years, for his expertise and for his support at every stage of this project.

Author's Note

Welcome, and thanks for embarking on this French journey with us! Whether you are a beginner in high school or a professional interested in learning a new language, you have come to the right place to start this exciting new journey. In this book, we will cover the essentials of French language and French culture—the **must knows** that will help you build grace and confidence as a language learner. And while learning a new language can seem intimidating, with enough patience and dedication, you'll master these fundamentals faster than you can say **c'est du gâteau**.

Le coin des créateurs

The creative exercises featured at the end of each chapter will help you master grammar, build your vocabulary, and increase your knowledge of common French expressions. It is through writing that we begin to understand the nuances that we often overlook when reading. Writing in French will unleash your creativity and help you develop your own voice in French.

Writing allows the French language to "stick." It will become deeply ingrained in your mind, increasing your fluency. Things you would never have thought of writing in your own language, you'll write in French! You'll amaze yourself!

Note culturelle

Language is an essential part of culture. Learning a language cannot be reduced to simply correct grammar and pronunciation. You cannot learn a language in a void. In this book, you'll discover the train stations in Paris than can take you to Bretagne or Occitanie. You'll learn about French newspapers, the environmental movement, and the importance of the French language around the world. You'll become familiar with French companies, if you ever want to apply for an internship, as well as with the National Center for Circus Arts, if you wish to be as famous as singer-acrobat Aloïse Sauvage. The cultural notes in this book are designed to give you insight into the heart of France and the French-speaking world and to increase your understanding of the language.

La culture ne s'hérite pas, elle se conquiert. (*Culture is not inherited, it is conquered.*)
—André Malraux

Contents

6 The Verb *Faire* and Using Prepositions

7 Pronominal Verbs

11 In Search of Lost Time...with French Past Tenses

12 Thinking About the World in the Conditional Mood

Introduction

Welcome to your new French book! Let us try to explain why we believe you've made the right choice. You've probably had your fill of books asking you to memorize lots of terms (such is school). This book isn't going to do that—although you're welcome to memorize anything you take an interest in. You may also have found that a lot of books make a lot of promises about all the things you'll be able to accomplish by the time you reach the end of a given chapter. In the process, those books can make you feel as though you missed out on the building blocks that you actually need to master those goals.

With *Must Know High School Basic French,* we've taken a different approach. When you start a new chapter, right off the bat you will immediately see one or more **must know** ideas. These are the essential concepts behind what you are going to study, and they will form the foundation of what you will learn throughout the chapter. With these **must know** ideas, you will have what you need to hold it together as you study, and they will be your guide as you make your way through each chapter.

To build on this foundation you will find easy-to-follow discussions of the topic at hand, accompanied by comprehensive examples that will increase your ability to communicate in French. Each chapter ends with review questions—more than 1,000 throughout the book—designed to instill confidence as you practice your new skills.

This book has other features that will help you on this French journey of yours. It has a number of sidebars that will both help provide helpful information or just serve as a quick break from your studies. The **BTW** sidebars ("by the way") point out important information as well as tell you what to be careful about French-wise. Every once in a while, an **IRL** sidebar ("in real life") will tell you what you're studying has to do with the real world; other IRLs may just be interesting factoids.

In addition, this book is accompanied by a flashcard app that will give you the ability to test yourself at any time. The app includes 100 "flashcards" with a review question on one "side" and the answer on the other. You can either work through the flashcards by themselves or use them alongside the book. In addition to the flashcards, the app includes extensive audio that will help you with the sounds of French. To find out where to get the app and how to use it, go to the next section, The Flashcard App—with Audio!

Before you get started, however, let us introduce you to your guide throughout this book. In addition to extensive experience as a French educator, Annie Heminway has written more than a dozen books on learning the language. Having had the opportunity to work together before, we know that Annie is unmatched in her enthusiasm for the French language (and culture!). She understands what you should get out of a French course and has developed strategies to help you get there. Annie has also seen the kinds of trouble that students run into, and she can show you how to overcome these difficulties. In this book, she applies her teaching experience to showing you the most effective way to learn a given concept, as well as how to extricate yourself from traps you may have fallen into. She will be your trustworthy guide as you expand your French knowledge and develop new skills.

Before we leave you to the author's surefooted guidance, let us give you one piece of advice. While we know that saying something "is the *worst*" is a cliché, if anything *is* the worst in French, it might be learning the pronunciation. Let Annie introduce you to French pronunciation and show you how to speak French confidently.

Good luck with your studies!

The Editors at McGraw-Hill

The Flashcard App–with Audio!

his book features a bonus flashcard app. Like other **Must Know** books, it includes a set of flashcards, but *High School Basic French* also features extensive audio.

The Flashcard App

To take advantage of this bonus feature, follow these easy steps:

Search for ***Must Know High School*** App from either Google Play or the App Store.

↓

Download the app to your smartphone or tablet.

↓

The flashcards will help you test yourself on what you've learned as you make your way through the book. You can access the 100+ "flashcards," both "front" and "back," in either of two ways.

↙   ↘

Just open the app and you're ready to go.	Use your phone's QR code reader to scan any of the book's QR codes.
You can start at the beginning, or select any of the chapters listed.	You'll be taken directly to the flashcards that match the chapter you chose.

↘   ↙

Be ready to test your French knowledge!

French Audio

The app also includes a ton (to use the technical term) of French-language audio. It has been designed to help with both your pronunciation and listening skills. On the app, you'll find the book's extensive French dialogues, along with the text so you can read along.

Each dialogue in the book is identified by the audio icon, 🔊. Follow the QR code at the end of a chapter to that chapter's app content. Or you can look at the app's easy-to-follow Contents and choose the section that interests you most. Listen closely, and we're confident your French skills will improve fast!

 # Meeting People

MUST ⚡ KNOW

⚡ In addition to **être**, *to be* in English can be **avoir** in French.

⚡ When you turn 21, you'll be **vingt <u>et</u> un ans**.

⚡ The **s** in **trois avions** is pronounced like a **z**.

⚡ Men are **chefs**, women are **cheffes**.

In this first chapter, you will come across some of the most commonly used verbs and expressions in the French language. You will learn how to count, how to greet a stranger, and how to introduce someone to your friend. And as you accumulate this new vocabulary, you'll be surprised at how many ideas you can express in such a short time.

Subject Pronouns

In order to refer to yourself and address others, it is essential both to know the proper pronouns and to conjugate the verb that goes *with* them. *I*, *you*, *he*, *she*, *it*, *one*, *we*, and *they* are the major personal pronouns in French and English, but there is one big difference: the word *you*. In French, there are two versions of *you*. When you are with your friends, relatives, peers, or children, the appropriate pronoun is **tu**. On the other hand, when you are speaking with an adult, a colleague, a person in a store, or a stranger, the appropriate pronoun is often **vous**. The subject pronouns are:

je	*I*	**nous**	*we*
tu	*you* (singular familiar)	**vous**	*you* (plural and singular formal)
il	*he, it*	**ils**	*they*
elle	*she, it*	**elles**	*they*
on	*one*		

BTW

In French, the first person **je** *drops the e when the verb begins with a vowel or before* **h**.

J'ai des amis. (I have friends.) **J'habite à Paris.** (I live in Paris.) *Note that the pronoun* **ils** *is also used as the subject pronoun when the subjects of a sentence are both masculine and feminine.*

Justin est américain. Il est américain.	Justin is American. He is American.
Alice et Loïc sont français. Ils sont français.	Alice and Loïc are French. They are French.
Alice et Clara sont amies. Elles sont amies.	Alice and Clara are friends. They are friends.
Le musée est ouvert. Il est ouvert.	The museum is open. It is open.
La lampe est à moi. Elle est à moi.	The lamp is mine. It is mine.

BTW

The subject pronoun **on** *literally means* one, *but it often replaces* **nous***, and can be translated as* we. *It can also refer to people in general:* one, everyone, people, they. *It all depends on the context.*

En France, on mange des croissants.	In France, they eat croissants.
Paul et moi, on est français.	Paul and I, we are French.
On dit que c'est un bon livre.	They say it is a good book.
On ne sait jamais.	One never knows.

The Verbs *être* and *avoir*

Two essential verbs are **être** (*to be*) and **avoir** (*to have*). They allow you to ask profound questions such as **Qui suis-je?** (*Who am I?*) By the time you have mastered **être** and **avoir**, you will have created a solid foundation for your studies of French.

être *to be*

je suis	*I am*	nous sommes	*we are*
tu es	*you are*	vous êtes	*you are*
il/elle/on est	*he/she/one is*	ils/elles sont	*they are*

Elle est française.	*She is French.*
Tu es en retard.	*You are late.*
Je suis psychologue.	*I am a psychologist.*
Qui êtes-vous?	*Who are you?*
On est vraiment désolés.	*We are really sorry.*

avoir *to have*

j'ai	*I have*	nous avons	*we have*
tu as	*you have*	vous avez	*you have*
il/elle/on a	*he/she/one has*	ils/elles ont	*they have*

J'ai un plan de Paris.	*I have a map of Paris.*
Nous avons un ami hollandais.	*We have a Dutch friend.*
Ils ont une voiture noire.	*They have a black car.*
Vous avez un dictionnaire bilingue?	*Do you have a bilingual dictionary?*

Idiomatic Expressions with *être* and *avoir*

Idiomatic expressions with **être** and **avoir** are staples of the French language. Let's take a look at idiomatic expressions with **être**.

être à l'heure	*to be on time*
être en retard	*to be late*
être en avance	*to be early*
être de retour	*to be back*
être en vacances	*to be on vacation*
être au régime	*to be on a diet*
être en forme	*to be in shape, to be fit*
être en bonne santé	*to be in good health*
être d'accord	*to agree*
être en colère	*to be angry*
être à l'aise	*to be comfortable*
être en train de	*to be in the process of (doing)*
être de bonne humeur	*to be in a good mood*
être de mauvaise humeur	*to be in a bad mood*

Alice est en retard pour le rendez-vous.	*Alice is late for the appointment.*
Les élèves sont en train de jouer dans la cour.	*The students are playing in the courtyard.*
Cet ordinateur est à Stéphanie.	*This computer is Stephanie's.*
C'est à toi de parler.	*It's your turn to speak.*

Idiomatic Expressions with *avoir*

avoir l'air de	*to seem/to appear*
avoir besoin de	*to need*
avoir de la chance	*to be lucky*
avoir chaud	*to be warm*
avoir froid	*to be cold*
avoir envie de	*to feel like*
avoir faim	*to be hungry*
avoir soif	*to be thirsty*
avoir raison	*to be right*
avoir tort	*to be wrong*
avoir sommeil	*to be sleepy*
avoir le temps	*to have time*
avoir l'occasion	*to have the opportunity*
avoir lieu	*to take place*
avoir mal à la tête	*to have a headache*

Ils ont le temps de visiter le musée Picasso.   *They have time to visit the Picasso Museum.*
Elle a besoin d'une carte Navigo pour le métro.   *She needs a Navigo Pass for the subway.*
Tu as toujours raison!   *You are always right!*
Roland a très faim.   *Roland is very hungry.*
Avez-vous besoin de quelque chose?   *Do you need anything?*

BTW

Idiomatic expressions cannot be translated literally. While in English we say "I am thirsty," French uses a different verb, **avoir***, to express the same thought:* **j'ai soif***.*

When stating someone's profession, you don't use the indefinite article **un** or **une** unless an adjective is added. In this case the third-person subject pronoun is changed to **ce** or **c'**.

Elle est ingénieure.	*She is an engineer.*
Il est médecin généraliste.	*He is an internist.*
Il est boulanger.	*He is a baker.*
C'est **un** très bon boulanger.	*He is a very good baker.*
Elle est créatrice de mode.	*She is a fashion designer.*
C'est **une** célèbre créatrice de mode.	*She is a famous fashion designer.*
Elles sont peintres.	*They are painters.*
Ce sont **des** peintres renommées.	*They are renowned painters.*

IRL In 2019, the Immortals of the Académie française finally abandoned years of opposition to the feminization of job titles. Now it is common to hear traditionally male occupations in the feminine form like Madame **la maire** (*mayor*), **la procureure** (*prosecutor*), **la juge** (*judge*). The feminine of **sapeur-pompier** (*fireman*) is **une sapeuse-pompière**. However, many prefer to be called **une pompière** or **une femme pompier**. **Un médecin** (*doctor*) and **une femme médecin** are used since **la médecine** refers to the field, not the person. Some women, however, don't want to become **une écrivaine** (*writer*) and prefer to remain **un écrivain;** others reject **une autrice** (*writer*) because of the mere sound of it. If in doubt, check with the person's office and ask if she wishes to be called **le chef** or **la cheffe**. The debate is far from over.

Cardinal Numbers

Cardinal numbers are the numbers used for counting and designating quantity. Let's explore basic counting in French from 1 to 60.

zéro	*zero*
un	*one*
deux	*two*
trois	*three*
quatre	*four*
cinq	*five*
six	*six*
sept	*seven*
huit	*eight*
neuf	*nine*
dix	*ten*
onze	*eleven*
douze	*twelve*
treize	*thirteen*
quatorze	*fourteen*
quinze	*fifteen*
seize	*sixteen*
dix-sept	*seventeen*
dix-huit	*eighteen*
dix-neuf	*nineteen*
vingt	*twenty*
vingt et un	*twenty-one*
vingt-deux	*twenty-two*
vingt-trois	*twenty-three*
vingt-quatre	*twenty-four*
vingt-cinq	*twenty-five*
vingt-six	*twenty-six*
vingt-sept	*twenty-seven*
vingt-huit	*twenty-eight*

vingt-neuf	*twenty-nine*
trente	*thirty*
trente et un	*thirty-one*
trente-deux	*thirty-two*
trente-trois	*thirty-three*
quarante	*forty*
quarante et un	*forty-one*
quarante-deux	*forty-two*
quarante-trois	*forty-three*
cinquante	*fifty*
cinquante et un	*fifty-one*
cinquante-deux	*fifty-two*
cinquante-trois	*fifty-three*
soixante	*sixty*

Benoît a trois dictionnaires.	*Benoît has three dictionaries.*
Mathilde parle quatre langues.	*Mathilde speaks four languages.*
Six Américains étudient à l'université de Caen.	*Six Americans study at the University of Caen.*
Il y a trente bureaux dans la classe.	*There are thirty desks in the classroom.*

BTW

When the following numbers precede a vowel, we use a liaison. It alters the pronunciation to make it more pleasing to the ear.

troi͟s Indonésiens	**s → z**
deu͟x ingénieurs, si͟x artistes	**x → z**
neu͟f ans	**f → v**

When the numbers 5, 6, 8, and 10 precede a word beginning with a consonant, their final consonant is mute. Here are some examples:

cinq livres	*five books*
six crayons	*six pencils*

huit tapis persans	*eight Persian rugs*
dix billets	*ten tickets*

Common Greetings and Expressions

Let's take a look at some common words and phrases that will help you start—and finish—talking with a French speaker.

bonjour	*hello/good morning/good afternoon*
Salut!	*Hi!*
coucou	*hey*
bonsoir	*good evening*
bonne nuit	*good night*
oui	*yes*
non	*no*
pas du tout	*not at all*
au revoir	*good-bye*
enchanté(e)	*nice to meet you*
ravi(e) de faire votre connaissance	*nice meeting you*
à tout de suite	*see you in a bit*
à tout à l'heure	*see you later*
à bientôt	*see you soon*
à demain	*see you tomorrow*
à la semaine prochaine	*see you next week*
merci	*thank you*
de rien	*you're welcome*
je t'en prie	*you're welcome*
je vous en prie	*you're welcome*
s'il vous plaît	*please*
s'il te plaît	*please*
excusez-moi	*excuse me*

DIALOGUE *Alice, je te présente Justin!*
Alice, meet Justin!

Alice runs into Loïc in the Monoprix supermarket. They chat about their weekend plans. Alice invites him to a picnic on l'Île aux Cygnes in Paris.

 **IRL** Founded in 1932, Monoprix is part of the French landscape. It is a major French retail chain offering a wide selection of food, clothing, household items, gifts, and hardware. And they are so widespread that you can find a Monoprix in every large town in France. With extended business hours, Monoprix can help you during those last-minute runs to buy some milk, a pair of yoga leggings, or a birthday gift for a friend.

ALICE: Bonjour, Loïc! — *Hi, Loïc!*

LOÏC: Alice fait ses courses! — *Alice is doing her shopping!*

ALICE: Eh oui... — *Well yes...*

LOÏC: Comment vas-tu? — *How are you?*

ALICE: Très bien et toi? — *Very well and you?*

LOÏC: Très bien. Mon correspondant Justin est à Paris en ce moment. — *Very well. My penpal Justin is in Paris right now.*

ALICE: Il est anglais? — *He is English?*

LOÏC: Non, il est américain. Nous sommes amis depuis trois ans. — *No, he is American. We have been friends for three years.*

ALICE: C'est sympa. Vous avez des projets pour le week-end? — *That's great. Do you have any plans for the weekend?*

LOÏC: Euh, j'ai... En fait non, pas vraiment. — *Uh, I have... In fact no, not really.*

ALICE: J'organise un pique-nique sur l'Île aux Cygnes dimanche. Et je vous invite! — *I am organizing a picnic on Swan's Isle on Sunday and I am inviting you!*

LOÏC: L'Île aux Cygnes? Pour dire bonjour à la statue de la Liberté?

On Swan's Isle? To say hello the Statue of Liberty?

ALICE: Loïc, tu es si drôle! Donc dimanche à 11 heures?

Loïc, you are so funny! So Sunday at 11 am?

LOÏC: D'accord, dimanche à 11h!

OK, Sunday at 11 am!

A few days later on Swan's Isle.

LOÏC: Alice, je te présente Justin. Justin, je te présente Alice.

Alice, meet Justin. Justin, meet Alice.

JUSTIN: Bonjour, Alice, ravi de te rencontrer.

Hi, Alice, nice to meet you.

ALICE: Moi aussi. Bienvenue sur l'île! Bienvenue à Paris!

Same here. Welcome to the island! Welcome to Paris!

LOÏC: Merci, Alice.

Thanks, Alice.

ALICE: Je vais vous présenter à mes amis et après on mange.

I am going to introduce you to my friends and after we'll eat.

JUSTIN: Nous avons très faim!

We are very hungry!

ALICE: Mes amis ont une faim de loup! Luc!

My friends are hungry as a wolf! Luc!

LUC: Oui?

Yes?

ALICE: Luc, je te présente Loïc et Justin.

Luc, let me introduce you to Loïc and Justin.

LUC: Salut!

Hi!

LOÏC: Salut! On est contents de faire ta connaissance.

Hi! We're happy to meet you.

As we've just read, Alice's picnic is on l'Île aux Cygnes in Paris. You will come across the word **cygnes** as the swans glide slowly on ponds and lakes in many parks. And you will probably hear about **Le lac des cygnes** (*Swan Lake*), a ballet composed by Tchaikovsky in 1875, featured during the ballet or opera season, often in creative modern adaptations. And if you ever read Victor Hugo's ***Notre-Dame de Paris***, do not miss:

Le corbeau ne vole que le jour,	*The raven flies only by day,*
Le hibou ne vole que la nuit,	*The owl flies only by night,*
Le cygne vole nuit et jour.	*The swan flies by day and by night.*

EXERCISES

EXERCISE 1.1

Conjugate the verb **être** *in the following sentences.*

1. Ils _____ à Nice.

2. Tu _____ le correspondant de Loïc.

3. Vous _____ dans les Arènes de Lutèce.

4. Elle _____ directrice.

5. Nous _____ contents de visiter Paris.

6. Il _____ professeur de français.

7. Je _____ avec Christian dans le parc.

8. Elles _____ américaines.

9. Je _____ dans la classe.

10. Ils _____ fans de football.

EXERCISE 1.2

Rewrite each sentence adding the adjective **compétent** *(masculine),* **compétente** *(feminine),* **compétents** *(masculine plural), or* **compétentes** *(feminine plural) after the profession.*

1. Il est infirmier.

2. Elle est dentiste.

3. Il est secrétaire de direction.

4. Ils sont coiffeurs.

5. Elles sont serveuses.

6. Elle est directrice de communication.

7. Il est serveur.

8. Elle est coach de vie.

9. Il est entraîneur sportif.

10. Elle est animatrice multimédia.

EXERCISE 1.3

Conjugate the verb **avoir** *in the following sentences.*

1. Caroline _____ froid en Sibérie.

2. Le professeur _____ le temps de visiter le musée d'Art moderne.

3. Marc _____ très soif, il demande un smoothie glacé.

4. Ils _____ faim, ils mangent une pizza.

5. Elle _____ raison.

6. Vous _____ besoin de contacter Luca.

7. On _____ le temps de regarder le film.

8. Vous _____ tort!

9. Dans le désert, nous _____ chaud.

10. Je _____ encore faim. Une autre pizza, s'il vous plaît!

EXERCISE 1.4

Complete with the appropriate subject pronoun. There may be more than one answer.

1. _____ avons une Peugeot 508 bleue.

2. _____ suis brésilien.

3. _____ sommes chinois.

4. _____ ont de la chance.

5. _____ a un dictionnaire français-anglais.

6. _____ es content de visiter le musée du Louvre.

7. _____ ont un correspondant anglais.

8. _____ êtes dans le parc André-Citroën.

9. _____ avons un iPad.

10. _____ sont devant la tour Eiffel.

EXERCISE 1.5

Translate the following sentences into English.

1. Elle a un dictionnaire.

2. Tu as froid.

3. Nous sommes américains.

4. Vous avez une bicyclette.

5. J'ai froid.

6. Je suis française.

7. Ils ont faim.

8. Tu as le temps de visiter le musée d'Orsay.

9. Il est espagnol.

10. Nous avons un chat persan.

EXERCISE 1.6

*Complete each sentence with the verb **avoir** or **être**, depending on the meaning.*

1. Tu _____ une caméra.

2. Vous _____ français.

3. On _____ le temps.

4. Ils _____ chaud.

5. Je _____ un ami à Toulouse.

6. Nous _____ à Nice.

7. Elle _____ un appartement à La Rochelle.

8. Je _____ besoin d'un nouveau dictionnaire.

9. Elle _____ une agence de voyages.

10. Vous _____ fatigué?

EXERCISE 1.7

Translate the following sentences into French using **vous** *when necessary.*

1. You have an apartment in La Rochelle.

2. We agree with Loïc.

3. They are on vacation in Nice.

4. My friend Adrien is very funny.

5. I am fifteen years old.

6. Anas is very hungry. He eats a croissant.

7. You have a black car.

8. We are lucky to be in Paris.

9. She is American, and he is Spanish.

10. I have a headache.

EXERCISE 1.8

Spell out the numbers in parentheses. Pay attention to the gender of the nouns.

1. Mon ami Pierre a (1) _____ voiture.

2. Paris a (20) _____ arrondissements.

3. Elle mange (2) _____ pains au chocolat.

4. Le professeur a (33) _____ élèves.

5. Étienne a (3) _____ paires de baskets.

6. Il a (1) _____ amie à Lyon.

7. Les (11) _____ _____ joueurs de football arrivent au Parc des Princes.

8. Sara a (4) _____ chats et (5) _____chiens.

9. (15) _____ plus (36) _____ font 51.

10. Le guide parle à un groupe de (28) _____ touristes coréens.

LE COIN DES CRÉATEURS

L'INVENTAIRE

Create a list of ten sentences with the verbs **avoir** or **être** using words you have learned in this chapter or words you already knew before you started. Example:

Zoé a un chat
Elle est sur une île à Paris
Elle est contente d'être à Paris
Son chat Mistigris a faim
Mais il est au régime
Il est de mauvaise humeur
Il a envie de manger le croissant de Zoé
...
...

À votre tour! (*Your turn!*)

Je suis un étudiant américain....
or
Il a un cousin à Paris...

NOTE CULTURELLE

PARIS—ISLANDS IN THE SEINE

At 482 miles, the Seine is France's fifth-longest river. Originating in Source-Seine, 19 miles northwest of the city of Dijon, it flows through Paris, dividing the city into the Right and Left Banks, before continuing to its ultimate destination of Le Havre and the English Channel. In Paris, the Seine is also home to three islands, two of them natural and one artificial: the Île de la Cité, the Île Saint-Louis, and the Île aux Cygnes.

The Île de la Cité is the oldest part of Paris. It was the center of Lutèce, as it was known in the Roman Empire. In the Christian era, it became the home of Notre-Dame Cathedral, on which construction began in AD 1160. The Île is truly the heart of Paris and of France itself, since all distances are measured from Paris Point Zero, a spot directly in front of the cathedral's front door. Victor Hugo's 1831 novel *Notre-Dame de Paris*, aka *The Hunchback of Notre-Dame*, made the cathedral internationally famous.

The Île Saint-Louis, the smaller of the Seine's two natural islands, is connected to Paris by four bridges and to the Île de la Cité by one, the Pont Saint-Louis. It consists of two natural islets—the larger Île Notre-Dame and the smaller Île aux Vaches, once used for grazing cattle and stocking wood for the city—joined together in 1614. It is named for Louis IX (Saint Louis), king of France from 1226 to 1270. Now an elegant, mostly residential neighborhood, it is a great place for a stroll, perhaps topped off with a *cornet de glace* (ice-cream cone) from Berthillon, a destination for ice-cream lovers from around the world.

The Île aux Cygnes, or Swan's Island, is a small artificial island that was built in 1827 to serve as a reinforcement point for the construction of three Parisian bridges. It connects the Pont de Bir-Hakeim to the Pont de Grenelle and is traversed by the Pont Rouelle. There are no residents on the island, but it is a popular place for visitors, and its main walkway, the Allée des Cygnes, is much appreciated by walkers, joggers, and runners alike. At the end of the walkway, at the southern point, stands the island's most notable feature: a replica of the Statue of Liberty. One-fourth the size of the original, it was a gift to the city from the American community of Paris in 1889 to commemorate the centennial of the French Revolution.

Languages and Nationalities

MUST ⚡ KNOW

 For winter, you'll need **un ou deux manteaux**, **une écharpe**, and **des gants**.

 In school, you'll study **le français**, **la géographie**, and **les sciences humaines**.

 Sa veste can mean *his* or *her* jacket.

 Ne… pas surrounds the conjugated verb.

Congrats on making it through the first chapter! Now it's time to dig a little more deeply into the mechanics of French nouns and verbs. Did you know that French nouns almost always use articles, even when we don't use them in English? Learning the articles is tricky business, especially when we have to take gender into account. Similarly, we'll explore how French sometimes changes a verb's conjugation to keep its original sound.

Speaking of sound, French is one of the most melodious languages. So it's no surprise that Gustave Flaubert had a special room in his house, the **gueuloir** (*shouting room*), where he would read out the latest draft of his novel at the top of his voice to adjust its rhythm and cadence. Even if you are not ready to write Volume II of *Madame Bovary*, read aloud each dialogue in the book to develop a greater intuition of French's flow.

Introduction to Indefinite and Definite Articles

All French nouns are gendered. They are either masculine or feminine whether they refer to a person, animal, thing, or abstract notion. This will be explored further in Chapter 4 when studying the gender of French nouns.

Indefinite Articles

In French, there are three indefinite articles: **un** (masculine singular), **une** (feminine singular), and **des** (plural). **Un** and **une** translate to *a* and *an*, and **des** translates to *some*. Notice, however, that in English the word *some* is often omitted.

Alice a **un** frère, **une** sœur, et **des** chats.	*Alice has a brother, a sister, and some cats.*
Nous avons **des** amis à Limoges.	*We have friends in Limoges.*

masculine singular		**feminine singular**	
un cahier	*a notebook*	une voiture	*a car*
un stylo	*a pen*	une chanson	*a song*

masculine plural		feminine plural	
des cahiers	*notebooks*	des voitures	*cars*
des stylos	*pens*	des chansons	*songs*

Definite Articles

In French, there are three definite articles: **le** (masculine singular), **la** (feminine singular), and **les** (plural). And they all translate to the word *the*.

Also, you should know how to make a noun plural. Usually this is done by adding an **-s**, so pay to attention to how words change from their singular form into plural.

Le garçon pose **les** livres sur **la** table.   *The boy is placing the books on the table.*

masculine singular		feminine singular	
le livre	*the book*	la pomme	*the apple*
le film	*the film*	la décision	*the decision*

J'écoute **la** radio.   *I am listening to the radio.*
Le livre est dans **la** cuisine.   *The book is in the kitchen.*

And notice that most of the time, you use an elision, the **le** and **la** become **l'** in front of nouns starting with a vowel or a mute **h**.

l'ordinateur	*the computer*	l'idée	*the idea*
l'hôtel	*the hotel*	l'hôtesse	*the hostess*

Here are some exceptions when there is no elision: **le haricot** (*bean*). It is oddly called an **h aspiré**, although it is not "aspirated." Don't worry about the label; just memorize some of these nouns in a sentence as you go along. In the plural form, you do *not* make a liaison between the definite article and the noun: **les haricots** (*beans*).

BTW

In most cases, to turn a singular noun into the plural form, one adds **-s**. *For example:* **un livre** *(a book),* **des livres** *(books);* **un vélo** *(a bicycle),* **des vélos** *(bicycles). Most nouns ending in* **-eau** *take an* **-x** *in the plural:* **un bateau** *(a boat),* **des bateaux** *(boats).*

la haine	hatred
le hamac	hammock
le hamburger	hamburger
le hameau	hamlet
la hanche	hip
le handicap	handicap
le harcèlement	harassment
le haricot	bean
le hasard	chance/randomness
le haut	top
la hauteur	height
le hibou	owl
la hiérarchie	hierachy
le hockey	hockey
la Hollande	Holland
le homard	lobster
la honte	shame
la housse	cover

Connais-tu la fable *L'aigle et **le** hibou* de Jean de la Fontaine?

Do you know the fable The Eagle and the Owl *by Jean de la Fontaine?*

Est-ce **le** hasard ou le destin?

Is it chance or fate?

Donnez-moi **la** housse de couette bleue.

Give me the blue duvet cover.

Le chat dort dans **le** hamac.

The cat is sleeping in the hammock.

Préfères-tu **les** haricots verts ou **les** haricots rouges?

Do you prefer green beans or red beans?

Let's look at the masculine and feminine plural of nouns:

masculine plural

les livres	*the books*
les films	*the films*

feminine plural

les pommes	*the apples*
les décisions	*the decisions*

| les ordinateurs | *the computers* | les idées | *the ideas* |
| les hôtels | *the hotels* | les hôtesses | *the hostesses* |

J'aime les films d'action.	*I like action films.*
Les ordinateurs de l'hôtel ne marchent pas.	*The computers in the hotel do not work.*
Les hôtels sont tous pleins.	*The hotels are all full.*

In the plural form, for nouns starting with a vowel or a mute **h**, you make a liaison between the definite article and the noun with a **z** sound.

| les idées | s → **z** |
| les hôtels | s → **z** |

Let's compare the plural forms of the definite and indefinite articles:

| Elle apporte **les** livres pour la classe. | *She brings the books for the class.* |
| Apporte-nous **des** livres et **des** cahiers. | *Bring us some books and notebooks.* |

| Aimes-tu **les** chansons de Dalida? | *Do you like Dalida's songs?* |
| Il chante **des** chansons romantiques. | *He sings romantic songs.* |

Possessive Adjectives

Possessive adjectives are used to express relationship and ownership. They agree in gender and number with the noun they modify.

masculine singular

mon livre	*my book*	notre livre	*our book*
ton livre	*your book*	votre livre	*your book*
son livre	*his/her book*	leur livre	*their book*

feminine singular

ma veste	*my jacket*	notre veste	*our jacket*
ta veste	*your jacket*	votre veste	*your jacket*
sa veste	*his/her jacket*	leur veste	*their jacket*

masculine and feminine plural

mes professeurs	*my teachers*	nos professeurs	*our teachers*
tes professeurs	*your teachers*	vos professeurs	*your teachers*
ses professeurs	*his/her teachers*	leurs professeurs	*their teachers*

Note that the masculine form (**mon**, **ton**, **son**) is used before singular feminine nouns beginning with a vowel or a mute **h**.

Mon avion part à 23 heures.	*My plane leaves at 11 pm.*
Ton adresse est toujours la même?	*Is your address the same?*
Son hélicoptère est prêt à partir.	*His/her helicopter is ready to leave.*
Son hôtel est dans le 15ᵉ arrondissement.	*His/her hotel is in the 15th arrondissement.*

Therefore **son**, **sa**, and **ses** can mean either *his* or *hers*. The context will usually prevent any ambiguity on the owner. Otherwise, the sentence will be reformulated.

son appartement	*his/her apartment*
sa chambre	*his/her room*
ses lunettes de soleil	*his/her sunglasses*

Another way of expressing possession is to use **à** + a noun or a pronoun.

À qui est ce livre?	*Whose book is it?*
C'est à qui?	*Whose is it?*
C'est à Alice?	*Is it Alice's?*
Non, ce n'est pas à Alice.	*No, it's not Alice's.*
C'est à moi.	*It's mine.*
Ce n'est pas à moi.	*It's not mine.*

Introducing -er Verbs

Unconjugated verbs are called *infinitives*, and the French infinitives are divided into three groups, each with its own endings. The first set ends in **-er** and includes verbs like **parler** (*to speak*), **habiter** (*to live*), and **danser** (*to dance*). To conjugate regular **-er** verbs, you need to memorize the ending for each person and attach it to the root of the verb. The root is obtained by dropping the **-er** and attaching the corresponding ending. For instance, the root of **parler** is **parl-** and the root of **habiter** is **habit-**. The endings for the regular **-er** verbs are as follows:

	singular	plural
1st person	e	ons
2nd person	es	ez
3rd person	e	ent

It's important to note that the **-e**, **-es**, and **-ent** endings are all silent. And the final **s** of **nous**, **vous**, **ils**, and **elles** links with verbs beginning with a vowel sound, making a z sound; this is called a *liaison*. Most **-er** verbs are regular and follow this pattern, though there are exceptions.

parler *to speak*

je parle	*I speak*	nous parlons	*we speak*
tu parles	*you speak*	vous parlez	*you speak* (plural and *you* singular formal)
il/elle/on parle	*he/she/one speaks*	ils/elles parlent	*they speak*

Parlez-vous italien?	*Do you speak Italian?*
Oui, je parle italien.	*Yes, I speak Italian.*
Ma mère parle **l'**italien couramment.	*My mother speaks Italian fluently.*
À l'ONU, on parle beaucoup de langues.	*Many languages are spoken at the UN.*

BTW

Notice how the definite article le is added when an adverb is used with the verb parler. Je parle suédois, but je parle très bien le suédois. Il parle le japonais couramment.

apporter   *to bring*

j'apporte	*I bring*	nous apportons	*we bring*
tu apportes	*you bring*	vous apportez	*you bring*
il/elle/on apporte	*he/she/one brings*	ils/elles apportent	*they bring*

Notice how **apporter** in the first person contracts to the form **j'apporte**.

Apportez-moi des bonbons!	*Bring me some candy!*
Les invités apportent des fleurs à l'hôtesse.	*The guests are bringing the hostess flowers.*
Leurs parents leur apportent du soutien.	*Their parents bring them support.*
Qu'est-ce que tu apportes pour le pique-nique?	*What are you bringing to the picnic?*

Verbs Ending in *-ger*

A few **-er** verbs are spelled differently in the present tense in order to maintain the sound of the infinitive. With verbs ending in **-ger**, as **voyager** (*to travel*), the **-g-** becomes **-ge-** before the first-person plural. Let's take a look at the verb **voyager**.

je voyage	*I travel*	nous voyageons	*we travel*
tu voyages	*you travel*	vous voyagez	*you travel*
il/elle/on voyage	*he/she/one travels*	ils/elles voyagent	*they travel*

Nous voya**ge**ons avec notre chien.	*We are traveling with our dog.*
Nous ne man**ge**ons jamais de hamburgers.	*We never eat hamburgers.*
Nous mélan**ge**ons le citron et le miel dans une tasse.	*We are mixing the lemon and the honey in a cup.*
Nous parta**ge**ons le même amour des langues.	*We share the same love for languages.*

Verbs Ending in -cer

Similar to verbs ending in **-ger**, verbs ending in **-cer** change spelling when in the present-tense first-person plural. The **c** is replaced with a **ç** (a soft sound that matches the infinitive form of the verb). Let's take a look at the verb **prononcer**.

je prononce	*I pronounce*	nous prononçons	*we pronounce*
tu prononces	*you pronounce*	vous prononcez	*you pronounce*
il/elle/on prononce	*he/she/one pronounces*	ils/elles prononcent	*they pronounce*

Nous effaçons le tableau à la fin de la classe.	*We erase the blackboard at the end of the class.*
Nous remplaçons toutes les fenêtres de la maison.	*We are replacing all the windows in our house.*
Nous avançons lentement mais sûrement.	*We are advancing slowly but surely.*
Nous plaçons beaucoup d'espoir en vous.	*We are placing a lot of hope in you.*

Accent-Changing Verbs

With some verbs composed of **-e** + consonant + **-er**, like the verb **enlever** (*to remove*), some accent changes occur. An *accent grave* is added in all but the first- and the second-person plural.

j'enlève	*I remove*	nous enlevons	*we remove*
tu enlèves	*you remove*	vous enlevez	*you remove*
il/elle/on enlève	*he/she/one removes*	ils/elles enlèvent	*they remove*

Il enlève son chapeau avant d'entrer dans la classe.	*He removes his hat before entering the classroom.*
Mon oncle congèle les framboises de son jardin.	*My uncle freezes the strawberries from his garden.*
J'emmène ma nièce au théâtre.	*I am taking my niece to the theater.*
Elle achète ses légumes au marché.	*She buys her vegetables at the market.*

But:

Nous ach**e**tons notre pain à la boulangerie artisanale.	*We are buying our bread at the artisanal bakery.*
Vous enl**e**vez l'étiquette.	*You are removing the label.*

Épeler

With some verbs composed of **-e + l + -er**, like the verb **épeler** (*to spell*), add an additional **l** in all but the first- and second-persons plural.

j'épelle	*I spell*	nous épelons	*we spell*
tu épelles	*you spell*	vous épelez	*you spell*
il/elle/on épelle	*he/she/one spells*	ils/elles épellent	*they spell*

Comment s'épe**ll**e ce mot?	*How is this word spelled?*
Tu t'appe**ll**es Caroline?	*Is your name Caroline?*
Diane renouve**ll**e son passeport.	*Diane is renewing her passport.*
Je te rappe**ll**e demain.	*I'll call you back tomorrow.*

This rule also applies to verbs like **jeter** and its derivatives, which require an additional **t** in all but the first- and second-persons plural.

Elle je**tt**e le journal dans la poubelle.	*She throws the newspaper in the trash bin.*
Je feuille**tt**e le roman.	*I am flipping through the novel.*
Il proje**tt**e un film sur un mur blanc.	*He is screening a film on a white wall.*
Ils reje**tt**ent notre proposition.	*They are rejecting our proposal.*

Countries and Languages

Here are some countries whose names you should know in French, along with their official languages. Do remember, however, that in some of these countries, many other languages are spoken.

Pays (*Countries*)   **Langue principale** (*Main Language*)

l'Allemagne	*Germany*	allemand	*German*
l'Argentine	*Argentina*	espagnol	*Spanish*
le Brésil	*Brazil*	portugais	*Portuguese*
le Canada	*Canada*	anglais/français	*English/French*
la Chine	*China*	mandarin	*Mandarin*
le Danemark	*Denmark*	danois	*Danish*
l'Espagne	*Spain*	espagnol	*Spanish*
les États-Unis	*United States*	anglais	*English*
l'Inde	*India*	hindi	*Hindi*
l'Indonésie	*Indonesia*	indonésien	*Indonesian*
l'Italie	*Italy*	italien	*Italian*
le Japon	*Japan*	japonais	*Japanese*
le Kenya	*Kenya*	swahili	*Swahili*
le Maroc	*Morocco*	arabe	*Arabic*
le Royaume-Uni	*United Kingdom*	anglais	*English*
la Russie	*Russia*	russe	*Russian*
le Sénégal	*Senegal*	wolof	*Wolof*
la Suède	*Sweden*	suédois	*Swedish*
la Turquie	*Turkey*	turc	*Turkish*
le Viêt Nam	*Vietnam*	vietnamien	*Vietnamese*

Interrogative and Negative Sentences

Could you imagine life without questions? Or life without the ability to say no? Let's learn how to craft sentences using the interrogative and negative forms.

Interrogative Sentences

Interrogative is a complex way to express the idea of asking questions. In French, there are three ways of asking a question:

- Inverting the subject and the verb

- Adding **est-ce que** to the beginning of the sentence

- Ending the unmodified sentence with an upward intonation

Parlez-vous français?	*Do you speak French?*
Est-ce que vous parlez français?	*Do you speak French?*
Vous parlez français?	*Do you speak French?*
Travailles-tu pour une ONG?	*Do you work for an NGO?*
Est-ce que tu travailles pour une ONG?	*Do you work for an NGO?*
Tu travailles pour une ONG?	*Do you work for an NGO?*

Each way of asking a question is subtly different. While the **est-ce que** form is widespread in spoken French, inversion is common in writing and is more formal. And in informal dialogue, ending an unmodified sentence with an upward intonation gets the job done.

BTW

*If the third-person singular of a verb ends in a vowel, a **t** is inserted to facilitate the pronunciation. This helps to make the sentence flow better.*

Il s'appelle Loïc.	His name is Loïc.
Comment s'appelle-t-il?	What is his name?
Elle parle finlandais.	She speaks Finnish.
Parle-t-elle finlandais?	Does she speak Finnish?
On déjeune au café aujourd'hui.	We are having lunch at the café today.
Déjeune-t-on au café aujourd'hui?	Are we having lunch at the café today?

The **t** is not needed in the third-person plural since the **-er** verb ending **-ent** already has one.

Ils organisent la cérémonie.	*They are organizing the ceremony.*
Organisent-ils la cérémonie?	*Are they organizing the ceremony?*

Elles regardent le film.	*They are watching the film.*
Regardent-elles le film?	*Are they watching the film?*

Negative Sentences

In French, a negative sentence has two components: **ne** and **pas**. To make a sentence negative, simply place the **ne** and **pas** around the conjugated verb.

Parle-t-elle suédois?	*Does she speak Swedish?*
Non, elle **ne** parle **pas** suédois.	*No, she does not speak Swedish.*

Étudiez-vous la musique baroque?	*Are you studying Baroque music?*
Non, je **n'**étudie **pas** la musique baroque.	*No, I am not studying Baroque music.*

Est-ce qu'il déménage ce week-end?	*Is he moving this weekend?*
Non, il **ne** déménage **pas** ce week-end.	*No, he is not moving this weekend.*

Vous travaillez dans le centre-ville?	*Do you work downtown?*
Non, je **ne** travaille **pas** dans le centre-ville.	*No, I don't work downtown.*

Est-ce qu'elles gèrent cette entreprise seules?	*Do they manage the company by themselves?*
Non, elles **ne** gèrent **pas** cette entreprise seules.	*No, they don't manage the company by themselves.*

DIALOGUE *Quelle langue parlez-vous?*
What language do you speak?

Justin and Alice are at the Anticafé Beaubourg in the third arrondissement.

JUSTIN: Alice, tu parles anglais?	*Alice, do you speak English?*
ALICE: Un peu. Je ne parle pas très bien.	*A little. I do not speak very well.*
JUSTIN: Tu as l'occasion de parler anglais?	*Do you have the opportunity to speak English?*
ALICE: Oui, je parle souvent avec mon amie Emilia sur WhatsApp.	*Yes, I often speak with my friend Emilia on WhatsApp.*
JUSTIN: Emilia parle français?	*Does Emilia speak French?*
ALICE: Oui, elle parle français et aussi un peu de cajun.	*Yes, she speaks French and also a bit of Cajun.*
JUSTIN: Cajun?	*Cajun?*
ALICE: Oui, elle chante dans un groupe de musique cajun.	*Yes, she sings in a Cajun music group.*

 IRL **Cajun** music is rooted in the songs of the Acadians who found refuge in Louisiana after being exiled from Nova Scotia and New Brunswick between 1755 and 1764. Cajun music is defined by three elements: the button accordion, the fiddle, and the French language. Cajun music and its hybrid offspring Zydeco, celebrated every year in New Orleans, attract music lovers from all over the world.

JUSTIN: Où habite-t-elle? · *Where does she live?*

ALICE: Elle habite à
La Nouvelle-Orléans, en Louisiane. · *She lives in New Orleans, in Louisiana.*

JUSTIN: Alors, vous parlez en
anglais ou en français? · *So do you speak in English or in French?*

ALICE: Ça dépend. Quand je suis
fatiguée, je parle en français. · *It depends. When I am tired, I speak in French.*

JUSTIN: Et quand tu n'es pas fatiguée? · *And when you are not tired?*

ALICE: Quand j'ai la pêche, je
parle en anglais! · *When I feel in top form, I speak in English!*

BTW

*We learned quite a few expressions with **avoir** in Chapter 1. **Avoir la pêche** is another familiar expression, commonly used, that means to be in top form or to be full of energy. The origin of this expression is subject to debate. Some think it comes from China, where the peach is a symbol of immortality and good health. Who knows? The most important is to **avoir la pêche!** Remember, it is a familiar expression you will only use with friends.*

JUSTIN: De quoi parlez-vous? · *What do you talk about?*

ALICE: Nous parlons de musique
et de cinéma. · *We talk about music and film.*

JUSTIN: Est-ce que tu parles une
autre langue étrangère? · *Do you speak another foreign language?*

ALICE: Je parle italien. Ma grand-mère maternelle est d'origine italienne. Et toi, Justin, combien de langues parles-tu?

I speak Italian. My grandmother is from Italian descent. And you, Justin, how many languages do you speak?

JUSTIN: Un peu de français, comme tu vois.

A little French, as you see.

ALICE: Pas mal...

Not bad...

JUSTIN: Mais j'aimerais aussi parler arabe, mandarin, portugais, mais mon objectif principal est de parler le français couramment.

But I would like to speak Arabic, Mandarin, Portuguese, but my main concern is to speak French fluently.

ALICE: Alors, parlons français!

So let's speak French!

BTW

Learning French isn't as hard as you think! Thanks to cognates, you have already mastered thousands of French words, including **la soupe**, **la salade**, **le sofa**, **le dictionnaire**, **le cinéma**, and **la musique**. Cognates are words that are spelled similarly and have the same meaning as in English—though the prounciation is different for each word. Because many of these words are derived from Latin, they share a common linguistic history, making your life as a language learner all the easier.

EXERCISES

EXERCISE 2.1

Fill in each blank with the appropriate possessive adjective.

1. Aimez-vous (*my*) _____ nouvelle veste?

2. Je connais (*his*) _____ grand-mère paternelle.

3. Que pensez-vous de (*our*) _____ professeur de maths?

4. (*His*) _____ voiture est une Citroën C-ZERO électrique.

5. (*Our*) _____ parents habitent à Carcassonne.

6. J'admire (*her*) _____ tableau.

7. (*Your, sing.*) _____ cousine a-t-elle des enfants?

8. Non, (*my*) _____ sœur est décoratrice.

9. Quel âge a (*their*) _____ fils?

10. (*His*) _____ question est importante.

EXERCISE 2.2

Conjugate the following verbs in the present tense.

1. Vous (penser) _____ à votre ami Henri.

2. Je (arriver) _____ au restaurant.

3. Nous (donner) _____ des chocolats à Alice.

4. Tu (entrer) _____ dans un café.

5. Elle (chercher) _____ un magasin.

6. Ils (porter) _____ un costume bleu.

7. Vous (parler) _____ français.

8. On (poser) _____ une question.

9. Je (aimer) _____ la glace à la framboise.

10. Il (fermer) _____ la porte.

EXERCISE 2.3

Conjugate the following verbs in the present tense.

1. Nous (nager) _____ dans l'océan Atlantique.

2. Nous (mélanger) _____ les ingrédients.

3. Nous (corriger) _____ les exercices.

4. Nous (changer) _____ la décoration.

5. Nous (partager) _____ les mêmes opinions.

6. Nous (ranger) _____ la salle de classe.

7. Nous (protéger) _____ l'environnement.

8. Nous (échanger) _____ des idées.

9. Nous (voyager) _____ en TGV.

10. Nous (télécharger) _____ un film.

EXERCISE 2.4

Conjugate the following verbs in the present tense.

1. Nous (commencer) _____ la nouvelle leçon.

2. Nous (remplacer) _____ l'équipement.

3. Nous (financer) _____ cette organisation.

4. Nous (effacer) _____ les erreurs sur le tableau.

5. Nous (prononcer) _____ le mot clairement.

6. Nous (avancer) _____ rapidement.

7. Nous (dénoncer) _____ l'injustice.

8. Nous (placer) _____ le vase sur la table.

9. Nous (lancer) _____ le ballon.

10. Nous (recommencer) _____ le chapitre.

EXERCISE 2.5

Conjugate the following verbs in the present tense.

1. Il (enlever) _____ sa veste en classe.

2. Je (acheter) _____ les légumes au marché.

3. Vous (emmener) _____ votre grand-mère en vacances.

4. Nous (lever) _____ la main pour répondre.

5. Elles (congeler) _____ les fruits rouges.

6. Vous (acheter) _____ un magazine.

7. Je (emmener) _____ mon amie Coralie au théâtre.

8. Ils (soulever) _____ une question difficile.

9. Il (geler) _____ en décembre.

10. Nous (enlever) _____ les étiquettes sur les fruits.

EXERCISE 2.6

Conjugate the following verbs in the present tense.

1. Il (appeler) _____ sa mère tous les jours.

2. Nous (appeler) _____ les enfants pour dîner.

3. Vous (jeter) _____ les papiers dans la corbeille.

4. Il (rejeter) _____ notre offre.

5. Je (projeter) _____ d'ouvrir un restaurant dans ce quartier.

6. Nous (projeter) _____ de voyager en Australie.

7. Tu (épeler) _____ son nom avec un ou deux « t »?

8. Nous (épeler) _____ son nom correctement.

9. Je (jeter) _____ mes vieilles baskets.

10. Elle (feuilleter) _____ le magazine.

EXERCISE 2.7

Complete the following answers with the verb used in the question. Watch out for spelling changes.

1. —Gérez-vous cette entreprise vous-même? —Oui, je la _____ moi-même.

2. —Déménagez-vous bientôt? —Oui, je _____ bientôt.

3. —Achètes-tu les oranges au marché? —Oui, je _____ les oranges au marché.

4. —Espérez-vous une amélioration? —Oui, je _____ une amélioration.

5. —Commencez vous demain? Oui, nous _____ demain.

6. —À quelle heure appelez-vous Xavier? —Je _____ Xavier à midi.

7. —Mangez-vous une pizza ce soir? —Oui, nous _____ une pizza ce soir.

8. —Emmenez-vous Éric au cinéma? —Oui, je _____ Éric au cinéma.

9. —Effacez-vous le tableau? —Oui, nous _____ le tableau.

10. —Répétez-vous la chanson? —Oui, je _____ la chanson.

EXERCISE 2.8

Complete the following statements with their corresponding language.

1. Micaelo habite en Argentine. Il parle _____.

2. Kristen habite au Danemark. Elle parle _____.

3. Aziz habite au Maroc. Il parle _____.

4. Kofi habite au Kenya. Il parle _____.

5. Liang habite en Chine. Il parle _____.

6. Akiko habite au Japon. Elle parle _____.

7. Wolfgang habite en Allemagne. Il parle _____.

8. Mei Lin habite en Indonésie. Elle parle _____.

9. Aylin habite en Turquie. Elle parle _____.

10. Alberto habite en Italie. Il parle _____.

EXERCISE 2.9

Turn the following sentences into questions using inversion.

1. Vous parlez mandarin.

2. Tu achètes les croissants chez Poilâne.

3. Elle habite dans un studio à Lille.

4. On mange dans le jardin ce soir.

5. Il pose une question en anglais.

6. Tu apportes les baguettes pour le pique-nique.

7. Elle prononce le mot correctement.

8. Elles chantent la chanson d'Angèle.

9. Ils dînent avec Agathe demain.

10. Vous commencez un nouveau projet.

EXERCISE 2.10

*Turn the following sentences into questions using the **est-ce que** form.*

1. Elle préfère jouer au golf. _____

2. Vous cherchez une maison dans ce quartier. _____

3. Nous invitons Julien. _____

4. Tu étudies le japonais. _____

5. Ils aiment étudier les langues étrangères. _____

6. Nous voyageons à l'Île Maurice cet été. _____

7. Tu m'appelles ce soir. _____

8. Elle emmène Justin à l'opéra. _____

9. Vous déménagez bientôt. _____

10. Tu gardes les enfants ce week-end. _____

EXERCISE 2.11

Make the following sentences negative.

1. Je chante une chanson de Renaud. _____

2. Elle s'appelle Christine. _____

3. Vous passez vos vacances au Danemark. _____

4. Ils déménagent dimanche. _____

5. Tu achètes le journal au kiosque. _____

6. Nous habitons dans un appartement. _____

7. Il apporte le dessert. _____

8. Vous regardez le match de tennis. _____

9. J'arrive en retard à la cérémonie. _____

10. Nous travaillons dans le centre-ville. _____

EXERCISE 2.12

*Translate the following sentences using the **vous** form when necessary. When asking a question, use inversion.*

1. Are you asking the questions in English?

2. I do not live in a studio. Alex and I share an apartment downtown.

3. We are traveling in Argentina with our friend Micaelo.

4. She is taking her friend Amélia to the theater.

5. Where do you buy the Chinese newspapers?

6. Does she like to speak French? Yes, she speaks French fluently.

7. Are you bringing dessert?

8. Babette and Clara work for an Italian company.

9. We start a new chapter.

10. We are not pronouncing this word properly!

Flashcard App

LE COIN DES CRÉATEURS

AUJOURD'HUI AVANT LE DÎNER...

Using vocabulary from Chapters 1 and 2, make a list of ten things that you are doing, in the present tense, before dinner. For example:

J'ai le temps de visiter un musée; je contacte Luca; j'étudie le chapitre deux; ...

À votre tour! *Your turn!*

NOTE CULTURELLE

FRENCH AND FRANCOPHONIE

"Francophone" is the term used to describe those who speak French, whether by birth or by choice, and "francophonie" the quality of speaking French. Did you know that, according to the French Ministry of Foreign Affairs, French is the fifth most spoken language in the world, after Mandarin Chinese, English, Spanish, and Arabic? In 2018, there were more than 300 million French speakers worldwide, up 9.6 percent since 2014.

Everyone has their own reasons for wanting to learn another language, but why French? Here are some reasons to consider:

French is an international language. It is the second most used language in diplomacy after English. It is one of the official languages of the United Nations and is a working language of the European Union and the African Union. Together with English, it is one of the two official languages of the Olympic Games and a number of other international sports federations.

French is a modern language. It is the fourth most used language on the internet and the fifth in terms of number of articles in Wikipedia. It is the third most used language in business, with francophone countries accounting for over 15 percent of global wealth. It is also the second language for international information in the media.

French is a living language. It is one of the rare languages taught in the education systems of almost every country. It ranks second in terms of number of learners, with more than 125 million people studying French around the world. And to teach them, there are more than 500,000 French teachers outside of France.

Why study a foreign language anyway? In the United States, we often assume that everyone speaks English. Of course that isn't true, but are there good reasons for learning French in the United States? Definitely! According to Fabrice Jaumont, author of *The Bilingual Revolution: The Future of Education Is in Two Languages,* there are more than nine million Americans who claim French ancestry, so French is certainly part of the United States' heritage.

Jaumont's revolution has provided an invaluable bilingual road map for parents and educators all over the world.

From its very foundation, the United States and France have shared strong ties. These historical bonds have proven robust over the years and continue to unite both countries as they face new global challenges.

There are, of course, more specific reasons to study French. For those interested in cooking, fashion, theater, cinema, the visual arts, dance, and architecture, knowledge of French is a must. And for some, there is simply the pleasure of learning a beautiful, rich, melodious language that is often called "the language of love."

Looking towards the future, it is estimated that by 2050 there will be more than 700 million French speakers in the world! If so, will you be one of them?

The Verb Aller and Speaking About Time

MUST KNOW

- To ask how someone is doing, use the verb **aller**.

- **Aller** + infinitive is used only for immediate actions.

- If you want to understand something, ask **pourquoi**.

- The official week starts **lundi**.

- Days and months are not capitalized.

Pick up your calendar because this chapter is all about making plans. To make plans, you'll need to know the days of the weeks and the months of the year. You'll also need to learn how to tell time using the 24-hour clock; otherwise, you might miss your flight!

Aller

The verb **aller** is one of the most frequently used verbs in French. While its literal translation is *to go*, **aller** is used in many idiomatic expressions.

je vais	*I go*	nous allons	*we go*
tu vas	*you go*	vous allez	*you go* (formal and plural of **tu**)
il/elle/on va	*he/she/one goes*	ils/elles vont	*they go*

BTW

*With the **nous** and **vous** forms of the verb **aller**, you must pronounce the **s** as a **z**. For example, you would say « **nouz allons** ». Remember that this is called a liaison.*

Julie va souvent au ballet.	*Julie often goes to the ballet.*
Allez-vous au travail en métro?	*Are you going to work by subway?*
Tu vas à la plage?	*Are you going to the beach?*
—Tu y vas? —Non, je n'y vais pas!	*Are you going? No, I am not going!*

With the verb **aller**, inverting in the first-person singular **je** requires a bit more attention than the other subject pronouns do. Doing this is considered formal, so it largely depends on the context.

Quand **vais-je** recevoir le nouveau contrat?	*When am I going to the receive the new contract?*
« Ciel! que **vais-je** lui dire [...]? » —*Phèdre*, Jean Racine	*"Heavens! What will I tell him [...]?" Phaedra*, Jean Racine

Notice that in the first example, we are using **vais-je** in a professional context, perhaps with an employer or an administrator. And in the second example, it is used with dramatic effect in *Phèdre*, a classic seventeenth-century play by Jean Racine.

Idiomatic Expressions with Aller

You cannot truly speak French without employing at least a few idiomatic expressions with the verb **aller**.

J'y vais.	*I'm going.*
Allons-y!	*Let's go!*
On y va!	*Let's go!*
Allez-y!	*Go!*
Comment allez-vous?	*How are you?*
Comment vas-tu?	*How are you?*
Ça va?	*How's it going?*
s'en aller	*to go away*
Ça va de soi.	*It goes without saying.*
aller chercher	*to fetch, to go pick up something or someone*
Ça te va bien.	*That suits you.*
Cette couleur te va à merveille.	*This color suits you really well.*

The Immediate Future

Aller is often paired with the infinitive of another verb to indicate that one is *going* to do something. With the immediate future, it is expected that the action be realized in the very near future; otherwise, you would use the **futur simple**. We'll see that in Chapter 10.

To form the immediate future tense, combine the present form of **aller** with the infinitive of the main verb, its unconjugated form. It should look something like this:

> subject pronoun + conjugation of **aller** + infinitive

Here is an example with the verb **partir**:

je vais partir	*I'm going to leave*	nous allons partir	*we are going to leave*
tu vas partir	*you are going to leave*	vous allez partir	*you are going to leave*
il/elle/on va partir	*he/she/one is going to leave*	ils/elles vont partir	*they are going to leave*

Elle va passer un examen.	*She is going to take a test.*
Sylvain va déménager samedi.	*Sylvain is going to move on Saturday.*
Ils vont faire du camping en Corse.	*They are going to go camping in Corsica.*
On va construire une maison dans la baie d'Arcachon.	*We are going to build a house in Arcachon Bay.*

Time Words and Expressions

Whether you want to see a movie, sign up for a course, invite someone to dinner, or all of the these things, memorizing these key time words will make your life much easier.

Basic Time Words

You cannot make plans without knowing when to meet. For this, time words are key.

la seconde	*second*
la minute	*minute*
l'heure	*hour*
le jour	*day*
la semaine	*week*
le mois	*month*
le semestre	*semester*
l'année	*year*
la décennie	*decade*
le siècle	*century*
le millénaire	*millennium*

Days of the Week

Notice how the week in French starts on Monday and how the words are not capitalized.

lundi	*Monday*
mardi	*Tuesday*
mercredi	*Wednesday*
jeudi	*Thursday*
vendredi	*Friday*
samedi	*Saturday*
dimanche	*Sunday*
le week-end	*weekend*

Lundi Pierre a une importante réunion.	*On Monday Pierre has an important meeting.*
Pierre va au club de sport le lundi et le mercredi.	*Pierre goes to the fitness club on Mondays and Wednesdays.*

| Félicie va dîner avec ses amis vendredi. | *Félicie is going to have dinner with her friends on Friday.* |
| Félicie anime un club de lecture le vendredi dans une bibliothèque. | *Félicie hosts a book club at the library on Fridays.* |

Another case where **le** is used with days is when referring to a specific date. It follows the format **le + nombre + mois**. That's why the famous French holiday Bastille Day is referred to as **le 14 juillet**!

| Son anniversaire est **le** 10 octobre. | *His birthday is on October 10th.* |
| Les Français célèbrent la fête du Travail **le** 1er mai. | *The French celebrate Labor Day on May 1st.* |

> **BTW**
>
> The definite article **le** is not used when referring to a particular event or action in time. However, when referring to a recurring activity, **le** is used before the day. In English, this is the equivalent of distinguishing between on Friday and on Fridays.

Months

En is the preposition that is used in front of the months. And like the days, the months of the year are not capitalized.

janvier	*January*
février	*February*
mars	*March*
avril	*April*
mai	*May*
juin	*June*
juillet	*July*
août	*August*
septembre	*September*
octobre	*October*
novembre	*November*
décembre	*December*

Émilie va passer un examen en mai.	*Émilie is going to take an exam in May.*
La famille Huard va louer sa villa à Pyla-sur-mer en juillet et en août.	*The Huard family is going to rent their villa in Pyla-sur-mer in July and in August.*

Seasons

Note that while we say **en été, en automne**, and **en hiver**, we say **au printemps**.

la saison	*the season*
le printemps	*spring*
l'été	*summer*
l'automne	*fall*
l'hiver	*winter*

There are three cases used with seasons: **en**, **le**, and **au**.

L'hiver est très froid en Finlande.	*Winter is very cold in Finland.*
Nous allons dans les Alpes suisses pour faire du ski **en** hiver.	*We go skiing in the Swiss Alps in the winter.*
L'été est la saison préférée d'Anna.	*Summer is Anna's favorite season.*
On va à la plage **en** été.	*We go to the beach in the summer.*
En France, **l'**automne est la saison des prix littéraires.	*In France, fall is the season of literary awards.*
En automne, je ramasse des champignons dans la forêt d'Amboise.	*In the fall, I go mushroom picking in the Amboise Forest.*
Le printemps est dans l'air.	*Spring is in the air.*
Les violettes fleurissent **au** printemps.	*Violets bloom in the spring.*

Time Adverbs

Now that we've seen the days, months, and seasons, let's take a look at some useful adverbial expressions of time. The following adverbial expressions are used when speaking directly to people in what is known as *direct speech*.

aujourd'hui	*today*
ce matin	*this morning*
cet après-midi	*this afternoon*
demain	*tomorrow*
hier	*yesterday*
après-demain	*the day after tomorrow*
avant-hier	*the day before yesterday*
dans trois jours	*in three days from today*
dans une semaine	*in a week*
dans une quinzaine	*in two weeks*
dans un mois	*in a month*
dans un an	*in a year*
la semaine prochaine	*next week*
la semaine dernière	*last week*

Guillaume va chez le médecin demain.

Guillaume is going to the doctor's tomorrow.

Il va célébrer son anniversaire dans une semaine.

He is going to celebrate his birthday in a week.

When narrating a past or future event, something known as *indirect speech* is used. It is "indirect" in the sense that one is describing the event as an outsider. Familiarize yourself with the following adverbial expressions.

la veille	*the day before, eve*
le jour même	*the very day*
le lendemain	*the day after*
l'avant-veille	*two days before*

le surlendemain	two days later
la semaine suivante	the following week
la dernière semaine	the last week (of a sequence)

Ma sœur va arriver la veille de mon mariage.

My sister is going to arrive on the eve of my wedding.

J'arrive à Hanoï le 14 mars et je repars le lendemain.

I'll arrive in Hanoi on March 14th, and I'll leave the following day.

Here are some additional adverbs or expressions of time:

chaque jour	every day
tous les jours	every day
maintenant	now
en ce moment	at this present time
actuellement	presently
à l'heure actuelle	at the present time
autrefois	formerly
d'habitude	usually
d'ordinaire	usually
toujours	always, still
souvent	often
parfois	sometimes
quelquefois	sometimes
de temps en temps	from time to time
de temps à autre	from time to time
rarement	seldom
longtemps	for a long time
tôt	early
tard	late
ne... jamais	never

Ils vont en Tunisie de temps en temps.	*They go to Tunisia from time to time.*
Actuellement il n'y a pas de places disponibles dans ce cours.	*At the present time, there are no spots available in this class.*
Elle loue une maison en Écosse chaque année.	*She rents a house in Scotland every year.*
Je t'appelle demain.	*I'll call you tomorrow.*
Ils voyagent rarement en hiver.	*They seldom travel in the winter.*

Telling Time

This is how you casually ask about and tell time in French.

Quelle heure est-il?   *What time is it?*

- On the hour:

Il est 9 heures.	*It is nine o'clock.*
Il est 11 heures.	*It is eleven o'clock.*
Il est midi.	*It is noon.*
Il est minuit.	*It is midnight.*

- On the half or quarter hour:

Il est huit heures et demie.	*It is eight thirty* (lit. *"and a half"*).
Il est midi et demi.	*It is half past twelve.*
Il est minuit et demi.	*It is half past twelve.*

Note that **midi** and **minuit** are masculine, so **demi** does not take the final **e**. But since **heure** is feminine, **demie** agrees.

Il est trois heures et quart.	*It is a quarter past three.*
Il est trois heures moins le quart.	*It is a quarter to three.*

Now let's go all the way around the clock!

Il est une heure.	*It is one o'clock.*
Il est une heure cinq.	*It is five past one.*
Il est une heure dix.	*It is ten past one.*
Il est une heure et quart.	*It is a quarter past one.*
Il est une heure vingt.	*It is twenty past one.*
Il est une heure vingt-cinq.	*It is twenty-five past one.*
Il est une heure et demie.	*It is half past one (one thirty).*
Il est deux heures moins vingt-cinq.	*It is twenty-five to two.*
Il est deux heures moins vingt.	*It is twenty to two.*
Il est deux heures moins le quart.	*It is a quarter to two.*
Il est deux heures moins dix.	*It is ten to two.*
Il est deux heures moins cinq.	*It is five to two.*
Il est deux heures.	*It is two o'clock.*

To make explicit whether am or pm is being referred to, add either **du matin** (*in the morning*), **de l'après-midi** (*in the afternoon*), or **du soir** (*in the evening*):

Thomas part à sept heures du matin.	*Thomas is leaving at seven in the morning.*
Nous rentrons à quatre heures de l'après-midi.	*We get back home at four o'clock in the afternoon.*
La réunion est à huit heures du soir.	*The meeting is at eight o'clock in the evening.*

Time with the 24-Hour Clock

In formal settings like at train stations and business offices, time is referred to as a 24-hour block (rather than merely going up to 12). To switch from the 12-hour clock to the 24-hour clock, add twelve hours to every hour past noon.

24-hour clock	12-hour clock	
12h00	12:00pm	midi (noon)
12h30	12:30pm	
13h00	1:00pm	
14h00	2:00pm	
15h00	3:00pm	
15h15	3:15pm	
16h00	4:00pm	
17h00	5:00pm	
18h00	6:00pm	
18h30	6:30pm	
19h00	7:00pm	
20h00	8:00pm	
21h00	9:00pm	
22h00	10:00pm	
23h00	11:00pm	
23h45	11:45pm	
0h00	12:00am	minuit (midnight)

L'avion part à vingt heures.	*The plane leaves at 8pm.*
Le concert commence à dix-neuf heures.	*The concert starts at 7pm.*
La cérémonie de remise des diplômes finit à seize heures.	*The graduation ceremony will end at 4pm.*
La réunion est prévue pour quinze heures trente.	*The meeting is planned for 3:30pm.*

Introducing -*re* Verbs

As you continue your French studies, you will inevitably come across **-re** verbs. And like all grammar concepts, there are regular **-re** verbs and irregular **-re** verbs. But don't worry, **vous allez très vite comprendre!** —*you will understand very quickly!*

Regular *-re* Verbs in the Present Tense

To conjugate regular **-re** verbs, remove the infinitive ending **-re** and add the following endings:

	singular	**plural**
1st person	**s**	**ons**
2nd person	**s**	**ez**
3rd person	**d**	**ent**

Here is how we conjugate the verb **attendre** (*to wait/to expect*):

j'attends	*I wait*	nous attendons	*we wait*
tu attends	*you wait*	vous attendez	*you wait*
il/elle/on attend	*he/she/one waits*	ils/elles attendent	*they wait*

Sandra attend le train à la gare de Lyon.	*Sandra is waiting for the train at the Lyon station.*
J'attends les résultats de mon examen.	*I am waiting for the results of my exam.*
Ils attendent votre réponse.	*They are waiting for your answer.*
Elle attend son premier enfant.	*She is expecting her first child.*
Qu'attendez-vous de moi?	*What do you expect from me?*

Below are some more regular **-re** verbs that are conjugated in the same way.

défendre	*to defend, to forbid*	→ je défends	*I defend, I forbid*
		nous défendons	*we defend, we forbid*
descendre	*to go down*	→ je descends	*I go down*
		nous descendons	*we go down*
entendre	*to hear*	→ j'entends	*I hear*
		nous entendons	*we hear*

mordre	*to bite*	→ je mords	*I bite*
		nous mordons	*we bite*
perdre	*to lose*	→ je perds	*I lose*
		nous perdons	*we lose*
prétendre	*to claim*	→ je prétends	*I claim*
		nous prétendons	*we claim*
rendre	*to give back, to return*	→ je rends	*I give back, I return*
		nous rendons	*we give back, we return*
répandre	*to spread, to spill*	→ je répands	*I spread, I spill*
		nous répandons	*we spread, we spill*
répondre	*to answer*	→ je réponds	*I answer*
		nous répondons	*we answer*
tendre	*to stretch, to hold out*	→ je tends	*I stretch, I hold out*
		nous tendons	*we stretch, we hold out*
tordre	*to twist*	→ je tords	*I twist*
		nous tordons	*we twist*
vendre	*to sell*	→ je vends	*I sell*
		nous vendons	*we sell*

Est-ce que Renaud va vendre sa collection de bandes dessinées?	*Is Renaud going to sell his comic book collection?*
Nous défendons nos propres intérêts.	*We defend our own interests.*
Le professeur nous rend nos devoirs cet après-midi.	*The teacher will give us back our homework this afternoon.*
Parlez plus fort, on ne vous entend pas.	*Speak up, we can't hear you.*

Some Irregular -re Verbs

French has many irregular **-re** verbs, so let's get acquainted with a few essential ones.

prendre   *to take*

je prends	*I take*	nous prenons	*we take*
tu prends	*you take*	vous prenez	*you take*
il/elle/on prend	*he/she/one takes*	ils/elles prennent	*they take*

Martin prend son petit déjeuner à sept heures.	*Martin has breakfast at 7am.*
Nous prenons le métro pour aller au travail.	*We take the subway to go to work.*
Est-ce que tu prends du sucre dans ton thé?	*Do you take sugar in your tea?*
Ils ne prennent pas de vacances en été.	*They don't go on vacation in the summer.*

Here are some derivatives of the verb **prendre**:

apprendre	*to learn*	→ j'apprends	*I learn*
		nous apprenons	*we learn*
comprendre	*to understand*	→ je comprends	*I understand*
		nous comprenons	*we understand*
entreprendre	*to undertake*	→ j'entreprends	*I undertake*
		nous entreprenons	*we undertake*
surprendre	*to surprise*	→ je surprends	*I surprise*
		nous surprenons	*we surprise*

Comprenez-vous l'explication du professeur?	*Do you understand the teacher's explanation?*
J'apprends les verbes irréguliers par cœur.	*I am learning the irregular verbs by heart.*
Elle va entreprendre la traduction d'un recueil de poèmes chinois.	*She is going to undertake the translation of a Chinese book of poetry.*
Sa décision ne vous surprend pas?	*Aren't you suprised by his/her decision?*

DIALOGUE *Vive les vacances!*
Long live vacations!

Émilie meets Julien, a neighbor in the hallway of their building, and talks about vacation destinations.

 IRL Vacation time is sacred to the French. In 1936, under Léon Bloom's *Front populaire*, the French government implemented a policy of 15 days of paid vacation. Over time, this period of paid vacation kept increasing until 1982, when it was extended to five weeks. Today, the average is 33 days, though it is not uncommon for people to stretch their vacation to six or even seven weeks. *Vive les vacances!*

ÉMILIE: Comment allez-vous? — *How are you?*

JULIEN: Je vais bien, merci. Et vous? — *I am doing well, thank you. What about you?*

ÉMILIE: Très bien. Le semestre est fini! — *Very well. The semester is over!*

JULIEN: Allez-vous prendre des vacances? — *Are you going to take a vacation?*

ÉMILIE: J'ai très envie d'aller au Portugal. — *I really feel like going to Portugal.*

JULIEN: Au Portugal? — *To Portugal?*

ÉMILIE: Oui, au Portugal, à Nazaré exactement, pour faire du surf. J'en rêve! — *Yes, to Portugal, in Nazaré to be precise, to go surfing. I am dreaming about it!*

JULIEN: C'est fantastique! — *It's fantastic!*

ÉMILIE: Oui, mais pas cet été … je vais rester à Paris. — *Yes, but not this summer… I am going to stay in Paris.*

JULIEN: Pourquoi? — *Why?*

ÉMILIE: J'ai un examen important la semaine prochaine.

I have an important exam next week.

JULIEN: C'est dommage!

What a shame!

ÉMILIE: Et vous? Avez-vous des projets?

What about you? Do you have any plans?

JULIEN: Je vais à Arcachon. Ma famille a une maison près de la dune du Pilat.

I am going to Arcachon. My family has a house close to the Dune of Pilat.

ÉMILIE: Vous avez de la chance!

You are lucky!

JULIEN: Je vais prendre une semaine de vacances. J'ai besoin de soleil et de repos.

I am going to take a week's vacation. I need some sun and rest.

ÉMILIE: Vous partez samedi?

Are you leaving on Saturday?

JULIEN: Non, la semaine prochaine. Je vais aider mon ami Sylvain à déménager ce week-end.

No, next week. I am going to help my friend Sylvain move this weekend.

ÉMILIE: Comme c'est gentil!

How nice of you!

JULIEN: Alors, bonne chance avec vos examens!

So, good luck with your exams!

ÉMILIE: Merci. Bonnes vacances!

Thank you. Enjoy your vacation!

JULIEN: Ne travaillez pas trop et prenez bien soin de vous! À bientôt!

Do not work too much and take good care of yourself! See you soon!

ÉMILIE: À bientôt!

See you soon!

EXERCISES

EXERCISE 3.1

Conjugate the verb **aller** *in the present tense.*

1. Je _____ chez le dentiste mardi.

2. Est-ce qu'elle _____ au cinéma ce soir?

3. Nous _____ chez Auchan une fois par mois.

4. Je ne _____ pas à la piscine sans toi!

5. Est-ce qu'il _____ chez le coiffeur aujourd'hui?

6. Nous _____ en Australie en avril.

7. —Comment _____ la mère de Céleste? —Elle _____ très bien.

8. Est-ce que tu _____ à l'école à bicyclette?

9. _____-vous à Angoulême en voiture ou en train?

10. Est-ce que vous _____ au Portugal cet été?

EXERCISE 3.2

Rewrite the following sentences as questions using inversion. Watch out for spelling changes.

1. Vous allez à Monoprix cet après-midi.

2. Tu vas au pique-nique d'Alice sur l'Île aux Cygnes.

3. Il va au Théâtre du Rond-Point.

4. Elles vont à l'Institut de Touraine pour apprendre le français.

5. Il va chez sa grand-mère samedi.

6. Nous allons faire une promenade sur un bateau-mouche.

7. Elle va au conservatoire de musique de Marseille.

8. Vous allez en Louisiane cet été.

9. Tu vas à Milan en avion.

10. Vous allez au bureau ce matin.

EXERCISE 3.3

Rewrite the following sentences in the immediate future tense.

1. J'invite mes voisins à prendre un verre.

2. Il téléphone à son coiffeur dans le Marais.

3. Elles étudient la musique baroque au conservatoire.

4. Elle travaille en Asie.

5. Vous jouez au tennis avec Maude.

6. Tu prends des photos pendant les vacances.

7. Guillaume déjeune avec sa patronne.

8. Je reste chez moi ce week-end.

9. Frédéric et Line préparent leurs valises.

10. Nous chantons une chanson pour son anniversaire.

EXERCISE 3.4

Put the following sentences in the negative form.

1. Nous allons visiter le château de Chambord aujourd'hui.

2. Je vais étudier le français dans une école à Perpignan.

3. Il va prendre une semaine de vacances en avril.

4. Elle va avoir le temps d'aller au supermarché ce soir.

5. Vous allez être en retard pour votre rendez-vous.

6. Ils vont être à l'aise en classe économique.

7. Elles vont parler anglais avec Justin.

8. Tu vas apporter le livre d'économie en classe.

9. Je vais mélanger le citron et le miel dans la tasse.

10. Ils vont financer l'organisation.

EXERCISE 3.5

*Translate the following sentences using the immediate future tense. When asking questions, use the **est-ce que** form.*

1. I am going to buy a Navigo Pass for the subway.

2. They are going to play in André Citroën Park.

3. Julien is going to be hungry after tennis.

4. We are going to start a new lesson today. (*nous*)

5. I am not going to work this weekend.

6. We are going to have lunch at noon. (*on*)

7. They are going to organize the reception for sixty people.

8. Are you going to ask difficult questions? (*vous*)

9. Pauline is going to be fifteen tomorrow.

10. Florent is going to call his mother after dinner.

EXERCISE 3.6

Match the items in the two columns. Choose the most logical answers.

1. Les tulipes poussent   a. en automne.

2. On ramasse les feuilles mortes   b. au printemps.

3. Elle a toujours froid   c. lundi.

4. On va à la plage   d. en été.

5. Le premier jour de la semaine est   e. en février.

EXERCISE 3.7

*Translate the following sentences using the **tu** form when necessary. When asking questions, use the **est-ce que** form.*

1. Marion is going to buy a Navigo Pass on Monday.

2. In March, Alexis is going to study French at Rennes University.

3. In the fall, Noémie's parents are going to the Canary Islands.

4. Is your birthday in September?

5. I play tennis with Matthias on Wednesday afternoons.

6. Thomas and Léa are going to meet Justin on Tuesday.

7. Is the reception on Saturday or Sunday?

8. We are going to the Fête de la Musique in June.

9. Winter is very long in Siberia.

10. I am going to travel to Louisiana in the spring.

EXERCISE 3.8

Translate the words in parentheses.

1. —Émilie passe un examen (*today*) _____? —Non, elle passe un examen (*tomorrow*) _____.

2. —Jean-Luc rentre (*this afternoon*) _____? —Non, il rentre (*tomorrow afternoon*) _____.

3. —Lucie travaille (*tomorrow*) _____? —Non, elle travaille (*the day after tomorrow*) _____.

4. —Tu es disponible (*this week*) _____? —Non, je suis disponible (*next week*) _____.

5. —Vous dînez (*often*) _____ avec Jean? —Non, je dîne avec Jean (*from time to time*) _____.

6. —Muriel part (*in a week*) _____? —Non, elle part (*in a month*) _____.

7. —Il arrive (*sometimes*) _____ en avance? —Non, il arrive (*always*) _____ en retard.

8. —Tu manges des légumes (*every day*) _____? —Oui, je mange des légumes (*every day*) _____.

9. Vous allez (*often*) _____ à Trouville? —Non, nous n'allons (*never*) _____ à Trouville.

10. —Elle va (*sometimes*) _____ au jardin du Luxembourg? —Non, elle va (*rarely*) _____ au jardin du Luxembourg.

EXERCISE 3.9

*Translate the following sentences using **vous** when necessary. When asking a question, use inversion.*

1. We are going to France next week.

2. Gérard is going to Australia in a month.

3. Today is Muriel's birthday.

4. We are going to meet François for the first time in Paris next week.

5. —Are you going to call Alice's friends tomorrow? —No, in two or three days.

6. She is taking her exam next week. The following week she is going to travel to India.

7. Tomorrow I am going to wear my blue suit.

8. The day before Daniel's birthday, it was my birthday.

9. Are you going to leave tomorrow? – No, I am leaving the day after tomorrow.

10. He is arriving in Strasbourg on Thursday, and he is going to Prague the following day.

EXERCISE 3.10

Write out the times in expanded form. Use the 24-hour clock.

1. 4:30pm

2. 5:45pm

3. 8:10pm

4. 9:40pm

5. 11:50pm

EXERCISE 3.11

Conjugate the following verbs in the present tense.

1. Je (entendre) _____ une chanson de Mika.

2. La skieuse (descendre) _____ la piste très rapidement.

3. Je (rendre) _____ un livre de science-fiction à la bibliothèque.

4. André (vendre) _____ sa moto.

5. Vous (attendre) _____ Zoé?

6. Il (prétendre) _____ en savoir plus que moi.

7. La presse à sensation (répandre) _____ des rumeurs sur la famille royale.

8. Nous (perdre) _____ trop de temps à vous attendre.

9. Le professeur me (tendre) _____ la main pour me dire bonjour.

10. Nous (répondre) _____ au questionnaire.

EXERCISE 3.12

Match the items in the two colums. Choose the most logical answers.

1. Nous entendons   a. mon dictionnaire bilingue.

2. J'attends   b. avant demain.

3. Réponds-moi   c. votre attitude.

4. Nous ne comprenons pas   d. de la musique dans la rue.

5. Paul me rend   e. l'autobus place de la République.

EXERCISE 3.13

Conjugate the following verbs in the present tense.

1. Nous (comprendre) _____ votre dilemme.

2. Ils (entreprendre) _____ un grand voyage.

3. Vous (apprendre) _____ à jouer de la flûte.

4. Est-ce que tu (prendre) _____ l'autobus ou le métro?

5. Joël (surprendre) _____ souvent ses collègues.

6. Ils (comprendre) _____ l'importance de ce sommet international.

7. Les rumeurs sur la famille royale ne me (surprendre) _____ jamais.

8. Boris ne (comprendre) _____ rien au manuel d'utilisation pour cet appareil.

9. Je (apprendre) _____ les paroles d'une chanson de Yannick Noah.

10. La France (entreprendre) _____ des réformes économiques essentielles.

EXERCISE 3.14

*Translate the following sentences in the present tense. When asking questions, use the **est-ce que** form.*

1. We are waiting for Janine's visit. (*on*)

2. Do you sell French magazines? (*vous*)

3. Why are you learning Japanese? (*tu*)

4. They rarely take the subway to go downtown.

5. I'll return the book to the library tomorrow morning! I promise!

6. We answer the teacher in French. (*nous*)

7. I don't understand why they are always late.

8. Pierre never loses anything on the train.

9. She claims to be my friend.

10. We are going down the Champs-Élysées. (*nous*)

LE COIN DES CRÉATEURS

L'ACROSTICHE

An acrostic is a series of lines in which the first letter in each line forms a name or a message when read in sequence.

Luca	**Sofia**
Lumineux	**S**érieuse
Ultra-chic	**O**bjective
Charmant	**F**rancophone
Aventureux	**I**ndépendante
	Avant-gardiste

Take a friend's name and find a series of adjectives or nouns that best describe him or her—with the help of another friend, your dictionary—to make a flattering portrait. Pay attention to the masculine or feminine form of the adjective according to the person you choose.

NOTE CULTURELLE

ARCACHON AND THE DUNE OF PILAT

Spend some time in France and you will most certainly hear reference made to *l'Hexagone*, "the hexagon," and you may wonder what it is. It is actually the nickname the French have for their country, which, when you look carefully at a map of France, does seem to be six-sided. Four of those six sides face the sea and, with 2,130 miles of coastline, there are many beautiful beaches and coastal areas to be visited and enjoyed. One such area, in southwest France, is the seaside resort town of Arcachon and the nearby Dune of Pilat, a 1.6-mile natural sand dune that is the tallest in Europe. At first glance, its very size makes it appear like a desert right off the coast of France, but it really is one of the most beautiful sandboxes in the world! With more than one million visitors per year, the Dune of Pilat and the nearby town of Arcachon are famous tourist destinations, beautiful in summer and winter alike. What makes them special?

Arcachon's history dates back to Louis XVI, who wanted to turn its bay into a military port. To do so, it was necessary to stop the sand in the dunes from moving. Civil engineers worked to resolve this problem and came up with the idea of planting trees and other vegetation as a way of creating a natural barrier. It was successful, but the military port was never built. However, in the early nineteenth century, the location was already known for the quality of its climate. With the building of the Bordeaux–La Teste railroad line, which brought in people from all over the region, it began to grow, and in 1823, the first bathing establishment, designed to serve a wealthy clientele, was opened.

In 1857, Arcachon, formerly a district of La Teste-de-Buch, was created as a separate community by imperial decree of Napoléon III. The Pereire brothers, bankers and railroad owners, decided to extend the railroad line as far as Arcachon, hoping to increase its importance as a commercial location and port. While they achieved only minimal success, they also worked to develop summer and winter tourism. Arcachon became known not just for the beauty of its beaches but also as destination for those seeking to improve their health. Its climate and natural springs were also a draw for those suffering from chronic diseases such as rheumatoid arthritis and tuberculosis. Some of the more wealthy decided to settle there permanently, building large villas and mansions in a variety of architectural styles.

Today Arcachon has four districts, named for the four seasons. The Ville d'Été, the summer district, is home to shopping streets, the town's sandy main beach, and a casino located in the nineteenth-century Château Deganne. The Ville d'Hiver, the winter district, is famous for its extravagant nineteenth-century villas. South of the town is the Dune de Pilat. Visitors come for the beach, for the dunes, and for the unique, picturesque architecture. Since 1985, the entire Ville d'Hiver district has been classified as a historic monument.

 **Nouns and Their Genders**

MUST KNOW

 Don't be fooled by **e** endings—**le problème** is masculine!

 A word's gender doesn't change when it gets abbreviated: **la photographie** and **la photo**.

 Countries have gender: **le Japon** and **la France**.

 Le bijou and **le bateau** become **les bijoux** and **les bateaux**.

Perhaps the most striking difference between French and English is that French words have gender. You'll be tempted to think that words like **bijou** (jewelry) and **parfum** (perfume) are feminine, but you'd be wrong to guess so. The point is that while all words have gender, it's nearly impossible to guess the gender for every single word. But as we will learn in this chapter, there arc clever rules to help us to identify masculine and feminine words; knowing the word endings will be the key for your success.

Indefinite and Definite Articles

The three types of indefinite articles (**un**, **une**, and **des**) depend on the gender and number of the noun that follows.

J'ai **un** dictionnaire.	*I have a dictionary.*
Elle a **une** voiture.	*She has a car.*
Ils ont **des** amis en France.	*They have friends in France.*

In the negative form, **un**, **une**, and **des** become **de** or **d'**.

Je n'ai **pas de** dictionnaire.	*She does not have a dictionary.*
Elle n'a **pas de** voiture.	*She does not have a car.*
Ils n'ont **pas d'**amis en France.	*They don't have friends in France.*

The definite articles (**le**, **la**, and **les**) depend on the gender and number of the noun as well. If there is a vowel sound or an **h**, **l'** is mostly used.

Il aime **le** fromage de Normandie.	*He likes cheese from Normandy.*
La mer est à cinq kilomètres d'ici.	*The sea is five kilometers from here.*
L'Occitanie, c'est la région que nous allons visiter!	*Occitanie is the region we are going to visit!*
Où se trouve **l'**hôtel de Michel?	*Where is Michel's hotel?*
Les États-Unis ont cinquante États.	*The United States has fifty states.*

There are two genders in French: masculine and feminine, both of which are preceded by a definite article or an indefinite article. It is tempting to assume that a word's gender is picked arbitrarily, though this is far from the case. In fact, many nouns have endings on which you can rely to figure out their gender, though not all do. For this reason, you should memorize the gender linked with each new noun you learn, as if they are together.

General Masculine Noun Endings

The following endings tend to indicate a masculine word:

- **-age**

le from**age**   *cheese*
le nu**age**   *cloud*
le gar**age**   *garage*

La Normandie est une grande région productrice de from**ages**.   *Normandy is a large producer of cheese.*
Le mari**age** de mon cousin est prévu le 20 septembre.   *My cousin's wedding is planned for September 20.*

But there are a few exceptions:

la cage	*cage*
l'image	*image*
la page	*page*
la plage	*beach*

■ **-eau, -ou**

le bat**eau**	*boat*
le gât**eau**	*cake*
le bij**ou**	*jewel*
le gen**ou**	*knee*

Certains ois**eaux** migrent vers l'Espagne et le Maroc en hiver.	*Certain birds migrate to Spain and Morocco in the winter.*
Nous allons visiter le chât**eau** de Versailles.	*We are going to visit the château of Versailles.*
Où achètes-tu tes bij**oux** fantaisie?	*Where do you buy your custom jewelry?*

Note that most of the time nouns ending in **-eau** and **-ou** take an **-x** in the plural form, not an **-s**, like **les bateaux** (*the boats*), **les choux** (*cabbages*).

■ **-on, -om**

le cray**on**	*pencil*
le torch**on**	*dish towel*
le blous**on** en cuir	*leather jacket*

le n**om**	*name*
le prén**om**	*first name*
le surn**om**	*nickname*

Le sal**on** de thé Mariage Frères est dans le 6ᵉ arrondissement.	*The Mariage Frères Tearoom is in the sixth arrondissement.*
À Royan, le festival *Un viol**on** sur le sable* attire un large public.	*In Royan, the festival* Un violon sur le sable *attracts a large crowd.*

But there are a few exceptions:

la boisson	*beverage*
la chanson	*song*
la façon	*manner*

| la leçon | lesson |
| la maison | house |

■ **-er**

le passag**er** *passenger*
le berg**er** *shepherd*
le dîn**er** *dinner*

Qu'est-ce qu'on mange pour le déjeun**er**?   *What are we eating for lunch?*

Ce boulang**er** vend des baguettes artisanales.   *This baker sells artisinal baguettes.*

■ **-el, -iel**

le caram**el** *caramel*
l'hôt**el** *hotel*
le tunn**el** *tunnel*

le ci**el** *sky*
le logici**el** *software*
le mi**el** *honey*

Ce matéri**el** est fabriqué en Corée du Sud.   *This equipment is made in South Korea.*

La Provence produit du mi**el** de lavande.   *Provence produces lavender honey.*

■ **-al**

l'anim**al** *animal*
le chev**al** *horse*
le mét**al** *metal*

Le can**al** du Midi relie l'océan Atlantique à la mer Méditerranée.   *The canal du Midi connects the Atlantic Ocean with the Mediterranean Sea.*

Dans le sud-est de la France, on lit le journ**al** quotidien *Nice-Matin*.	*In the southeast of France, one reads the daily* Nice-Matin *paper.*

Generally, the plural form of words ending in **-al** is **-aux**, like **les animaux** and **les chevaux**. Still, there are several exceptions:

le festiv**al** (*festival*)	→ les festiv**als** (*festivals*)
le b**al** (*ball*)	→ les b**als** (*balls*)
le carnav**al** (*carnival*)	→ les carnav**als** (*carnivals*)

Chaque année, la Bretagne offre de nombreux festiv**als** littéraires.	*Each year, Brittany offers numerous literary festivals.*

■ **-ant**, **-ent**

le ch**ant**	*singing, song*
le diam**ant**	*diamond*
le restaur**ant**	*restaurant*

l'arg**ent**	*money*
le réchauffem**ent** climatique	*global warming*
le tal**ent**	*talent*

Le mistral est un **vent** très violent.	*The mistral is a very strong wind.*
La bague de ma sœur est un diam**ant** de 24 carats.	*My sister's ring is a 24-carat diamond.*

There is one main exception:

la d**ent**	*tooth*

■ **-ment**

l'équipe**men**t	*equipment*
l'événe**ment**	*event*
le traite**ment**	*treatment*

À quelle heure commence l'entraîne**ment**?

At what time does the training start?

Merci pour le compli**ment**.

Thank you for the compliment.

■ **-ail**, **-eil**, **-euil**, **-ouil**

le trav**ail**	*work*
le dét**ail**	*detail*
le vitr**ail**	*stained-glass window*

le fen**ouil**	*fennel*
l'écur**euil**	*squirrel*
le faut**euil**	*armchair*
le recu**eil**	*collection, anthology*

Elle apporte toujours son évent**ail** à l'opéra.

She always brings her fan to the opera.

Des millions de personnes vivent sous le s**euil** de pauvreté.

Millions of people live below the poverty line.

Je vous remercie pour l'accu**eil** chaleureux que vous nous avez réservé.

I thank you for the warm welcome you extended to us.

■ **-at**, **-et**, **-t**

le chocol**at**	*chocolate*
le déb**at**	*debate*
l'anonym**at**	*anonymity*
le gil**et**	*vest*
le tabour**et**	*stool*
l'alphab**et**	*alphabet*
le li**t**	*bed*
le circui**t**	*circuit, tour*
le frui**t**	*fruit*

La restauration de l'édifice a été réalisée grâce au mécén**at** de Louis Vuitton.	*The building was restored thanks to Louis Vuitton's sponsorship.*
Tu as ton bill**et** de train pour Annecy?	*Do you have your train ticket for Annecy?*
Son nouveau film est un nav**et**.	*His new film is a flop.*

There are some key exceptions:

la basket	sneaker
la dot	dowry
la forêt	forest
la mort	death
la nuit	night

■ -ac, -ak, -ic, -oc, -uc

le ham**ac**	*hammock*
le kay**ak**	*kayak*
le diagnost**ic**	*diagnosis*
le bl**oc** de papier	*block, writing pad*
l'aqued**uc**	*aqueduct*

Ils vont faire un bivou**ac** dans le désert du Maroc.	*They are going to bivouac in the Moroccan desert.*
En Italie, le basil**ic** est un ingrédient de base.	*In Italy, basil is a basic ingredient.*

■ -e

Attention! Many nouns ending in **-e** are masculine, despite the common misconception that an **-e** ending makes the word feminine. Here are some examples of masculine nouns that end in **-e**:

le beurr**e**	*butter*
l'espac**e**	*space*
le group**e**	*group*

le peign**e**	*comb*
le magazin**e**	*magazine*
le post**e**	*position/job*
le problèm**e**	*problem*
le verb**e**	*verb*
le verr**e**	*glass*

Le problèm**e** principal est que l'espac**e** est trop petit.	*The main problem is that this space is too small.*
Le group**e** d'artistes argentins va arriver à midi.	*The group of Argentinean artists is going to arrive at noon.*

Of course, many nouns ending in **-e** are feminine, but they often belong to another ending category, like **la balançoire** (*swing*), **la revue** (*review*), etc. Double check...always!

■ **-eur**

The **-eur** ending usually renders a noun feminine. But when the name of a profession or machine/tool ends in **-eur**, the noun becomes masculine. Let's take a look:

le composit**eur**	*composer*
l'ingéni**eur**	*engineer*
le dessinat**eur**	*designer*
l'aspirat**eur**	*vacuum cleaner*
le climatis**eur**	*air conditioner*
le réfrigérat**eur**	*refrigerator*

Avez-vous un ordinat**eur** portable?	*Do you have a laptop?*
Prends des glaçons dans le congélat**eur**!	*Take some ice cubes from the freezer!*

■ **-o, -op, -ort, -os, -ot, -ours, -us**

le lavab**o**	*bathroom sink*
le sir**op**	*syrup*
l'eff**ort**	*effort*
le d**os**	*back*
le coquelic**ot**	*poppy*
le c**ours**	*cours*
le j**us** de fruit	*fruit juice*

Quel est votre numér**o** de téléphone?	*What is your phone number?*
Quel est le plus gros paqueb**ot** du monde?	*What is the largest cruise ship in the world?*

Remember that gender does not change when a word is abbreviated:

la météo	*weather forecast*
la photo	*photography*
la philo	*philosophy*
la psycho	*psychology*
la stéréo	*hi-fi/stereo system*
la vidéo	*video*

That's a lot of word endings! Let's quickly review the masculine endings:

-age
-eau, -ou
-on, -om
-er
-el, -iel
-al
-ant, -ent
-ail, -eil, -euil, -ouil
-at, -et, -t

−ac, -ak, -ic, -oc, -uc
-e
-eur
−o, -op, -ort, -os, -ot, -ours, -us

Still, there are many more word endings to study, and to list them all would require countless more pages. Here are few of them: **-a**, **-ain**, **-ard**, **-g**, **-ien**, **-ier/-yer**, **-is**, **-oir**, **-oin**, **-phone**, **-scope**, and **-sme**. The important thing is to learn them step by step, gradually adding new endings to your arsenal as you come across them. And remember to focus on the exceptions, learning them in context. You can do this by memorizing a made-up sentence, the verse of a poem, or a line from your favorite French novel. While this may seem daunting, the more you can commit to noticing these patterns and spotting exceptions, the more natural this process will become.

General Feminine Noun Endings

There are many endings that indicate that a word is feminine; but, as usual, beware the treacherous exceptions.

■ **-ence**, **-ance**

la ch**ance**	*luck, chance*
la puiss**ance**	*power, authority*
l'indépend**ance**	*independence*
la présid**ence**	*presidency*

Cette assiette est en faï**ence** de Quimper.	*This plate is made of Quimper faience.*
Léo a passé son enf**ance** en Dordogne.	*Léo spent his childhood in Dordogne.*

A key exception to remember is **le silence** (*silence*).

■ **-ure**

la nat**ure**	*nature*
la peint**ure**	*paint/painting*
l'écrit**ure**	*writing*

Avez-vous la broch**ure** du club nautique d'Ajaccio?	*Do you have the flyer for the Ajaccio Nautical Club?*
La lect**ure** est un moyen de voyager dans le monde.	*Reading is a way of traveling the world.*

■ **-eur** (excluding nouns denoting professions and machines)

la chal**eur**	*heat*
la coul**eur**	*color*
la douc**eur**	*sweetness*

Quelle est la **fl**eur préférée de ta mère?	*What is your mother's favorite flower?*
Il y a une lu**eur** d'espoir.	*There is a glimmer of hope.*

Here are some exceptions:

le bonheur	*happiness*
l'honneur	*honor*
le malheur	*misfortune/ordeal*

■ **-sion, -tion**

la compréhen**sion**	*understanding*
l'occa**sion**	*chance/opportunity*

| la popula**tion** | *population* |
| l'informa**tion** | *information* |

| Elle va prendre une importante déci**sion**. | *She is going to make an important decision.* |
| La généra**tion** Z défend la cause environnementale. | *Generation Z is defending environmental causes.* |

■ **-ude**

l'ét**ude**	*study*
l'inquiét**ude**	*anxiety*, *worry*
la solit**ude**	*solitude/loneliness*

| Ils ont l'habit**ude** de randonner dans les gorges du Verdon. | *They are used to hiking the Gorges du Verdon.* |
| Il y a une multit**ude** d'activités à partager en famille. | *There is a multitude of family activities.* |

Here are a few exceptions:

| l'interlude | *interlude* |
| le prélude | *prelude* |

■ **-ie, -rie**

| la mag**ie** | *magic* |
| la poés**ie** | *poetry*, *poem* |

| la pâtisse**rie** | *pastry* |
| la tapisse**rie** | *tapestry*, *wallpaper* |

| C'est la v**ie**! | *That's life!* |
| Nous allons visiter la gale**rie** Sapone à Nice. | *We are going to visit the Sapone Gallery in Nice.* |

There are several important exceptions:

le génie	genius
l'incendie	fire
le parapluie	umbrella
le sosie	double
le zombie	zombie

■ **-ise**

la cer**ise**	cherry
la chem**ise**	shirt, folder
la cr**ise**	crisis, attack, fit

J'ai une surpr**ise** pour toi!	*I have a surprise for you!*
Ma val**ise** est prête pour mon voyage en Sicile.	*My suitcase is ready for my trip to Sicily.*

■ **-aille**, **-ille**, **-ouille**

la méd**aille**	medal, disk
la p**aille**	straw

la fam**ille**	family
la myrt**ille**	blueberry

la citr**ouille**	pumpkin
la gren**ouille**	frog

Quelle est la t**aille** de cette chemise?	*What is the shirt size?*
On va manger de la ratat**ouille** et une glace à la van**ille**.	*We are going to eat some ratatouille and then vanilla ice cream.*

■ **-ique**

la botan**ique**   *botany*
la polém**ique**   *polemics*
la polit**ique**   *politics, policy*

Tu vas à la Fête de la Mus**ique** à
Toulouse?

*Are you going to the Fête de la
Musique in Toulouse?*

Le président de la Républ**ique** est élu
pour cinq ans.

*The president of the Republic is
elected for five years.*

Here are a few exceptions:

le lexique	*glossary*
le moustique	*mosquito*
le pique-nique	*picnic*
le plastique	*plastic*
le téléphérique	*cable car*

■ **-ette**

l'assi**ette**   *plate, basis*
la d**ette**   *debt*
la servi**ette**   *napkin*

Cette nois**ette** est utilisée pour la
fabrication de l'huile.

This hazelnut is used to make oil.

Avez-vous une fourch**ette** à huîtres?

Do you have an oyster fork?

Here are some noteworthy exceptions:

le squelette	*skeleton*
le casse-noisette	*nutcracker*
le porte-serviette	*napkin holder*
le quartette	*quartet*

■ **-ée**

l'araign**ée**	*spider*
l'id**ée**	*idea*
la journ**ée**	*day*

Il aime faire la grasse matin**ée** le dimanche.	*He likes to sleep in on Sundays.*
Cette pièce de théâtre est présentée en matin**ée**.	*This play is performed in the afternoon.*

Here are a few exceptions:

le lycée	high school
le musée	museum
le rez-de-chaussée	main floor
le mausolée	mausoleum
le trophée	trophy

Additionally, words indicating quantity are often feminine:

une assiettée	plateful
une bouchée	mouthful
une brassée	armful
une poignée	handful

Ajoutez une cuillér**ée** d'huile!	*Add a spoonful of oil!*
Mangez une poign**ée** de mûres chaque jour!	*Eat a handful of blackberries every day!*

■ **-té**

You'll be be glad to know that most French words ending in **-té** carry the same meaning as their English counterparts ending in -*ty*, a suffix that was borrowed from French. For this reason, many words ending in **-té** are cognates.

l'identi**té**	*identity*
l'illégali**té**	*illegality*
la liber**té**	*freedom/liberty*
la vani**té**	*vanity*

Lucie a la nationali**té** française et américaine.	*Lucie has both French and American nationalities.*
Leur propri**été** donne sur la baie d'Agde à Sète.	*Their property faces the Agde Bay in Sète.*

Here are a few exceptions:

le comité	*committee*
le comté	*county*
le traité	*treaty*

■ **-esse, -osse, -ousse**

la polit**esse**	*politeness*
la jeun**esse**	*youth*
la sag**esse**	*wisdom*
la br**osse**	*brush*
la tr**ousse**	*case*

J'ai une nouvelle tr**ousse** à maquillage.	*I have a new makeup bag.*
Quelle belle h**ousse** de couette!	*What a beautiful duvet cover!*

Here are a few exceptions:

le carrosse	*coach*
le pamplemousse	*grapefruit*

Again, that's a lot of word endings! Let's quickly review the feminine endings:

-ence, -ance
-ure
-eur
-tude
-ie, -rie
-ise
-aille, -ille, -ouille
-ique
-ette
-ée
-té
-esse, -osse, -ousse

Once again, the list of word endings could go on and on. Learn them step by step.

Geographic Names

The names of most cities are considered proper nouns and do not require definite articles.

J'adore Paris.   *I love Paris.*
Lyon est la troisième ville la plus   *Lyon is the third biggest city in France.*
grande de France.

A few cities have a definite article as part of their name: **Le Caire**, **La Havane**, **Le Havre**, **Le Mans**, **La Nouvelle-Orléans**, **La Rochelle**, etc. For this reason, you should memorize both components together.

Countries

Generally speaking, countries that end in **e** tend to be feminine, while other endings tend to be masculine. And as mentioned before, always watch out for the exceptions. Let's look at some feminine countries.

l'Albanie	Albania	la Hongrie	Hungary
l'Algérie	Algeria	l'Inde	India
l'Allemagne	Germany	l'Irlande	Ireland
l'Angleterre	England	l'Italie	Italy
l'Arabie saoudite	Saudi Arabia	la Jordanie	Jordan
l'Argentine	Argentina	la Malaisie	Malaysia
l'Australie	Australia	la Mauritanie	Mauritania
l'Autriche	Austria	la Mongolie	Mongolia
la Belgique	Belgium	la Namibie	Namibia
la Biélorussie	Belarus	la Norvège	Norway
la Bolivie	Bolivia	la Pologne	Poland
la Bulgarie	Bulgaria	la Roumanie	Romania
la Chine	China	la Russie	Russia
la Côte d'Ivoire	Ivory Coast	la Suède	Sweden
la Croatie	Croatia	la Syrie	Syria
l'Égypte	Egypt	la Tanzanie	Tanzania
l'Espagne	Spain	la Thaïlande	Thailand
l'Éthiopie	Ethiopia	la Tunisie	Tunisia
la Finlande	Finland	la Turquie	Turkey
la France	France	la Sierra Leone	Sierra Leone
la Grèce	Greece	l'Ukraine	Ukraine
la Guyane	Guyana	la Zambie	Zambia

Ils vont assister à un mariage **en** Inde.

They are going to attend a wedding in India.

Here are a few exceptions. Although they end in **e**, these countries are in fact masculine:

le Cachemire   *Kashmir*
le Cambodge   *Cambodia*
le Mexique   *Mexico*

Elle va visiter des galeries d'art **au** Mexique.

She is going to visit art galleries in Mexico.

Now let's take a deeper look at some masculine countries:

l'Afghanistan	*Afghanistan*	le Kenya	*Kenya*
le Bangladesh	*Bangladesh*	le Laos	*Laos*
le Bénin	*Benin*	le Liban	*Lebanon*
le Bhoutan	*Bhutan*	le Maroc	*Morocco*
le Brésil	*Brazil*	le Mali	*Mali*
le Canada	*Canada*	le Nigéria	*Nigeria*
le Chili	*Chile*	le Pakistan	*Pakistan*
le Congo	*Congo*	le Pérou	*Peru*
le Danemark	*Denmark*	le Portugal	*Portugal*
l'Équateur	*Ecuador*	le Rwanda	*Rwanda*
le Gabon	*Gabon*	le Sénégal	*Senegal*
l'Iran	*Iran*	le Togo	*Togo*
l'Irak	*Iraq*	le Venezuela	*Venezuela*
le Japon	*Japan*	le Viêt Nam	*Vietnam*

Elle va tourner son prochain film **au** Maroc.

She is going to shoot her next film in Morocco.

Furthermore, some countries, like **Israël,** do not use articles. For most, they are islands that are political entities, either countries or states like **Cuba**, **Haïti**, **Hawaï**, **Chypre**, **Taiwan**, etc.

Leur groupe va participer à un festival de danse **à** Cuba.	*Their band is going to be part of a dance festival in Cuba.*
Nous randonnons autour des volcans **à** Hawaï.	*We hike around volcanoes in Hawaii.*

French Regions and Departments

Let's look at the 18 administrative regions that Ashley mentions in the dialogue below. The first 13 are located on the European continent, while the last 5 are located overseas.

la région Auvergne-Rhône-Alpes
la région Bourgogne-Franche-Comté
la Bretagne
le Centre-Val de Loire
la Corse
le Grand Est
les Hauts-de-France
l'Île-de-France
la Normandie
la Nouvelle-Aquitaine
l'Occitanie
le Pays de la Loire
la région Provence-Alpes-Côte d'Azur

la Guadeloupe
la Martinique
la Guyane
La Réunion
Mayotte

In addition to administrative regions, there are entities called **départements**, whose names are often denoted by those of rivers and mountains.

Here are some departments that take the masculine form:

Le Cher
Le Jura
Le Var

And here are some departments that take the feminine form:

La Charente-Maritime
La Loire
La Vendée

Finally, here are departments that take the plural form:

Les Alpes-Maritimes
Les Bouches-du-Rhône
Les Hauts-de-Seine

U.S. States

In French, the names of most states do not change, except for a few whose spelling is modified. Here are some examples of feminine states:

la Californie	California
la Floride	Florida
la Louisiane	Louisiana
la Virginie	Virginia
la Caroline du Sud	South Carolina
la Géorgie	Georgia
la Pennsylvanie	Pennsylvania

Nous allons **en** Californie en juin.   *We are going to California in June.*

Il cherche un emploi **en** Pennsylvanie.   *He is looking for a job in Pennsylvania.*

And here are some examples of masculine states:

le Colorado	Colorado
le New Hampshire	New Hampshire
le Texas	Texas
le Kansas	Kansas
le Nouveau-Mexique	New Mexico
le Vermont	Vermont
le Maine	Maine
le Wyoming	Wyoming
le Michigan	Michigan
le Montana	Montana

Ma correspondante habite **au** Nouveau-Mexique.	*My penpal lives in New Mexico.*
Une partie du parc national Glacier est **au** Montana.	*One part of Glacier National Park is in Montana.*

Prepositions with Geographic Names

Now that we've seen the names of countries, regions, departments, and states, let's learn their respective prepositions. And depending on the context, geographic names will use different prepositions.

Cities

With cities, two main prepositions are used, **à** and **de**. When describing being *in* a city, use **à**.

Mélanie habite **à** Buenos Aires.	*Mélanie lives in Buenos Aires.*
Nous assistons au festival de musique **à** La Havane.	*We are attending the music festival in Havana.*

And when describing being *from* or *of* a city, use the preposition **de**.

Mélanie revient **de** Buenos Aires.	*Mélanie is coming back from Buenos Aires.*
Ils sont originaires **de** La Havane.	*They are from Havana.*

Countries

Similarly, we can refer to countries both by being *in* a country and being *from* or *of* a country. When describing being *in* or going *to* a country, there are four main prepositions.

preposition	condition
au	masculine singular
en	masculine singular and in front of vowel or mute **h**
en	feminine singular
aux	plural

Je travaille **au** Canada.	*I work in Canada.*
Il habite **en** Iran.	*He lives in Iran.*
Elle vit **en** Grèce.	*She lives in Greece.*
Ils sont installés **aux** États-Unis.	*They settled in the United States.*

And when describing being *from* or *of* a country, there are four main prepositions. *From* is expressed by **de (d')** for continents, feminine countries, provinces, regions, and states. For masculine and plural entities, the definite article is retained (**du**, **des**).

preposition	condition
de	feminine singular
du	masculine singular
d'	singular and in front of vowel or mute **h**
des	plural

Il est originaire **du** Texas.	*He is originally from Texas.*
Je suis rentré **de** Finlande hier.	*I came back from Finland yesterday.*
À quelle heure arrive le vol **de** Guyane?	*What time is the flight from Guyana arriving?*
Elle vient **de** Thaïlande.	*She is from Thailand.*

BTW

*When coming back from a state, the same rule applies as with countries: **de** if the place you are coming from is feminine; **du**, masculine; **des**, plural—**Je reviens de Californie; elle est originaire d'Arizona; il vient du Texas; ça provient du Montana.***

Provinces and Departments

With French provinces and departments, the preposition may vary. In front of feminine nouns or masculine nouns starting with a vowel, **en** is used. However, in front of the masculine nouns, **dans le** often replaces **au**. When in doubt, check the official local newspapers or a reliable dictionary. Be careful with material posted online!

Il y a des centaines de kilomètres de plage **en** Charente Maritime.	*There are hundreds of kilometers of beach in Charente Maritime.*
Ils vivent **dans le** Lubéron et travaillent **dans le** Lot.	*They live in the Lubéron and work in the Lot.*
On va assister à un mariage **en** Indre-et-Loire.	*We are going to attend a wedding in Indre-et-Loire.*
Marie a une ferme **dans les** Cévennes.	*Marie has a farm in the Cévennes.*
Nous allons voyager **en** Nouvelle-Aquitaine.	*We are going to travel around Nouvelle-Aquitaine.*
Ils passent l'été **en** Occitanie.	*They spend the summer in Occitanie.*

U.S. States

Finally, with state names, **en** is used in front of feminine states or states starting with a vowel. For masculine states, the pattern is less strict, and you may hear **au**, **dans le**, or **dans l'État de**, depending on the state. For states starting with a vowel, the preposition **en** is often used: elle habite **en** Arizona, **en** Arkansas, **en** Alaska, **en** Indiana, although you'll hear **dans l'**Ohio, **dans l'**Utah for a smoother sound with less vowels. When not sure, you can always say **dans l'État d'**Illinois, **dans l'État d'**Arkansas.

Elle fait du surf **en** Californie du Sud.	*She surfs in Southern California.*
Nous allons tourner un film **au** Colorado.	*We are going to shoot a film in Colorado.*

It is important to be precise when referring to regions that have repeated names. For instance, you should say **l'État de New York** when referring to New York State, and **New York** when referring to New York City. Similarly, you should say **l'État de Washington** when referring to Washington State, and **Washington** when referring to Washington, D.C.

So let's recap. As you will see in the dialogue below, Florent is teasing Ashley about the gender of the nouns in French. He tells her that some nouns like **après-midi** can take on both masculine and feminine forms. You might also run into **un oasis** or **une oasis** and **un parka** or **une parka**.

And remember that for some nouns, changing the gender changes their meaning. They are homographic homonyms. Had Ashley known this, she might have prevented the confusion caused by *le* champagne and *la* Champagne!

Here are a few examples of these homonyms whose meaning depends on gender:

masculine		feminine	
le champagne	*champagne*	la Champagne	*Champagne region*
le crêpe	*crepe/fabric*	la crêpe	*pancake/crêpe*

le critique	*critic*	la critique	*review/criticism*
le légume	*vegetable*	la grosse légume	*big shot/big wig*
le livre	*book*	la livre	*pound/pound sterling*
le mode	*mode/way*	la mode	*fashion*
le poste	*job/position*	la poste	*post office*

Try to memorize some of them as you go along, using them in full sentences to keep out of trouble. Maybe you'll test your friends and be able to show off just a little.

DIALOGUE *18 et 101*
18 and 101

Florent is with Ashley, one of his American friends who is having trouble remembering the names of the 18 regions and 101 departments of France and their genders.

ASHLEY: Auvergne-Rhône-Alpes, Bourgogne-Franche-Comté, Bretagne, Centre-Val de Loire, Corse, Grand Est, Hauts-de-France, Île-de-France, Normandie, Nouvelle-Aquitaine, Occitanie, Pays de la Loire, Provence-Alpes-Côte d'Azur.

FLORENT: Qu'est-ce que tu fais?	*What are you doing?*
ASHLEY: Chut! Guadeloupe, Martinique, Guyane, La Réunion, Mayotte.	*Shh! Guadeloupe, Martinique, Guyane, La Réunion, Mayotte.*
FLORENT: Mais tu délires!	*But you're out of your mind!*
ASHLEY: Non, j'apprends les nouvelles régions françaises!	*No, I'm learning the new French regions!*
FLORENT: Ça, c'est un sujet très controversé!	*That's a very controversial topic!*

ASHLEY: Oui, je sais, le Champagne n'est pas content.

Yeah, I know, champagne is not happy.

FLORENT: (rires) Ashley! Ce n'est pas **le** Champagne, mais **la** Champagne!

*(laughter) Ashley! It's not **le** Champagne, but **la** Champagne!*

ASHLEY: C'est un nom féminin?

Is it a feminine noun?

FLORENT: Féminin et masculin! On boit **le** champagne et on visite **la** Champagne.

*Feminine and masculine! One drinks **le** champagne and one visits **la** Champagne.*

ASHLEY: C'est vrai que la région Champagne-Ardenne a été obligée de fusionner avec l'Alsace et la Lorraine?

Is it true that the region Champagne-Ardenne was forced to merge with Alsace and Lorraine?

FLORENT: Oui, c'est la même chose pour la région Languedoc-Rousillon-Midi-Pyrénées qui est aujourd'hui l'Occitanie.

Yes, it is the same thing for the Languedoc-Rousillon-Midi-Pyrénées region, which today is called Occitanie.

ASHLEY: C'est bizarre...

That's weird...

FLORENT: C'est une question à la fois politique et économique.

It's both a political and economic question.

ASHLEY: Et comment expliques-tu **la** Manche, **la** manche et **le** manche?

*And how do you explain **la** Manche, **la** manche, and **le** manche?*

BTW

*Ashley is referring to a kind of homonym that has the same spelling, the same pronunciation, sometimes a different gender, but definitely a different meaning: **la Manche** (the Channel), **la manche** (sleeve), and **le manche** (handle of a tool). Another example: **le livre** (book), **la livre** (pound).*

FLORENT: Quand tu apprends un mot, tu apprends son genre: **le** département, **la** région, **le** livre, **la** maison. Les terminaisons des mots permettent la plupart du temps d'identifier le genre.

*When you learn a word, you learn its gender: **le** département, **la** région, **le** livre, **la** maison. Most of the time, the word endings allow you to identify the gender.*

ASHLEY: Quel travail!

So much work!

FLORENT: N'oublie pas qu'il y a 101 départements, treize régions métropolitaines et cinq régions ultramarines!

Don't forget that there are 101 departments, 13 mainland regions, and 5 overseas regions.

ASHLEY: Bon, je vais étudier le genre des noms cet après-midi. « Après-midi »? Masculin ou féminin?

Ok, I'm going to study the genders of nouns this afternoon. "Après-midi"? Masculine or feminine?

FLORENT: Les deux! « Après-midi » est un nom épicène. Il est masculin et féminin. Un après-midi ou une après-midi. À toi de choisir.

Both! "Après-midi" is a nom épicène. *It is masculine and feminine.* Un après-midi *or* une après-midi. *It's up to you to choose.*

ASHLEY: **Le** Finistère, **la** Provence, **les** Côtes-d'Armor! **Le** Calvados, **la** Savoie, **les** Pyrénées-Orientales! Masculin, féminin, pluriel...

***Le** Finistère, **la** Provence, **les** Côtes-d'Armor! **Le** Calvados, **la** Savoie, **les** Pyrénées-Orientales! Masculine, feminine, plural...*

BTW

*Notice how, most of the time, French nouns are written in lowercase. While in English we write Monday and December by capitalizing the first letter, as we saw in Chapter 3, **lundi** and **décembre** are written in lowercase. On the other hand, in French, while geographic names like **la Champagne** and **le Calvados** are capitalized, their respective regional products **le champagne** and **le calvados** take lowercase form.*

EXERCISES

EXERCISE 4.1

Put the following sentences in the negative form.

1. Nous avons une maison en France.
2. Elle aime le silence à la campagne.
3. Il a une villa sur la Côte d'Azur.
4. Nous achetons des croissants.
5. J'ai un compte en banque en France.
6. Vous connaissez la route pour aller à Cahors.
7. Nous avons un chien.
8. J'ai des amis à Paris.
9. Il lit le journal chaque matin.
10. J'achète des journaux en vacances.

EXERCISE 4.2

*Indicate the gender by adding the definite article, **le** or **la**.*

1. _____ fréquence
2. _____ culture
3. _____ ventilateur
4. _____ bouteille
5. _____ fromage
11. _____ petit déjeuner
12. _____ fauteuil
13. _____ classement
14. _____ mouton
15. _____ liberté

6. _____ courage

7. _____ couteau

8. _____ saveur

9. _____ vedette

10. _____ travail

16. _____ plage

17. _____ peur

18. _____ chapeau

19. _____ prénom

20. _____ poésie

EXERCISE 4.3

Indicate the gender of these nouns by adding the indefinite article, **un** *or* **une.**

1. _____ numéro

2. _____ couleur

3. _____ musée

4. _____ idée

5. _____ feuille

6. _____ ordinateur

7. _____ page

8. _____ pâtisserie

9. _____ travail

10. _____ animal

11. _____ chanson

12. _____ parapluie

13. _____ kayak

14. _____ fourchette

15. _____ bateau

16. _____ forêt

17. _____ lycée

18. _____ boulanger

19. _____ peinture

20. _____ motel

EXERCISE 4.4

Match the items in the two columns and add the corresponding prepositions.

1. La tour Eiffel est   a. _____ Chine.

2. Le Machu Picchu est   b. _____ Inde.

3. Le Taj Mahal est   c. _____ États-Unis.

4. La Grande Muraille est   d. _____ Pérou.

5. L'Empire State Building est   e. _____ Paris.

EXERCISE 4.5

Fill in the blanks first with the appropriate definite article and then with the corresponding preposition.

1. Il aime _____ Japon. Il voyage _____ Japon.

2. Il aime _____ Danemark. Il voyage _____ Danemark.

3. Il aime _____ Thaïlande. Il voyage _____ Thaïlande.

4. Il aime _____ Brésil. Il voyage _____ Brésil.

5. Il aime _____ Inde. Il voyage _____ Inde.

6. Il aime _____ Suède. Il voyage _____ Suède.

7. Il aime _____ Sénégal. Il voyage _____ Sénégal.

8. Il aime _____ Hongrie. Il voyage _____ Hongrie.

9. Il aime _____ Mexique. Il voyage _____ Mexique.

10. Il aime _____ Angleterre. Il voyage _____ Angleterre.

EXERCISE 4.6

Following the model, build sentences with the words below.

Marie/aller/Japon/avril. <u>**Marie va au Japon en avril.**</u>

1. Jeanne/aller/Amazonie/février.

2. Carole/aller/Florence/mai.

3. Marc et Claude/aller/Rwanda/printemps.

4. Victor et moi/aller/Pérou/septembre.

5. Henri/aller/Roumanie/été.

6. Sylvain/aller/Chili/automne.

7. Nathalie/aller/Namibie/janvier.

8. Odile/aller/Tunisie/hiver.

9. Michel/aller/Laos/mars.

10. Carl/aller/Pays-Bas/juin.

EXERCISE 4.7

Fill in the blanks with the appropriate prepositions.

1. (la Normandie) Elle étudie _____ Normandie.

2. (la Haute-Savoie) Elle étudie _____ Haute-Savoie.

3. (le Colorado) Elle étudie _____ Colorado.

4. (la Dordogne) Elle étudie _____ Dordogne.

5. (le Texas) Elle étudie _____ Texas.

6. (la Corse) Elle étudie _____ Corse.

7. (la Louisiane) Elle étudie _____ Louisiane.

8. (l'Occitanie) Elle étudie _____ Occitanie.

9. (la Floride) Elle étudie _____ Floride.

10. (la Bretagne) Elle étudie _____ Bretagne.

EXERCISE 4.8

Translate the following sentences using **vous** *and the* **est-ce que** *form if necessary.*

1. Every year we go hiking in Canada.

2. Is he living in Brazil or in Argentina?

3. She is originally from Italy.

4. Are you going to visit the Picasso Museum?

5. Marc's high school is in Normandy.

EXERCISE 4.9

Let's end on a poetic note with a famous poem by Guillaume Apollinaire (1880–1918). Restore the missing masculine or feminine definite articles, **le, la, l',** *or* **les,** *with the help of the translation below.*

Le Pont Mirabeau

Sous _____ pont Mirabeau coule _____ Seine
Et nos amours
Faut-il qu'il m'en souvienne
_____ joie venait toujours après _____ peine
Vienne _____ nuit sonne l'heure
Les jours s'en vont je demeure

____ mains dans ____ mains restons face à face

Tandis que sous

____ pont de nos bras passe

Des éternels regards ____ onde si lasse

Vienne ____ nuit sonne ____ heure

____ jours s'en vont je demeure

____ amour s'en va comme cette eau courante

____'amour s'en va

Comme ____ vie est lente

Et comme ____ Espérance est violente

Vienne ____ nuit sonne ____ heure

____ jours s'en vont je demeure

Passent ____ jours et passent ____ semaines

Ni temps passé

Ni ____ amours reviennent

Sous ____ pont Mirabeau coule ____ Seine

Vienne____ nuit sonne ____ heure

____ jours s'en vont je demeure

Mirabeau Bridge

Under the Mirabeau bridge flows the Seine

And our loves

Must I remember them

Joy always followed pain

The night falls and the hours ring

The days go away I remain

Hand in hand let us stay face to face

While underneath the bridge

Of our arms passes

The water tired of the eternal looks

The night falls and the hours ring

The days go away I remain

Love goes away like this flowing water
Love goes away
Life is so slow
And hope is so violent
The night falls and the hours ring
The days go away I remain
Days pass by and weeks pass by
Neither past time
Nor past loves will return
Under the Mirabeau bridge flows the Seine
The night falls and the hours ring
The days go away I remain

LE COIN DES CRÉATEURS

À LA DÉCOUVERTE DU MONDE

Choose five countries and describe a site worth visiting, then add some historical or cultural details following the examples below. Review the vocabulary you have learned so far in the four chapters.

Je vais aller **à** Venise, **en** Italie, pour voir le pont des Soupirs (*Bridge of Sighs*). Le pont des Soupirs a inspiré un opéra, un film, et une chanson par Charles Aznavour « Que c'est triste Venise ».

En mars, nous allons **à** Kyoto, **au** Japon, pour admirer les cerisiers en fleurs. Nous aimons marcher dans les parcs, contempler la nature, et pique-niquer sous les arbres.

À votre tour! Rome, Angkor, le Grand Canyon, Grenade, etc.

NOTE CULTURELLE

REGIONS OF FRANCE

As you travel through France, you will learn that each part of the country has its own character and, as is the case in Corsica, its own separate language. France today is a republic that is divided into 18 regions, 13 located on the European continent and 5 overseas.

The 13 metropolitan regions are: Grand Est, Nouvelle-Aquitaine, Auvergne-Rhône-Alpes, Bourgogne-Franche-Comté, Brittany, Centre-Val de Loire, Île-de-France, Occitanie, Hauts-de-France, Normandy, Pays de la Loire, Provence-Alpes-Côte d'Azur, Corsica.

The legal definition of a region was adopted in 1982. At that time, there were 27 regions, but in 2016 a number of regions were combined, not always willingly, reducing the number to 18. The idea was to streamline and centralize certain administrative functions and to save money. The combining of some regions was not always welcomed and in some cases was met with protest and accusations of "forced marriage." This was particularly true in regions when a name change was involved. Of the 13 metropolitan regions, only 6 retained their historic name.

The five overseas regions have similar powers to those of the 13 metropolitan regions. As integral parts of the French Republic, they are represented in the National Assembly, Senate and Economic and Social Council, elect a Member of the European Parliament (MEP), and use the euro as their currency.

The five overseas regions are: French Guiana, Guadeloupe, Martinique, Mayotte, Réunion.

There are also five overseas communities. These have a semiautonomous status and are not to be confused with the overseas regions. The five overseas communities are: Saint-Pierre and Miquelon, Wallis and Futuna, French Polynesia, Saint Barthélemy, Saint Martin.

What are the responsibilities of the regions? They do not have any legislative authority, so they cannot enact their own laws. Their most important assignment is building and managing the country's high schools.

They also make spending decisions on regional infrastructure, transport, and environmental planning. They promote regional tourism and oversee natural parks and economic development. They are able to levy their own taxes and receive a portion of this revenue back from the central government. Each region is further broken down into **départements**, the next level down on the ladder of administrative structure.

While it may seem complicated, these regions and communities are a reflection of France's history, both the fact that it was not always a single, unified country and that it was once a major colonial power with a presence outside of continental France.

Regions of Metropolitan France

Source: BonjourLaFrance.com

Asking Questions and Talking About the Immediate Past

MUST ⚡ KNOW

 Où is *where* and **ou** is *or*. Accent marks change everything!

 In most cases, negations need **ne**.

 If you're surprised, say **tiens tiens**.

 Quatre-vingt-dix is **quatre** × **vingt** + **dix**.

Your French journey would be not nearly as much fun if you couldn't ask precise questions. Whether you're at the market, at a friend's house, or in a restaurant, you'll want to have a variety of question words at your disposal. The following list is a comprehensive overview of the most commonly used question words, known as *interrogatives*, and they will help you jump into any conversation.

This chapter is also a treasure trove of verbs, verbs that will help you answer questions, as well as ask them. **Allons-y!**

Question Words

Like in English, questions words are placed at the start of a question. Here are some question words that will come in handy:

comment	*how*
combien	*how much/many*
pourquoi	*why*
pour quelle raison	*for what reason*
de quelle manière	*in what manner*
de quelle façon	*in what way*
dans quelle mesure	*to what extent*
où	*where*
quand	*when*
à quelle heure	*at what time*
que	*what*
qui	*who*

Comment allez-vous?	*How are you?*
Comment faire une mousse au chocolat?	*How is chocolate mousse made?*
Combien coûte un billet de train Paris–Marseille?	*How much is a train ticket from Paris to Marseille?*
Combien coûtent ces baskets?	*How much do these sneakers cost?*

Pourquoi aimez-vous voyager en Italie?	*Why do you like to travel to Italy?*
Pour quelle raison va-t-il à Dubaï en septembre?	*For what reason does he go to Dubai in September?*
Où habitez-vous?	*Where do you live?*
D'où viens-tu?	*Where are you from?*
Où se trouve la patinoire?	*Where is the skating rink located?*
Quand part-elle en vacances?	*When is she leaving for vacation?*
À quelle heure commence le film?	*At what time does the film start?*
Que mange-t-on ce soir?	*What are we eating tonight?*
Qui est la directrice de cette entreprise?	*Who is the head of this company?*

The -*ir* Verbs

The **-ir** verbs use two different conjugation patterns. One type of **-ir** verb drops the **-ir** of the infinitive; adds an **-iss** to the **nous**, **vous**, **ils**, and **elles** forms; and then adds the appropriate ending.

choisir   *to choose*

je choisis	*I choose*	nous choisissons	*we choose*
tu choisis	*you choose*	vous choisissez	*you choose*
il/elle/on choisit	*he/she/one chooses*	ils/elles choisissent	*they choose*

Many other verbs follow the same type of conjugation; so try your best to memorize them.

abolir	*to abolish*	→ nous abolissons	*we abolish*
accomplir	*to accomplish*	→ nous accomplissons	*we accomplish*
adoucir	*to soften*	→ nous adoucissons	*we soften*
agir	*to act*	→ nous agissons	*we act*
agrandir	*to enlarge*	→ nous agrandissons	*we enlarge*
applaudir	*to applaud*	→ nous applaudissons	*we applaud*
bâtir	*to build*	→ nous bâtissons	*we build*
bénir	*to bless*	→ nous bénissons	*we bless*

démolir	*to demolish*	› nous démolissons	*we demolish*
éclaircir	*to lighten*	→ nous éclaircissons	*we lighten*
épanouir (s')	*to bloom*	→ nous nous épanouissons	*we bloom*
établir	*to establish*	→ nous établissons	*we establish*
évanouir (s')	*to faint*	→ nous nous évanouissons	*we faint*
finir	*to finish*	→ nous finissons	*we finish*
grandir	*to grow up*	→ nous grandissons	*we grow up*
guérir	*to heal*	→ nous guérissons	*we heal*
investir	*to invest*	→ nous investissons	*we invest*
maigrir	*to lose weight*	→ nous maigrissons	*we lose weight*
mincir	*to slim down*	→ nous mincissons	*we slim down*
obéir	*to obey*	→ nous obéissons	*we obey*
pâlir	*to turn pale*	→ nous pâlissons	*we turn pale*
rafraîchir	*to refresh*	→ nous rafraîchissons	*we refresh*
ralentir	*to slow down*	→ nous ralentissons	*we slow down*
remplir	*to fill*	→ nous remplissons	*we fill*
réussir	*to succeed*	→ nous réussissons	*we succeed*
rougir	*to blush*	→ nous rougissons	*we blush*
saisir	*to seize*	→ nous saisissons	*we seize*
vieillir	*to grow old*	→ nous vieillissons	*we grow old*

Nous choisissons un gâteau.	*We choose a cake.*
Je vais agrandir cette photo.	*I am going to enlarge this picture.*
Nous ralentissons au carrefour.	*We slow down at the intersection.*
Les fleurs s'épanouissent dans le jardin.	*Flowers blossom in the garden.*
Ils saisissent l'occasion.	*They seize the opportunity.*
La musique adoucit les mœurs.	*Music soothes the soul.*

The second type of **-ir** verb drops the **-ir** of the infinitive then adds the appropriate ending. Let's take a look at an example:

sortir   *to go out*

je sors	*I go out*	nous sortons	*we go out*
tu sors	*you go out*	vous sortez	*you go out*
il/elle/on sort	*he/she/one goes out*	ils/elles sortent	*they go out*

Some other common irregular **-ir** verbs are:

courir	*to run*	→ je cours	*I run*	→ nous courons	*we run*
dormir	*to sleep*	→ je dors	*I sleep*	→ nous dormons	*we sleep*
fuir	*to flee*	→ je fuis	*I flee*	→ nous fuyons	*we flee*
mentir	*to lie*	→ je mens	*I lie*	→ nous mentons	*we lie*
partir	*to leave*	→ je pars	*I leave*	→ nous partons	*we leave*
sentir	*to feel/ to smell*	→ je sens	*I feel/I smell*	→ nous sentons	*we feel/ we smell*
servir	*to serve*	→ je sers	*I serve*	→ nous servons	*we serve*

Qu'est-ce qu'on sert dans La boîte à Meuh?	*What do they serve in La boîte à Meuh?*
Est-ce que tu dors bien dans cette chambre?	*Do you sleep well in this room?*
Nous fuyons les conflits.	*We are fleeing from conflicts.*
Dominique ment comme il respire.	*Dominique lies through his teeth.*
Sentez-vous un courant d'air?	*Do you feel a draft?*
Nous courons le risque de perdre le match.	*We are running the risk of losing the game.*

Verbs that End in *-llir, -frir,* or *-vrir*

Most verbs that end in **-llir** and all that end in **-frir** or **-vrir** are conjugated like regular **-er** verbs.

offrir   *to offer*

j'offre	*I offer*	nous offrons	*we offer*
tu offres	*you offer*	vous offrez	*you offer*
il/elle/on offre	*he/she/one offers*	ils/elles offrent	*they offer*

Here are some similar common verbs:

bouillir	*to boil*	→ je bous	*I boil*	→ nous bouillons	*we boil*
couvrir	*to cover*	→ je couvre	*I cover*	→ nous couvrons	*we cover*
cueillir	*to pick*	→ je cueille	*I pick*	→ nous cueillons	*we pick*
offrir	*to offer*	→ j'offre	*I offer*	→ nous offrons	*we offer*
ouvrir	*to open*	→ j'ouvre	*I open*	→ nous ouvrons	*we open*
souffrir	*to suffer*	→ je souffre	*I suffer*	→ nous souffrons	*we suffer*

Le musée ouvre à 10h.	*The museum opens at 10 am.*
Fais bouillir de l'eau!	*Boil some water!*
Il souffre d'une maladie rare.	*He suffers from a rare disease.*
Je bous de rage.	*I am boiling with rage.*
Qui est-ce qui va faire bouillir la marmite?	*Who is going to put food on the table?*
Ils accueillent des étudiants étrangers chez eux.	*They welcome foreign students in their home.*

The Verbs *Tenir* and *Venir*

Tenir and **venir** are not only incredibly useful by themselves, but they are the building blocks of countless verbs and idiomatic expressions.

The Verb *Tenir*

Tenir (*to hold*) is an irregular **-ir** verb. It is used in many idiomatic expressions and can be followed by **à** or **de**. Additionally, it has several key derivatives, like **soutenir** (*to support*), **maintenir** (*to maintain*), **entretenir** (*to upkeep*), and **contenir** (*to to hold, to contain*).

je tiens	*I hold*	nous tenons	*we hold*
tu tiens	*you hold*	vous tenez	*you hold*
il/elle/on tient	*he/she/one holds*	ils/elles tiennent	*they hold*

Ils ne tiennent jamais leurs promesses.	*They never keep their promises.*
Elle tient une épicerie près de Narbonne.	*She runs a small grocery store near Narbonne.*
Ça ne va pas tenir dans le coffre.	*It is not going to fit in the car.*
Ils se tiennent par la main.	*They are holding hands.*
Vous devez tenir compte de notre situation.	*You must take our situation into account.*
Cette tasse de thé noir va vous tenir éveillé.	*This cup of black tea is going to keep you awake.*
Tenez-moi au courant!	*Keep me posted!*
Tiens-toi droit.	*Sit up/stand up straight.*
Cette histoire ne tient pas debout.	*This story does not make any sense.*

■ Tenir à

Elle tient à ce collier.	*She is attached to this necklace.*
Il tient à ses amis de lycée.	*He is attached to his high school friends.*
Je tiens à vous parler immédiatement.	*I need to talk to you immediately.*
Je tiens à m'excuser.	*I really want to apologize.*
Elle tient à faire votre connaissance.	*She is eager to meet you.*

■ Tenir de

Le bébé tient de sa mère.	*The baby takes after his/her mother.*
De qui tient-elle?	*Whom does she take after?*
Tiens, tiens, c'est étrange…	*Well, well, this is strange…*
Tiens, prends ce plan de Paris pour ton voyage.	*Here, take this map of Paris for your trip.*

The Verb *Venir*

The verb **venir** (*to come*) is another irregular **-ir** verb. And it has several key derivatives, like **devenir** (*to become*), **se souvenir** (*to remember*), **intervenir** (*to intervene*), **prévenir** (*to inform, to prevent*), and **provenir** (*to originate, to derive*).

je viens	*I come*	nous venons	*we come*
tu viens	*you come*	vous venez	*you come*
il/elle/on vient	*he/she/one comes*	ils/elles viennent	*they come*

Elle vient du Québec et lui, il vient de Guinée.	*She comes from Quebec and he comes from Guinea.*
Cela devient de plus en plus facile.	*It's getting easier and easier.*
Qu'est-ce que tu deviens?	*What have you been up to?*
À quelle heure revenez-vous?	*At what time are you coming back?*
Savez-vous d'où provient ce bijou?	*Do you know where this piece of jewelry comes from?*

The Immediate Past Tense

Similar in structure to the **futur immédiat**, the **passé immédiate** uses an infinitive after the conjugated form of **venir**. With **venir**, however, you need the preposition **de** to link the conjugated verb with the infinitive. And it expresses an action that has just taken place.

> **BTW**
>
> Although **venir** takes the present tense in French, it still refers to a past event.

Je viens de l'appeler.	*I just called him.*
Nous venons d'acheter un nouvel ordinateur.	*We just bought a new computer.*
Vous venez de vous inscrire à un cours de Pilates.	*You just signed up for a Pilates class.*
Tu viens de manger un autre yaourt glacé!	*You just ate another frozen yogurt!*

Negation Words

When you don't agree with somebody or want to contest the veracity of one's claim, you'll use negation words.

ne... pas

Je regarde cette nouvelle série.	*I am watching this new series.*
Je **ne** regarde **pas** cette nouvelle série.	*I am not watching this new series.*

If the **ne** precedes a verb starting with a vowel sound or a mute **h**, **ne** becomes **n'**.

J'aime les yaourts glacés.	*I like frozen yogurts.*
Je n'aime pas les yaourts glacés.	*I do not like frozen yogurts.*
Il habite à Rennes.	*He lives in Rennes.*
Il n'habite pas à Rennes	*He does not live in Rennes.*

Additional Negation Words

Negations can be used in many other ways. Let's take a look at the possibilities:

ne... pas	*not*
ne... rien	*nothing*
ne... jamais	*never*
ne... plus	*no longer*
ne... aucun	*not a single one*
ne... guère	*hardly*
ne... nulle part	*nowhere*
ne... personne	*nobody*
ne... point	*not (literary)*

Ils ne sortent jamais le lundi soir.	*They never go out on Monday evenings.*
Je ne joue plus aux échecs.	*I no longer play chess.*
Il n'a jamais fait de la voile.	*He has never gone sailing.*
Ce n'est guère le cas.	*It is hardly the case.*

Je ne l'ai trouvé nulle part.	*I could not find it/him anywhere.*
Elle ne connaît personne qui sait danser la zumba.	*She does not know anyone who can dance Zumba.*

The negation **ni… ni** (*neither…nor*) precedes each of the nouns it negates. When the definite articles **le**, **la**, and **les** are used, they remain in the sentence.

Il aime le jardinage et la pêche.	*He likes gardening and fishing.*
Il n'aime ni le jardinage ni la pêche.	*He likes neither gardening nor fishing.*

Elle aime le foot et les jeux vidéo.	*She likes football and video games.*
Elle n'aime ni le foot ni les jeux vidéo.	*She likes neither football nor video games.*

When the indefinite article is used in the original sentence, it gets dropped in the negative form.

Elle mange des mangues et des kiwis.	*She eats mangoes and kiwis.*
Elle ne mange ni mangues ni kiwis.	*She eats neither mangoes nor kiwis.*

Il achète des skis et un casque.	*He buys skis and a helmet.*
Il n'achète ni skis ni casque.	*He buys neither skis nor a helmet.*

Demonstrative Adjectives

Sometimes you need to be very specific in identifying items, and to do so, you have to use demonstrative adjectives (*this, that, these, those*). Like all adjectives in French, they agree in gender and number with the noun they modify.

masculine singular

ce vélo	*this bicycle*
cet avion	*this plane*
cet hôpital	*this hospital*

Note that the singular demonstrative adjective **ce** adds a **t** when a vowel or an **h** sound follows.

feminine singular

cette patinoire	*this skating rink*
cette école	*this school*

masculine and feminine plural

ces pays	*these countries*
ces chaussures	*these shoes*
ces hôtels	*these hotels*

To make a distinction between two elements, **-ci** and **–là** are added to the demonstrative adjectives.

Préférez-vous cette chemise-**ci** ou cette chemise-**là**?	*Do you prefer this shirt or that shirt?*
Quelle est la différence entre cet iPad-**ci** et cet iPad-**là**?	*What's the difference between this or that iPad?*

The Cardinal Numbers 60 to 100

We have learned zero to sixty and are now ready to keep counting. Cardinal numbers are the numbers used for counting and designating quantity.

soixante	*sixty*
soixante et un	*sixty-one*
soixante-deux	*sixty-two*
soixante-neuf	*sixty-nine*
soixante-dix	*seventy*

From seventy to seventy-nine, you add the teen numbers:

soixante et onze	*seventy-one*
soixante-douze	*seventy-two*
soixante-treize	*seventy-three*
soixante-quatorze	*seventy-four*
soixante-quinze	*seventy-five*

soixante-seize	*seventy-six*
soixante-dix-sept	*seventy-seven*
soixante-dix-huit	*seventy-eight*
soixante-dix-neuf	*seventy-nine*

Eighty is really four times twenty. So from eighty to eighty-nine, you'll keep adding to **quatre-vingts**. Note that **quatre-vingts** has an **s**. But once you attach another number to **quatre-vingts**, the **s** will drop.

quatre-vingts	*eighty*
quatre-vingt-un	*eighty-one*
quatre-vingt-deux	*eighty-two*
quatre-vingt-huit	*eighty-eight*
quatre-vingt-neuf	*eighty-nine*
quatre-vingt-dix	*ninety*
quatre-vingt-onze	*ninety-one*
quatre-vingt-douze	*ninety-two*
quatre-vingt-treize	*ninety-three*
quatre-vingt-dix-huit	*ninety-eight*
quatre-vingt-dix-neuf	*ninety-nine*
cent	*hundred*

Now we have reached one hundred! Let's keep going.

cent	*hundred*
cent un	*hundred and one*
cent deux	*hundred and two*
cent trois	*hundred and three*

Add an **s** to **cent** for numbers above one hundred except when **cent** is followed by another number.

deux cents	*two hundred*
trois cents	*three hundred*
neuf cents	*nine hundred*
deux cent douze	*two hundred and twelve*
quatre cent vingt	*four hundred and twenty*

mille	thousand
deux mille	two thousand
dix mille	ten thousand

Never add an **s** to **mille**.

un million	a million
un milliard	a billion

 DIALOGUE *Quel est votre passe-temps favori?*
What's your favorite hobby?

Benoît, Alexandra, and Quentin meet in Nantes at La boîte à Meuh, a trendy frozen yogurt establishment renowned for its organic milk from Brittany. They discuss their hobbies and try to come up with a plan for the weekend.

 IRL Similar to how the **Île de la Cité** in Paris is carved by the Seine, Nantes is beautifully shaped by the Loire. Often called **La Venise de l'Ouest**, Nantes is one of the most desirable places to live—especially for cookie lovers; it is renowned for its **Petits LU**, a delicious butter cookie with the line « LU PETIT-BEURRE NANTES » written on top.

BENOÎT: Je te retrouve avec Alexandra à La boîte à Meuh à 17h?

I'll meet you with Alexandra at La boîte à Meuh at 5 o'clock?

QUENTIN: Toi et tes yaourts glacés!

You and your frozen yogurt!

BENOÎT: Ces yaourts glacés bio sont délicieux! OK, on se retrouve à la Meuh! Meuh, meuh...

This organic frozen yogurt is delicious! Ok, we'll meet at la Meuh! Moo, moo...

(Benoît imite le meuh des vaches.

Benoît imitates a cow's moo.)

BTW

*As we see with **meuh**, onomatopoeia commonly occurs in French. Here are some other fun examples of onomatopoeia: **miaou** (meow), **toc-toc-toc** (knock-knock), **plouf** (splash), **vroum** (vroom), **pouah** (ugh), **aïe** (ouch), **ouf** (whew), **youpee** (yippee), **ouah** (wow), **hourrah** (hooray).*

Une demi-heure plus tard...	*A half-hour later...*
BENOÎT: Mangue ou framboise?	*Mango or raspberry?*
ALEXANDRA: Mangue avec des graines de tournesol. Et toi, Quentin, quel parfum?	*Mango with some sunflower seeds. And what about you, Quentin, what flavor?*

 IRL The word **parfum** has two meanings, flavor and perfume. **Quel parfum préférez-vous?** (*What flavor would you like?*) **N'oublie pas de rapporter un flacon de parfum.** (*Don't forget to bring back a bottle of perfume.*)

QUENTIN: Non merci.	*No thanks.*
ALEXANDRA: Tu as tort. Ces yaourts sont faits avec du lait de Bretagne sans crème et sans colorant!	*You are mistaken. This yogurt is made out of milk from Brittany without cream and without coloring!*
QUENTIN: Je sais, mais je vais courir dans le jardin des Plantes avec Arnaud à 19h.	*I know, but I am going for a run in the jardin des Plantes with Arnaud at seven o'clock.*
ALEXANDRA: Et qu'est-ce que tu fais vendredi soir?	*And what are you doing Friday night?*
QUENTIN: Je vais peut-être aller au cinéma ou sortir avec mes copains de ping-pong. Et toi?	*I may be going to the movies or going out with my ping-pong buddies. What about you?*
ALEXANDRA: Je vais regarder la nouvelle saison de *Dix pour cent*. Et toi, Benoît?	*I am going to watch the new season of* Call My Agent. *What about you, Benoît?*
BENOÎT: Je vais regarder un documentaire.	*I am going to watch a documentary.*
ALEXANDRA: Quel est le sujet?	*What's the topic?*

BENOÎT: Celui sur l'intimidation à l'école et le harcèlement. Je dois écrire un essai sur le sujet.

The one on bullying and harassment at school. I have to write an essay about it.

ALEXANDRA: C'est bien que votre prof vous en parle.

That's good that your teacher is talking to you about it.

BENOÎT: Oui, c'est un phénomène si répandu.

Yes, it is a widespread phenomenon.

QUENTIN: C'est horrible. Heureusement que ce n'est plus un sujet tabou.

That's horrible. Fortunately, it's no longer a taboo subject.

BENOÎT: Bon, changeons de sujet! Qu'est-ce que vous faites samedi soir?

Ok, let's change the topic! What are you doing Saturday night?

ALEXANDRA: Rien.

Nothing.

QUENTIN: Euh...rien.

Uh...nothing.

BENOÎT: Cela vous tente d'aller à la patinoire demain soir? Antoine Garrel sera le DJ.

Do you feel like going to the skating rink tomorrow night? Antoine Garrel will be the DJ.

ALEXANDRA: Un DJ à la patinoire?

A DJ at the skating rink?

BENOÎT: Oui, c'est génial de patiner en écoutant des percussions! Et dans le noir!

Yes, it's awesome to skate while listening to the beats. And in the dark!

QUENTIN: Dans l'obscurité? Mais comment vous orientez-vous dans le noir?

In the dark? But how do you navigate in the dark?

BENOÎT: Avec des accessoires fluo! Ils sont compris dans le prix d'entrée: 4,75 euros.

With glow-in-the-dark accessories. They are included in the admission fee: 4.75 euros.

IRL While in English we use periods to indicate decimals, French uses commas. In the amount 4,75 €, for example, one would say **quatre euros soixante-quinze** but without saying **comma**.

QUENTIN: Ah, toi tu adores le froid! Les yaourts glacés et maintenant, le patinage!

Huh, you do love the cold! Frozen yogurt and now ice skating!

ALEXANDRA: Bientôt tu vas faire de la plongée sous-marine en Islande!

Soon you are going to go scuba diving in Iceland!

QUENTIN: Ou du ski de fond au pays des Vikings!

Or cross-country skiing in the land of the Vikings!

ALEXANDRA: Pas de patinoire dans le noir pour moi.

No ice rink in the dark for me.

QUENTIN: Ah, tu rimes...

Oh, you are rhyming.

ALEXANDRA: Samedi je vais rester à la maison et regarder un autre épisode de *Dix pour cent*!

Saturday I am going to stay home and watch another episode of Call My Agent!

QUENTIN: Pas de patinoire dans le noir pour moi non plus. Je vais jouer de la guitare puis je vais dormir.

No ice rink in the dark for me either. I am going to play the guitar, and then I am going to sleep.

BENOÎT: Trouble-fête! Trouble-fête!

Killjoy! Killjoy!

QUENTIN ET ALEXANDRA: Meuh... Meuh...

Moo... Moo...

EXERCISES

EXERCISE 5.1

*Translate the following questions using inversion and the **vous** form when necessary.*

1. How much does a frozen yogurt cost?

2. Where is the Nantes skating rink?

3. What are you doing on Saturday?

4. How are you doing?

5. Why do you want to skate in the dark?

6. When is she arriving in Nantes?

7. At what time are they going to the movies?

8. Who is playing the guitar?

9. Why are you listening to Benoît?

10. How much do the accessories cost?

EXERCISE 5.2

Conjugate the following verbs in the present tense.

1. Il (choisir) _____ un yaourt glacé à la pistache.

2. Je (agir) _____ avec prudence.

3. Ils (bâtir) _____ une grande maison.

4. Nous (finir) _____ notre essai.

5. Elle (agrandir) _____ sa boutique.

6. Nos enfants (grandir) _____ vite.

7. Vous (choisir) _____ un parfum de glace différent.

8. Nous (applaudir) _____ le DJ à la patinoire.

9. Je (réfléchir) _____ à nos projets pour le week-end.

10. Elles (réussir) _____ tout ce qu'elles entreprennent.

EXERCISE 5.3

Match the items in the two columns. Choose the most logical answer.

1. Ils n'agissent pas	a. le mystère.
2. Elle remplit	b. prudemment.
3. Je finis	c. de l'argent.
4. Il éclaircit	d. la bouteille.
5. Nous investissons	e. le roman.

EXERCISE 5.4

Conjugate the following verbs in the present tense.

1. Nous (sortir) _____ avec nos copains ce soir.

2. Qu'est-ce que je vous (servir) _____?

3. On (sentir) _____ un parfum délicat.

4. Nous (dormir) _____ la fenêtre ouverte.

5. À quelle heure (partir) _____ -vous?

6. Ils (mentir) _____ trop souvent.

7. Pourquoi est-ce que tu (courir) _____? Tu es pressé?

8. Ils (fuir) _____ leur pays en guerre.

9. Ils (servir) _____ un plateau de fromages.

10. Je (partir) _____ ce soir pour Genève.

EXERCISE 5.5

Match the items in the two columns. Choose the most logical answer.

1. Je cours   a. huit heures par nuit.

2. Il nous sert   b. en vacances demain.

3. Nous dormons   c. une bonne odeur.

4. Vous sentez   d. du café.

5. Ils partent   e. tous les matins dans le parc.

EXERCISE 5.6

Conjugate the following verbs in the present tense.

1. On (découvrir) _____ toujours de nouvelles étoiles dans le ciel.

2. En général, est-ce que tu (offrir) _____ des tournesols ou des orchidées?

3. Est-ce qu'ils (souffrir) _____ à cause de la pauvreté?

4. Qui (ouvrir) _____ le bal cette année?

5. Ils nous (accueillir) _____ toujours chaleureusement.

6. La nouvelle saison d'*Hippocrate* commence ce soir. Je (bouillir) _____ d'impatience!

7. Je (recueillir) _____ le maximum dc documents.

8. Quentin (découvrir) _____ un magasin de yaourt glacé tous les jours.

9. Vers quelle date est-ce que vous (cueillir) _____ vos mirabelles?

10. Les journalistes qui (couvrir) _____ l'ONU jouent un rôle important.

EXERCISE 5.7

Match the items in the two columns. Choose the most logical answer.

1. Elle ouvre   a. une nouvelle espèce de mammifère.

2. Vous découvrez   b. une e-carte-cadeau IKEA.

3. Je cueille   c. une mangue.

4. Tu bous   d. un compte en banque.

5. Il offre   e. de colère.

EXERCISE 5.8

Conjugate the following verbs in the present tense.

1. Nous (cueillir) _____ des champignons dans la forêt.

2. Je (ouvrir) _____ les fenêtres quand il fait chaud.

3. Vous (sortir) _____ ce soir?

4. Ils (démolir) _____ l'édifice en ruine.

5. Nous (grossir) _____ toujours un peu en vacances.

6. On (vieillir) _____ moins vite si on fait du sport.

7. À quelle heure (finir) _____ -ils ce soir?

8. Elles (mentir) _____ tout le temps!

9. Qu'est-ce que vous nous (servir) _____ ce soir?

10. Je (courir) _____ plus vite que Quentin.

EXERCISE 5.9

Conjugate the following verbs in the present tense.

1. Nous (tenir) _____ à notre vieille voiture.

2. Je (revenir) _____ dans un instant.

3. Ces mangues (venir) _____ du Burkina Faso.

4. Namous (tenir) _____ sa fille par la main.

5. Ils (tenir) _____ à leurs idées.

6. Ces informations (provenir) _____ d'une source sûre.

7. Est-ce que tu (tenir) _____ de ta mère ou de ton père?

8. Ce qu'elle (tenir) _____ dans sa main, c'est un vase égyptien.

9. D'où (venir) _____ -tu?

10. Ce journal nous (tenir) _____ au courant de l'actualité.

EXERCISE 5.10

*Rewrite the following sentences using the **passé immédiat**.*

1. Ils commencent un nouveau livre.

2. Je fais un jogging dans le bois de Boulogne.

3. Elle prononce un discours.

4. J'écoute le nouvel album de Mika.

5. Vous révélez la vérité.

6. Nous remplaçons les meubles de son bureau.

7. Il place un vase de fleurs sur la table.

8. Ils découvrent un morceau de météorite.

9. Nous achetons un sofa bleu nuit.

10. Elle chante une chanson.

EXERCISE 5.11

Translate the following sentences. When appropriate, use the **vous** *form.*

1. It is hot. I just opened the window.

2. We just picked some raspberries.

3. You just called Benoît.

4. I just read an article in *Le Monde*.

5. They just chose a restaurant for the wedding.

6. Cécile just bought a Navigo Pass.

7. She just filled out the form.

8. I just finished my essay.

9. He just served us a delicious pizza.

10. They just celebrated Quentin's birthday.

EXERCISE 5.12

*Rewrite the following sentences using **ne... pas**.*

1. Je vais au cinéma ce week-end.

2. Elle parle espagnol.

3. Il dort huit heures par nuit.

4. Vous jouez de la guitare.

5. Ils vont à la patinoire.

6. Tu cherches la rue des Carmes.

7. Nous écoutons le nouvel album.

8. Elle aime le froid.

9. Nous nageons dans la mer.

10. Nous restons à la maison le samedi soir.

EXERCISE 5.13

*Translate the following sentences using the **tu** form when necessary.*

1. He does not know anyone in Paris.

2. They do not do anything to help Jean-Claude.

3. I never eat French fries.

4. You no longer play ping-pong with your friends.

5. They sell neither ice cream nor frozen yogurt.

EXERCISE 5.14

Fill in the blanks with the correct demonstrative adjective.

1. Je n'aime pas _____ sport. C'est trop violent.

2. Est-ce que vous aimez _____ lunettes de soleil?

3. Ne prends pas_____ veste! Prends l'autre!

4. _____passe-temps est mon favori.

5. Je préfère réserver dans _____ hôtel.

6. Connais-tu _____ ancien album de Cœur de pirate?

7. Je ne vais pas acheter _____ ordinateur aujourd'hui.

8. J'ai du mal à écrire _____ essai.

9. Ils vont aimer _____ pâtisseries marocaines.

10. Connaissez-vous _____ deux écrivains?

EXERCISE 5.15

Write out the following numbers in word form.

1. 88

2. 76

3. 100

4. 101

5. 246

6. 80

7. 1000

8. 91

9. 99

10. 2010

LE COIN DES CRÉATEURS

LES AMOUREUX DU MODE INFINITIF

Create a story line using as many **-ir** verbs you learned in this chapter as possible, following the example below:

Travailler, c'est...
agrandir
démolir
bâtir
investir
courir
remplir
réussir
et vieillir...

Try to make up a similar list with:

Voyager, c'est...
Déménager, c'est...
Chanter, c'est...
Danser, c'est...
Écrire, c'est...

NOTE CULTURELLE

FRANCE AND SPORTS: IT'S NOT JUST *BOULES*

The game of *boules* used to be the stereotypical image of French sports. A relative of lawn bowling, it is typically played by two teams of one, two, or three people who take turns throwing or rolling a ball (*boule*) as close as possible to a target ball. The team that comes closest is the winner. While the game is still popular, it is far from defining French sports.

Much like the United States, France is a country that is crazy for sports, both professional and amateur. In team sports, it is a powerful presence in major world and European competitions. The French have a national team, known as *les Bleus* (for the blue color of their uniforms) for rugby, basketball, ice hockey, and, of course, soccer. France is the current holder of the World Cup in men's soccer, known as *le football* or *le foot*. Individual French athletes are also world famous, numbering among the medal winners in both the winter and summer Olympics and other international sporting events.

The French are also recreational athletes, frequenting gyms and jogging paths with great enthusiasm, and they engage in a wide variety of activities. France's varied topography includes extensive coastline and beaches on the Atlantic and Mediterranean as well as rugged mountains in the Alps and Pyrenees. As a result, sports like surfing and paragliding are as accessible as skiing and snowboarding.

For those who are more daring, extreme sports are also practiced, with two that are particularly notable for having been invented in France: parkour and flyboarding.

Parkour is a sport in which practitioners, known as *traceurs* in French, overcome barriers or obstacles, both artificial or natural, using agile movements, to get from one point to another as quickly and efficiently as possible. It includes running, free-running, climbing, swinging, vaulting, jumping, rolling, crawling, and other movements, all without the use of equipment. The word "parkour" comes from the term *parcours du combattant*, the French term for the type of obstacle course typically used in military training. Its origin as a sport dates back to the 1990s and to one man, David Belle, who is considered by many to be its originator. He developed it based on a system for building strength and endurance pioneered by his father, Raymond Belle, and used the media exposure he received as an actor and stuntman to help popularize it.

Parkour is an activity that can be practiced alone or with others and is usually carried out in urban spaces, though it can be done anywhere. It requires seeing one's environment in a new way and imagining the potential for navigating it by movement around, across, through, over, and under its features. Avid parkour practitioners can now be found running up walls in Paris, London, Boston, and New York, jumping off and around them, and vaulting their way over obstacles. In July and August every year, Parkour Generations, one of the sport's leading professional organizations, conducts a camp in the French Alps to teach and train parkour practitioners at the beginner and advanced levels. What better way to learn a truly French extreme sport than in the country where it was invented?

Flyboard is the commercial name for a type of hoverboard that uses hydrojet propulsion to drive the board into the air to perform a sport known as hydroflying or flyboarding. The rider stands on a board connected to a watercraft by a long hose. Water is forced through the hose under pressure to a pair of boots with jet nozzles underneath, which provide thrust and propel the rider into the air. Invented in France in 2012 by watercraft rider Franky Zapata, it became world famous when he flew over the parade on Bastille Day in July 2019. Less than one month later, on August 4, 2019, Zapata made history when he became the first person to cross the English Channel on a hoverboard powered by a backpack full of fuel. He did so in just over 20 minutes.

For those wishing to try the sport on a more modest scale, several flyboard rental companies have recently been established in the city of La Rochelle, in southwestern France. Boards can be rented by the hour. Instruction is, of course, a must. As it is still relatively new, it can be expensive, but with time and more practitioners, it will certainly become less so.

The Verb *Faire* and Using Prepositions

MUST KNOW

 Y a-t-il takes two hyphens.

 We use **faire** to talk about the weather.

 Faire + infinitive is the causative form.

 Put in the time to memorize each verb and its corresponding preposition.

 Changing a verb's preposition can change its meaning.

Faire is one of the most versatile verbs in the French language. With just one verb, you can talk about cooking, chores, hobbies, travel plans, and the weather. Almost as important as **faire**, prepositions are the glue that holds the language together. And if you want to pass as a native French speaker, you'll have to use the right prepositions at the right times —otherwise, you might blow your cover!

Il y a

Il y a (*there is*, *there are*) is an adverbial expression that states the existence of people and things. While in English we distinguish between *there is* and *there are*, **il y a** encompasses both the singular and plural form.

Il y a près de huit milliards d'êtres humains sur la Terre.	*There are nearly eight billion human beings on Earth.*
Combien y a-t-il d'espèces animales en danger en Afrique?	*How many endangered animal species are there in Africa?*
Est-ce qu'il y a de l'espoir?	*Is there any hope?*
Il n'y a pas assez d'eau potable dans le monde.	*There is not enough drinking water in the world.*

Faire

The verb **faire** is another essential part of the French language. Its literal translation is *to do* or *to make*, though it is used in countless idiomatic expressions. For example, **faire** allows us to both articulate the weather (**Quel temps fait-il?**) and get others' attention (**Faites attention!**). But for now, let's start with its present-tense conjugation.

je fais	*I do*	nous faisons	*we do*
tu fais	*you do*	vous faites	*you do*
il/elle/on fait	*he/she/one does*	ils/elles font	*they do*

Qu'est-ce que vous faites ce soir?   *What are you doing tonight?*
Elle fait ses devoirs l'après-midi.   *She does her homework in the afternoon.*

Weather Expressions

Whether it's the winter or the summer, being able to talk about the weather will certainly serve you throughout your language endeavors.

Quel temps fait-il aujourd'hui?   *What's the weather today?*

Il fait beau.	*It is nice.*
Il fait chaud.	*It is hot.*
Il fait froid.	*It is cold.*
Il fait frais.	*It is cool.*
Il fait doux.	*It is mild.*
Il fait du soleil.	*It is sunny.*
Il fait du vent.	*It is windy.*
Il fait gris.	*It is gray out.*
Il fait un temps splendide.	*The weather is beautiful.*
Il fait un sale temps.	*The weather is lousy.*
Il fait un temps affreux.	*The weather is horrible.*
Il fait un temps radieux.	*It's bright and sunny out.*
Il fait vingt degrés.	*It's twenty degrees out.*
Il fait jour.	*It's light out.*
Il fait nuit.	*It's dark out.*

> **BTW**
>
> *As we know from earlier chapters, the conjugated verb's final consonant in the first-, second-, and third-person singular is usually silent. The important thing to note about* **faire,** *however, is that the* **nous** *form has a tricky pronunciation. The "fai" of* **nous faisons** *is pronounced as a* **feh** *sound, and the* **s** *takes on a* **z** *sound.*

A lot of weather expressions use **faire**, but not all do. Here are some examples:

Il pleut.	*It is raining.*
Il pleut à verse.	*It is pouring down.*

Il pleut des cordes.	*It is raining cats and dogs.*
Il bruine.	*It is drizzling.*
Il neige.	*It is snowing.*
Il grêle.	*It is hailing.*
Il y a des nuages.	*It is cloudy.*
Il y a de la brume.	*It is misty.*
Il y a du brouillard.	*It is foggy.*

Climatologists and geologists are constantly on the lookout for powerful seismic and weather events. Let's take a look at some of the vocab they commonly come across in this realm:

un orage	*thunderstorm*
une tempête de neige	*snowstorm*
le tonnerre	*thunder*
les éclairs	*lightning*
la foudre	*lightning bolt*
une tornade	*tornado*
un ouragan	*hurricane*
un cyclone tropical	*tropical cyclone*
un typhon	*typhoon*
une inondation	*flood*
la canicule	*heat wave*
la sécheresse	*drought*
une vague de froid	*cold spell*
un blizzard	*blizzard*
une avalanche	*avalanche*
une éruption volcanique	*volcanic eruption*
un incendie de forêt	*forest fire*
un tremblement de terre/un séisme	*earthquake*
un raz-de-marée	*tidal wave*
un tsunami	*tsunami*
un météore	*meteor*

La météo prévoit des orages dans le nord de la France.

The forecast is calling for thunderstorms in the north of France.

La canicule sévit dans toute l'Europe.

The heat wave is rampant across all of Europe.

But, unfortunately, many events are caused or exacerbated by humans, and these are the issues that keep many up at night:

la pollution de l'air et de l'eau	*air and water pollution*
la pluie acide	*acid rain*
l'érosion du sol	*ground erosion*
la déforestation	*deforestation*
la marée noire	*oil spill*
un accident nucléaire	*nuclear accident*

La Montagne d'or en Guyane française est touchée par la déforestation.

The Gold Mountain in French Guyana is affected by deforestation.

La marée noire met en danger la faune et la flore au large des côtes de la Nouvelle-Zélande.

The oil spill is endangering flora and fauna off the coast of New Zealand.

Idiomatic Expressions with *Faire*

Faire is also used in expressions related to chores, activites, and sports, among other things.

faire attention	*to pay attention*
faire de son mieux	*to do one's best*
faire des progrès	*to make progress*
faire semblant de	*to pretend*
faire la queue	*to wait in line*
faire les courses	*to go shopping*

faire le marché	*to go to the market*
faire des économies	*to save money*
faire le ménage	*to do housework*
faire un voyage	*to take a trip*
faire sa toilette	*to wash up*
faire des projets	*to make plans*
faire partie de	*to be a part of/to be a member*
faire la sieste	*to take a nap*
faire la grasse matinée	*to sleep in*
faire la bise	*to kiss on the cheek*
faire des grimaces	*to grimace*
faire la tête	*to sulk*
faire mal	*to hurt*
faire peur	*to frighten*
faire plaisir	*to be happy to do something for somebody*
faire des bêtises	*to make mischief*
faire exprès	*to do something on purpose*
faire un tabac	*to have a huge success*
faire de l'exercice	*to exercise*
faire une promenade	*to go for a walk*
faire un tour	*to take a stroll/to go for a ride*
faire une randonnée	*to go for a hike*
faire du ski	*to ski*
faire du vélo	*to go biking*

Le réchauffement climatique nous fait peur. — *Global warming scares us.*

Il fait de plus en plus chaud en Alaska. — *It is getting warmer and warmer in Alaska.*

Il fait pousser ses plantes pour contrôler l'érosion du sol. — *He is growing plants to control ground erosion.*

Je fais de mon mieux pour réduire ma consommation de plastique. — *I am doing my best to reduce my consumption of plastic.*

Cela me fait plaisir de vous revoir.	*I am pleased to see you again.*
Il ne sait pas quoi inventer pour faire plaisir à ses amis.	*He doesn't know what to do to make his friends happy (to please his friends).*

Note that **faire plaisir** and **plaire** are often confused. **Faire plaisir** implies someone is happy to do something for somebody. **Plaire** means to like, to enjoy, to please. Make a mental note of these two verbs, as you'll come across them again in this book. Let's look at a few examples:

Cela me fait plaisir de t'offrir cette montre connectée.	*I am happy to give you this smartwatch.*
—J'espère que la montre te plaît. —Elle me plaît beaucoup!	*—I hope you like the watch. —I like it a lot!*
Cela lui fera plaisir de pouvoir les aider.	*He is happy to be able to help them.*
Je suis sûr que le nouveau film de Guillaume Nicloux va te plaire.	*I am sure you are going to enjoy Guillaume Nicloux's new film.*

Faire + **Infinitive:** *La forme causative*

When the conjugated verb **faire** is followed by an infinitive (e.g., **faire signer**), it is expressing the idea that one person causes another person to act. Often, this action is delegated or prompted by the main subject, who is having something done for him or her. For this reason, the preposition **par** may be used to emphasize the new actor stepping in for the main subject.

Léa arrose le jardin elle-même.	*Léa waters the garden herself.*
Léa **fait arroser** le jardin par le jardinier.	*Léa has the garden watered by the gardener.*

Christian signe la pétition.	*Christian signs the petition.*
Christian **fait signer** la pétition par un de ses amis.	*Christian has one of his friends sign the petition.*
Ils classent leurs documents eux-mêmes.	*They file the documents themselves*
Ils **font classer** leurs documents par le stagiaire.	*They have their documents filed by the intern.*
Décorez-vous votre appartement vous-même?	*Are you decorating your apartment yourself?*
Faites-vous **décorer** votre appartement par un architecte d'intérieur?	*Are you having your apartment decorated by an interior designer?*

Verbs with Prepositions

In French, you'll often want to link two verbs together, and to do this, you'll want to use prepositions. While not all verbs need a preposition to connect to an infinitive, many do, and so you'll want to memorize their corresponding prepositions; unfortunately, there is no secret recipe for this.

Verbs Followed by the Preposition *à* + a Verb in the Infinitive

Let's take a look at the first set of verbs that are followed by **à**.

accoutumer (s')	*to get accustomed to*
aider	*to help*
amuser (s')	*to enjoy*
apprendre	*to learn/to show how*
arriver	*to manage*

aspirer	*to aspire*
attendre (s')	*to expect*
autoriser	*to authorize*
chercher	*to try/to attempt*
commencer	*to start*
continuer	*to continue/to keep on*
décider (se)	*to make up one's mind*
encourager	*to encourage*
faire (se)	*to get used to*
faire attention	*to pay attention*
habituer (s')	*to get used*
hésiter	*to hesitate*
inciter	*to encourage*
intéresser (s')	*to get interested in*
inviter	*to invite*
mettre (se)	*to start/to begin*
parvenir	*to manage*
préparer (se)	*to get ready*
renoncer	*to give up*
résigner (se)	*to resign oneself*
réussir	*to succeed/to manage*
songer	*to think*
tenir	*to insist/to be eager*

J'hésite **à** le contacter.	*I hesitate to contact you.*
Ils s'attendent **à** un changement majeur.	*They expect a major change.*
France se fait **à** son nouveau poste.	*France is getting used to her new job.*
L'entreprise fait attention **à** ne pas polluer l'atmosphère.	*The company is careful to not pollute the atmosphere.*

Verbs Followed by the Preposition *de* | a Verb in the Infinitive

Now that we've seen some of the verbs followed by the preposition **à**, let's look at those followed by the preposition **de**.

accepter	to accept
accuser	to accuse
arrêter (s')	to stop
avoir besoin	to need to
avoir envie	to feel like
avoir l'intention	to intend to
avoir peur	to be afraid of
cesser	to stop/to cease
choisir	to choose
conseiller	to advise
contenter (se)	to content oneself with
défendre	to forbid
efforcer (s')	to try hard
empêcher	to prevent
empêcher (s')	to refrain from
envisager	to consider/contemplate an idea
essayer	to try
éviter	to avoid
excuser (s')	to apologize
faire semblant	to pretend
finir	to finish/to end
interdire	to forbid
menacer	to threaten
mériter	to deserve
offrir	to offer
oublier	to forget
permettre	to allow/to permit
persuader	to persuade/to convince
plaindre (se)	to complain

projeter	to plan
promettre	to promise
refuser	to refuse
regretter	to regret
remercier	to thank
reprocher	to reproach
souvenir (se)	to remember
tâcher	to try

Ils envisagent **d'**installer une éolienne.	*They are thinking about installing a wind turbine.*
Il a oublié **d'**acheter du quinoa.	*He forgot to buy some quinoa.*
Nous essayons **de** consommer moins d'énergie.	*We are trying to consume less energy.*
Ils ont l'intention **de** retourner sur la lune.	*They are planning to go back to the moon.*

Verbs that Are Followed by Multiple Prepositions

Some verbs can stand on their own without a preposition, and can still be followed by different prepositions. Note, however, that each variation carries a different meaning. For example:

Comment peut-on commencer **à** lutter contre le réchauffement climatique? On commence **par** changer ses habitudes.	*How do we start fighting climate change? We start by changing our habits.*

Let's look at another example:

Elle a commencé un nouveau travail.	*She started a new job.*
Elle a commencé **à** décorer sa maison.	*She started decorating her house.*
Elle a commencé **par** la cuisine.	*She started by the kitchen.*

Other verbs can follow the same pattern:

- **finir**

J'ai fini mes devoirs.	*I finished my homwork.*
J'ai fini **de** payer ma maison.	*I finished paying for my house.*
J'ai fini **par** comprendre son point de vue.	*I finally understood her point of view.*

- **parler**

Vous voulez me parler?	*Do you want to speak to me?*
Vous parlez **à** l'agent.	*You are talking to the agent.*
De quoi parlez-vous?	*What are you talking about?*
Elle parle **de** son affaire.	*She is talking about her business.*

- **penser**

À quoi pense-t-il?	*What is he thinking about?*
Il pense **à** ses vacances.	*He is thinking about his vacation.*
Que pensez-vous **de** ce documentaire?	*What do you think about this documentary?*

- **jouer**

Quel personnage jouez-vous?	*What character do you play?*
Je joue Harpagon.	*I play Harpagon.*
Je joue **au** tennis.	*I play tennis.*
Je joue **de** la guitare et **du** saxophone.	*I play the guitar and the saxophone.*

Verbs that Don't Need Prepositions in French

After learning about all these prepositions, it might be tempting to think that all verbs require a preposition. But remember that some verbs can be used directly before the infinitive without **à**, **de**, **par**, etc.

In French, when a conjugated verb is followed by another verb in the same clause, the second verb *must* be in the infinitive; this follows from the rule that two conjugated verbs cannot be directly next to each other.

aimer	*to like, to love*
aller	*to go*
avouer	*to admit*
compter	*to intend/to plan*
désirer	*to desire/to wish*
détester	*to hate*
devoir	*must*
écouter	*to listen*
espérer	*to hope*
faire	*to do*
falloir	*must*
laisser	*to let*
oser	*to dare*
paraître	*to appear*
penser	*to think*
pouvoir	*can*
préférer	*to prefer*
prétendre	*to claim*
savoir	*to know*
sembler	*to seem*
sentir	*to feel, to think*
souhaiter	*to wish*
venir	*to come*
voir	*to see*
vouloir	*to want*

Margot veut sensibiliser le public.   *She wants to raise public awareness.*
Vous désirez faire bouger les gens.   *You wish to mobilize people.*

Il faut prendre une décision.	*We must make a decision.*
Il déteste trier les déchets.	*He hates sorting out waste.*

As you've probably noticed, the subject of the first verb is the same as the one of the second verb; that's why the infinitive form is used. When the subjects are different, a dependent clause introduced by **que** is needed.

Elle espère changer le monde.	*She hopes to change the world.*
Elle espère que Noah changera le monde.	*She hopes Noah will change the world.*
Il prétend être un prince.	*He claims he is a prince.*
Il prétend que tout va bien.	*He pretends everything is fine.*

When the infinitive clause is in the negative, the negation stays combined in front of the infinitive.

Je préfère **ne pas** interrompre leur discussion.	*I prefer not to interrupt their discussion.*
Il aimerait **ne pas** en parler.	*He'd rather not talk about it.*

BTW

In some cases, a French verb does not need a preposition when its English counterpart requires one, and vice versa. You will notice this confusion the next time you hear a French person forget to use the correct preposition when speaking English—and this is a common problem among language learners.

J'écoute la présentatrice télé de France 24.	I am listening **to** the *France 24* anchorwoman.
Nous cherchons une solution.	We are looking **for** a solution.
Elle est entrée.	She walked **in**.
Ils attendent la pluie.	They are waiting **for** rain.

DIALOGUE *Le réchauffement climatique te fait peur?*
Does climate change scare you?

Margot attended the One Planet summit on climate change in Paris with her high school classmates and her geography teacher. Her friend Noah wants to know all about it.

NOAH: Alors, Margot, tu es prête à faire la révolution climatique?

So, Margot, are you ready to start the climate revolution?

MARGOT: Ça, c'est sûr! C'est maintenant ou jamais!

That's for sure. It's now or never!

NOAH: Comment peut-on commencer à lutter contre le réchauffement climatique?

How can we start to fight against global warming?

MARGOT: C'est facile. On commence par changer ses habitudes.

It's easy. We can start by changing our habits.

NOAH: Par exemple?

For example?

MARGOT: Manger moins de viande et plus de légumes et de céréales comme le quinoa.

Eating less meat and more vegetables and whole grains like quinoa.

NOAH: J'ai mangé une salade de quinoa avec de l'avocat à Marseille cet été. C'est pas mauvais...

I ate a quinoa salad with avocado this past summer in Marseille. It's not bad...

MARGOT: C'est délicieux! Vous allez à Marseille en avion, par le train, ou en voiture?

It's delicious! Do you go to Marseille by plane, by train, or by car?

NOAH: Euh... en avion. Les billets ne sont pas chers.

Um...by plane. The tickets aren't expensive.

MARGOT: Oui, mais tu sais que les émissions de CO_2 sont énormes. Le TGV relie Paris à Marseille en trois heures.

Yes, but you know that CO_2 emissions are massive. The TGV connects Paris to Marseille within a three-hour trip.

NOAH: Seulement trois heures?

Only three hours?

MARGOT: Oui, et les billets ne sont pas chers si tu les achètes à l'avance.

Yes, and the tickets aren't pricey if you buy them in advance.

BTW

You buy your tickets **à l'avance** (early/in advance), *and if you pay the rent in advance,* **vous payez le loyer à l'avance**. *However, if you arrive early for an appointment,* **vous arrivez en avance,** *not* **à l'heure** (on time), *or* **en retard** (late). *Make a note of the difference* **between à l'avance** *and* **en avance**.

NOAH: C'est vrai. Mais tu sais, à la maison, nous faisons très attention; nous recyclons nos déchets, nous compostons.

It's true. But, you know, at home, we are very careful; we recycle our trash and we compost.

MARGOT: Vous n'utilisez pas de plastique?

You don't use any plastic?

NOAH: Non, nous avons des sacs en toile recyclables pour le marché et ma sœur fait le savon et le shampooing solide pour toute la famille.

No, we have recyclable cloth bags for shopping, and my sister makes soap and solid shampoo for the whole family.

MARGOT: Elle fait du savon et du shampooing solide?

She makes soap and solid shampoo?

NOAH: Oui, son mantra est « Objectif zéro déchet ».

Yes, her mantra is the "zero waste objective."

MARGOT: Félicitations à ta sœur! On doit apprendre à tout recycler et à consommer moins. La planète est en danger.

Congrats to your sister! We must learn to recycle everything and to consume less. The planet is in danger.

NOAH: Et le niveau de la mer augmente sans cesse.

And the sea level keeps rising.

MARGOT: Entre 1900 et 2010, le niveau des mers et des océans a augmenté de presque 20 cm.

Between 1900 and 2010, the sea level has risen almost 20 cm.

NOAH: Les mers sont polluées et il y a de moins en moins de poisson.

The seas are polluted and there are fewer and fewer fish.

MARGOT: Pollution, canicule, pénurie d'eau et de nourriture, etc., la génération Z doit se mobiliser et agir.

Pollution, heat waves, water and food scarcities, etc., Generation Z must come together and take action.

NOAH: Comment faire bouger les gens?

How do we mobilize people?

MARGOT: Nous avons besoin de sensibiliser le public.

We need to raise public awareness.

NOAH: Et de lui faire comprendre la gravité de la situation. Il y a urgence!

And to make people understand the gravity of the situation. It is urgent!

MARGOT: Chacun a la responsabilité de calculer sa propre empreinte écologique et d'agir!

Each person is responsible for calculating their carbon footprint and taking action!

NOAH: Alors faisons bouger les gens!

So let's mobilize people!

EXERCISES

EXERCISE 6.1

Translate the following sentences into French. When asking a question, use inversion.

1. There is a skating rink in our town.

2. Is there soap in the kitchen?

3. There is water on the table.

4. There are no tickets for tonight.

5. There are vegetables in the refrigerator.

EXERCISE 6.2

Answer the following questions using the natural disaster words above.

1. Quelle catastrophe naturelle a dévasté la Louisiane en 2005?

2. Quelle catastrophe naturelle a eu lieu à Agadir, au Maroc, en 1960?

3. Quelles catastrophes ont eu lieu en Indonésie en 2004?

4. Quelle catastrophe naturelle a eu lieu à Londres en 1666?

5. Quelle catastrophe naturelle a eu lieu en Martinique en 1902?

EXERCISE 6.3

Conjugate the verb **faire** *in the present tense.*

1. Nous (faire) _____ une randonnée dans les Alpes-Maritimes.

2. En juillet, il (faire) _____ froid au Chili.

3. (faire) _____ -vous partie d'une association écologique?

4. Les fermiers bio (faire) _____ des progrès en matières environnementales.

5. Certains (faire) _____ semblant d'ignorer le réchauffement climatique.

6. Est-ce que tu (faire) _____ du vélo dans les Landes?

7. Je (faire) _____ des économies pour financer mon voyage en Antarctique.

8. Élisabeth ne (faire) _____ pas assez attention à sa consommation d'énergie.

9. Les scientifiques (faire) _____ un voyage au Groenland pour étudier le mouvement des glaciers.

10. —Qu'est-ce que tu (faire) _____ dans la vie? —Je suis climatologue.

EXERCISE 6.4

Match the items in the two columns. Choose the most logical answers.

1. Elle a un billet d'avion,   a. elle va faire le marché.

2. Elle aime dormir tard le dimanche, b. elle fait le grand ménage.

3. Elle est à Albertville,   c. elle fait la grasse matinée.

4. Le frigo est vide,   d. elle va faire du ski.

5. Sa mère arrive ce soir,   e. elle va faire un voyage.

EXERCISE 6.5

Translate the following sentences using the verb **faire.** *When asking a question,*
use the inversion form.

  1. They are hiking in the Alps.

  2. I like to bike in Martinique.

  3. He pretends not to see me.

  4. She is a member of an environmental association.

  5. Climate change scares me.

  6. What's the weather like this morning?

  7. It is cold, and it is misty.

  8. We are saving to go to France next year.

  9. You exercise every day. (*vous*)

  10. Aloïse Sauvage's new album is a big hit.

EXERCISE 6.6

Using the causative form, rewrite the following statements.

  1. Il répare la moto. (par le mécanicien)

  2. Je repeins mon appartement. (par mon frère)

  3. Nous faisons un gâteau. (par le pâtissier)

  4. Vous préparez le dossier. (par votre collègue)

  5. Est-ce que tu laves ta voiture? (par ton neveu)

  6. Ils envoient les paquets. (par leur stagiaire)

7. Elle tape le rapport. (par son assistant)

8. Thomas fait le ménage. (par un étudiant)

9. Je fais mes robes moi-même. (par un couturier)

10. Carole se coupe les cheveux elle-même. (par le coiffeur)

EXERCISE 6.7

Fill each blank with the appropriate preposition.

1. Elle s'intéresse _____ cette nouvelle source d'énergie.

2. Margot essaie _____ sensibiliser Noah à sa cause.

3. Nous vous invitons _____ devenir membre.

4. Il menace _____ quitter l'organisation.

5. Ils nous aident _____ planter des arbres.

6. Elle apprend _____ fabriquer son propre shampooing solide.

7. Je me souviens _____ l'ouragan de 2005.

8. Penses-tu que tu vas réussir _____ le convaincre?

9. Il n'arrive pas _____ se faire _____ nouveau travail.

10. Ils ont l'intention _____ faire le tour du monde en voilier.

EXERCISE 6.8

*Translate the following sentences using the **vous** form when applicable. When asking a question, use inversion.*

1. I need to water the garden.

2. Noah is helping clean the kitchen.

3. He remembers the date of the hurricane.

4. They are afraid of another oil spill.

5. I am interested in this series.

6. Do you feel like hiking in Brittany?

7. We are expecting a major change in our company.

8. I often forget to buy a frozen yogurt for Benoît.

9. She is encouraging me to make progress in French.

10. He always manages to water his garden in one hour.

EXERCISE 6.9

Fill in each blank with the appropriate preposition.

1. Quand vas-tu commencer _____ jouer _____ piano?

2. Elle veut jouer _____ tennis et _____ volleyball.

3. Margot nous parle _____ son nouveau projet.

4. _____ quoi penses-tu? Je pense _____ la mort de Marie-Antoinette.

5. Que pensez-vous _____ dernier film de François Ozon?

6. Nous pensons _____ nos amis qui sont en vacances en France.

7. _____ quoi parlez-vous?

8. Quand allez-vous finir _____ repeindre la maison de Xavier?

9. Je vais commencer _____ le salon et je vais finir _____ le bureau.

10. Ils parlent _____ la pluie et _____ beau temps.

EXERCISE 6.10

*Translate the following sentences using the **vous** form when applicable.*
When asking a question, use inversion.

1. I don't like to bike when it rains.

2. I know how to prepare Indian dishes.

3. We must sign the petition.

4. Are you planning to invest in Rwanda?

5. I dare not promise you the moon.

6. They can go to Bruxelles by train.

7. We hope to meet them soon.

8. I must learn how to make solid soap.

9. She claims to be a princess.

10. The Z generation is going to mobilize people.

LE COIN DES CRÉATEURS

DERRIÈRE LA PORTE...

Doors have always been intriguing. You may have seen doors from Greece, from Morocco, or French castle doors. What possibly is there behind this door? Get a postcard of a door on the Internet, or take your own picture of a door, whatever city, whatever country, and imagine what could be behind the door.

Example: Derrière la porte, il y a un chef japonais qui prépare un repas pour un enfant qui est passionné d'astronomie. Le chef... L'enfant...

À votre tour!

Derrière la porte, il y a...

NOTE CULTURELLE

LIBERTY, FRATERNITY, EQUALITY, AND...ECOLOGY?

In France, there is a long tradition of activism on behalf of environmental and ecological issues. For the French, "being green" and "green politics" are based on a political ideology that seeks to create an ecologically sustainable society by promoting environmentalism, nonviolence, and social justice, both on the individual and societal level.

Green political activism dates back to the first Earth Day, or *Jour de la Terre*, celebrated in the United States on April 22, 1970. An international event by 1990, it has mobilized more than 200 million people in 141 countries and raised awareness of environmental issues throughout the world. These issues are both general and local, and national Green political parties began to develop in many countries as a way of dealing with them. There were several such parties in France, the largest of which were The Greens and Europe Ecology. In November 2010, these two parties decided to join forces and form a single new party, *Europe Écologie Les Verts*, Europe Ecology—The Greens, abbreviated in French as EELV.

The mobilization of young people has played an important role in the EELV's spectacular rise, as voters reject traditional political parties and push government leaders to take quick action against climate change and other environmental issues. The party is now the primary political force among 18- to 34-year-old voters, as the results of recent French and European elections have shown. In a country committed to protecting the planet with environment-friendly practices, the EELV has been responsible for pushing France to the forefront in promoting sustainable practices and in combating climate change.

France supports efforts and initiatives by the United Nations (UN) and other international organizations to deal with environmental issues and problems of global concern, including climate change. The Paris Climate Agreement, also referred to as the Paris Climate Accord, is a pact sponsored by the UN. Negotiated in Paris, it brings together a majority of the world's nations with the goal of combating climate change and creating strategies to adapt to its effects. France has been an enthusiastic supporter of the agreement and was one of the first countries to sign it.

For the French, "being green" isn't just a color, it's an ideology. As *The Urban Dictionary* says: "To be green does not mean to dip yourself in green paint! To be green is to help the environment in every way possible." In France, people are doing just that.

Pronominal Verbs

rom when you get out of bed to when you fall asleep, and all throughout the day, you'll need to use pronominal verbs; your diary is probably chock full of them. You'll also run into them when your French friends talk about etiquette, or when you want to ask for a word's meaning. For this we say, **Comment ça se traduit?**

Pronominal verbs are preceded by the pronouns **me**, **te**, **se**, **nous**, **vous**, and **se**. There are four kinds of pronominal verbs: the reflexive, the reciprocal, the passive, and the subjective.

Reflexive Pronominal Verbs

The action of a reflexive verb is reflected back on the subject, the action being done to oneself. For example: **se promener** (*to walk*), **s'amuser** (*to have fun*), **se lever** (*to get up*).

se promener (*to walk*)

je me promène	*I walk*	nous nous promenons	*we walk*
tu te promènes	*you walk*	vous vous promenez	*you walk*
il/elle se promène	*he/she walks*	ils/elles se promènent	*they walk*

Attention! Note that the pronouns **me**, **te**, and **se** drop the **e** before **h** or a vowel.

s'habiller (*to dress oneself*)

je m'habille	*I dress myself*	nous nous habillons	*we dress ourselves*
tu t'habilles	*you dress yourself*	vous vous habillez	*you dress yourselves*
il/elle s'habille	*he/she/dresses himself/herself*	ils/elles s'habillent	*they dress themselves*

Here are some sample sentences:

Elle s'habille pour aller à la soirée.	*She gets dressed to go to the party.*
L'actrice se maquille dans sa loge.	*The actress does her makeup in the dressing room.*
Nous nous réveillons très tôt.	*We wake up very early.*
Il s'appelle Thomas.	*His name is Thomas.*

In the negative form, the **ne** is placed after the subject pronoun and before the reflexive pronoun. The **pas** is placed after the conjugated verb.

Elle ne se lève pas tôt le weekend.	*She does not get up early on the weekend.*
Il ne se rase pas tous les jours.	*He does not shave every day.*
Tu ne te coupes pas les cheveux tous les mois.	*You do not cut your hair every month.*
Je ne me couche pas avant minuit le samedi.	*I don't go to bed before midnight on Saturdays.*
Vous ne vous reposez jamais!	*You never rest!*

As we saw in Chapter 2, there are three ways of asking questions.

Vous vous couchez tard en vacances?	*Do you go to bed late during vacation?*
Est-ce que vous vous couchez tard en vacances?	*Do you go to bed late during vacation?*
Vous couchez-vous tard en vacances?	*Do you go to bed late during vacation?*
Te reposes-tu l'après-midi?	*Do you rest in the afternoon?*
Vous asseyez-vous au balcon au Palais Garnier?	*Do you sit in the balcony at the Palais Garnier?*

BTW

When using inversion, the reflexive pronoun remains in front of the verb.

When using inversion in the third-person singular (**il**, **elle**, **on**), if the conjugated verb is an **-er** verb ending in an **e** in the present tense, remember to link the verb and the subject with a **-t-**: **Comment s'appelle-t-il?** (What is his name?); **S'entraîne-t-elle tous les jours au club de forme?** (Does she train every day at the gym?) The added **t** will be used with other verb endings in other tenses that will be featured in future chapters. Note that it is only used for the singular since there is already a final **t** in the plural form: **Comment s'appellent-ils?**

Reciprocal Pronominal Verbs

Another type of pronominal verb is called a reciprocal verb. The word *reciprocal* means that the action is done unto two or more people. It has the same effect as using the phrase "each other." For example:

s'embrasser	to kiss each other
se téléphoner	to call each other
s'écrire	to write to each other

Here are some sample sentences:

On se retrouve à la gare?	*Shall we meet at the train station?*
Rose et Julien s'écrivent de longues lettres.	*Rose and Julien write each other long letters.*
Nous nous téléphonons tous les jours.	*We call each other every day.*
Pourquoi vous disputez-vous toujours?	*Why are you always arguing?*

Passive Pronominal Verbs

Then we have another kind of pronominal verb called passive. With the passive pronominal verbs, the subject is not a person or an animal and does not perform the action of the verb, but is subjected to it. Here are some sample sentences:

Ça ne se fait pas.	*That is just not done.*
Ça ne se dit pas.	*That is just not said.*
La cuisine chinoise se mange avec des baguettes.	*Chinese food is eaten with chopsticks.*
Le Perrier citron se boit frais.	*Lemon Perrier is drunk chilled.*
Comment ça se traduit?	*How is it translated?*

 IRL Passive verbs can help us understand the norms and etiquette of a culture or situation. In particular, the expression **ça ne se fait pas** is used to indicate that an action is atypical.

Parler très fort dans un restaurant, ça ne se fait pas!	*Speaking loudly at a restaurant, that is just not done!*
Appeler un serveur « garçon », ça ne se fait pas!	*Calling a waiter "garçon," that is just not done!*
Tutoyer une personne que tu ne connais pas, ça ne se fait pas!	*Using the* tu *form to a person you don't know, that is just not done!*
Commencer à manger avant l'hôte ou l'hôtesse, ça ne se fait pas!	*Beginning to eat before the host or hostess, that is just not done!*
Mettre ses coudes sur la table, ça ne se fait pas!	*Putting your elbows on the table, that is just not done!*
Parler la bouche pleine, ça ne se fait pas!	*Talking with your mouth full, that is just not done!*
Couper la salade avec un couteau, ça ne se fait pas!	*Cutting salad with a knife, that is just not done!*
Klaxonner la nuit, ça ne se fait pas!	*Honking at night, that is just not done!*
Ne pas laisser de pourboire, ça ne se fait pas!	*Not leaving a tip, that is just not done!*

Fumer dans un magasin, ça ne se fait pas!

Smoking in a store, that is just not done!

Resquiller au cinéma, ça ne se fait pas!

Cutting in line at the movie theater, that is just not done!

Subjective Pronominal Verbs

The final type of pronominal verb is called subjective. These verbs are neither reflexive nor reciprocal; they just happen to use the pronominal form. Here are some sample sentences:

À quelle heure est-ce que tu t'en vas?

What time are you leaving?

Tu te souviens des paroles de la chanson d'Aloïse Sauvage?

Do you remember the lyrics to Aloïse Sauvage's song?

De quoi te plains-tu?

What are you complaining about?

Jean ne se rend pas compte des conséquences de son comportement.

Jean does not realize the consequences of his behavior.

Here is a list of commonly used subjective verbs:

s'apercevoir de	to realize
s'attendre à	to expect
se débarrasser de	to get rid of
s'écrouler	to collapse
s'effondrer	to collapse
s'emparer de	to seize
s'enfuir	to flee
s'envoler	to fly away/to vanish
s'évanouir	to faint
se fier à	to trust
s'habituer à	to get used to
s'inquiéter de	to worry

se méfier de	to mistrust
se moquer de	to make fun of
se passer de	to do without
se servir de	to use
se tromper	to make a mistake

Disjunctive Pronouns

There are many ways to use disjunctive pronouns, also known as stressed or tonic pronouns.

moi	*me*	nous	*us*
toi	*you*	vous	*you*
lui	*him*	eux	*them*
elle	*her*	elles	*them* (feminine)

The disjunctive pronouns can be used to add extra *emphasis* to a thought.

Moi, je pense que le jardin botanique de Brest a les plus belles fleurs.	I *think that the Brest Botanical Gardens has the prettiest flowers.*
Toi, tu n'es jamais content!	You *are never happy!*
Lui, il m'impressionne toujours!	He *always impresses me!*
Eux, ils ont vraiment de la chance!	They *are really lucky!*

 IRL French people love to debate, and it is greatly reflected in their language. For instance, you will commonly hear them begin their sentences with « Moi, je… » to assert their position in discourse.

While in English we simply stress the subject pronoun, disjunctive pronouns used after **c'est** or **ce sont** help to stress identification.

C'est moi qui suis le meilleur jardinier!	I *am the best gardener!*
C'est toi qui vas ramasser les feuilles!	You *are going to pick up the leaves!*

C'est lui qui explique comment faire un herbier.	He *is explaining how to make an herbarium.*
C'est vous qui avez cueilli les fleurs tropicales?	*Did* you *pick the tropical flowers?*

Disjunctive pronouns are also used when different subjects are combined. Remember that there are the first-person, second-person, and third-person perspectives. We can combine these, though doing so requires that we change the subject pronouns into disjunctive pronouns. And we often restate the new subject for emphasis.

Anaïs et moi, nous allons visiter les serres tropicales.	*Anaïs and I are going to visit the tropical greenhouse.*
Elle et sa mère, elles ont la main verte.	*She and her mother have a green thumb.*
Toi et ton collègue, vous avez fait un super boulot!	*You and your colleague have done a great job!*
Toi et moi, nous formons une bonne équipe.	*You and I make a good team.*

Disjunctive pronouns are also used as one-word questions or answers when there isn't a verb present.

—Qui a teint c'est chemise en lin en bleu indigo? —Moi!	—*Who dyed the linen shirt blue indigo? —I did!*
—Qui veut se balader avec moi parmi les champs de bruyère? —Nous!	—*Who wants to walk with me through the heather fields? —We do!*
—J'adore le parfum de l'eucalyptus. — Moi aussi.	—*I love the smell of eucalyptus. —Me too.*
—Il n'aime pas les tissus synthétiques. —Elle non plus.	—*He does not like synthetic fabrics. —Neither does she.*

Disjunctive pronouns are also used after prepositions. To review the prepositions, see the list in Chapter 6.

Cet horticulteur travaille **pour** eux.	*This horticulturist is working for them.*
Tu veux participer à cet atelier **avec** moi?	*Do you want to participate in this workshop with me?*
Pourquoi ont-ils planté ce lilas **sans** nous?	*Why did they plant the lilac tree without us?*
La directrice du jardin botanique est assise **à côté d**'elle.	*The director of the botanical garden is sitting next to her.*

Additionally, you can use disjunctive pronouns to make comparisons.

Bastien est plus adroit que moi.	*Bastien is more skilled than me.*
Raphaël est moins efficace que toi.	*Raphaël is less efficient than you are.*
Vous êtes aussi douée qu'eux.	*You are as gifted as they are.*

Finally, you can use disjunctive pronouns with **même** (*self*) to reinforce the pronoun. And remember to make **même** agree with the subject pronoun.

Michelle a planté ce potager elle-même.	*Michelle planted this vegetable garden all by herself.*
Je ne vais jamais chez le médecin parce que je me soigne moi-même avec des plantes médicinales.	*I never go to the doctor because I treat myself with medicinal plants.*
Ramasse-les toi-même!	*Pick them up yourself!*
Les enfants ont fait l'herbier eux-mêmes.	*The kids make the herbarium themselves.*

DIALOGUE *Dessine-moi une fleur...*
Draw me a flower...

Camélia, who teaches sciences at the Lycée Sainte-Anne in Brest, is talking with Mathéo, who hosts workshops in the Jardin du Conservatoire botanique national de Brest.

CAMÉLIA: Je m'intéresse à vos ateliers pédagogiques. Combien y en a-t-il?

I am interested in your educational workshops. How many of them are there?

MATHÉO: Il y en a cinq. Je m'occupe de deux ateliers qui s'appellent « Quel est donc cet arbre? » et « L'homme et les plantes ».

There are five of them. I am in charge of two workshops that are called "So what is this tree?" and "Humans and plants."

CAMÉLIA: L'atelier « Quel est donc cet arbre? » semble fascinant. De quoi s'agit-il?

The workshop "So what is this tree?" sounds fascinating. What's it about?

MATHÉO: Les élèves se promènent dans le jardin et ils essaient d'identifier les arbres.

Students walk around the garden and try to identify the trees.

CAMÉLIA: Comment se préparent-ils pour l'atelier?

How do they prepare for the workshop?

MATHÉO: Ça, c'est vous qui vous en occupez!

You are in charge of that!

CAMÉLIA: Comme d'habitude...

As per usual...

MATHÉO: Mais je peux vous fournir nos fiches pédagogiques pour le collège et le lycée.

But I can give you our middle school and high school worksheets.

CAMÉLIA: Génial ! Et « L'hommes et les plantes », de quoi s'agit-il?

Awesome! And what is "Humans and plants" about?

MATHÉO: On montre que les plantes sont indispensables à la survie des animaux et des êtres humains.

We show that plants are indispensable to the survival of animals and human beings.

CAMÉLIA: Mes élèves s'inquiètent de l'avenir de la planète. Ça va les intéresser.

My students are worried about the future of the planet. This will interest them.

MATHÉO: Les êtres humains utilisent les plantes pour se nourrir, se soigner, se loger, et s'habiller, et aussi pour s'amuser et même se chauffer.

Human beings use plants to feed, heal, and dress themselves, and also to have fun and even to keep warm.

CAMÉLIA: Se chauffer? Vous pensez au miscanthus?

To keep us warm? Are you thinking of miscanthus?

MATHÉO: C'est exact. C'est une des énergies renouvelables qui attire l'attention du public.

That's right. It is one of the renewable energies that attracts the public's attention.

CAMÉLIA: Certains de mes élèves aiment s'habiller en fibres naturelles. Pourriez-vous leur parler des tissus écologiques?

Some of my students like wear natural fiber clothing. Could you talk to them about eco-friendly fabrics?

MATHÉO: Avec plaisir. L'industrie de la mode est la deuxième plus polluante au monde.

My pleasure. The fashion industry is The second largest polluter in the world.

CAMÉLIA: Je sais. J'espère que les innovations textiles vont changer notre façon de nous habiller.

I know. I hope textile innovations will change the way we dress.

MATHÉO: Pour créer des tissus, on utilise des techniques ancestrales pour fabriquer de nouveaux textiles à base de produits alimentaires.	*To create fabrics, we use ancestral techniques to make food-based textiles.*
CAMÉLIA: Ah oui, j'ai vu une pub « L'ortie est le nouveau coton ».	*Oh yeah, I saw an ad titled "Nettle is the new cotton."*
MATHÉO: Et aussi le lait, la banane, la noix de coco, le soja, et les algues.	*And milk, banana, coconut, soy, and seaweed.*
CAMÉLIA: Quels travaux pratiques les élèves vont-ils faire?	*What field exercises are the students going to do?*
MATHÉO: Ils rédigent un rapport de deux pages et ils dessinent une fleur ou une plante.	*They write a two-page report and draw a flower or a plant.*
CAMÉLIA: Parfait. Je vais choisir cet atelier. Je suis sûre de ne pas me tromper.	*Perfect. I am going to choose this workshop. I know I won't be wrong.*
MATHÉO: Très bien. Avant de fixer une date, voulez-vous aller jeter un coup d'œil aux serres tropicales?	*Good. Before setting a date, do you want to glance at the tropical greenhouses?*
CAMÉLIA: Désolée, mais je n'ai pas le temps aujourd'hui.	*Sorry, I don't have time today.*
MATHÉO: La prochaine fois. Dans nos serres, nous avons la plus forte concentration en France de plantes en voie de disparition!	*Next time. In our greenhouses, we have the highest concentration of endangered plants!*

CAMÉLIA: J'ai hâte de les voir. Voici ma carte de visite.

I am looking forward to seeing them. Here's my business card.

MATHÉO: Merci, Camélia. Je vais vous envoyer un mail avec des dates pour l'atelier.

Thank you, Camélia. I am going to send you an email with dates for the workshop.

CAMÉLIA: Merci, Mathéo. Ravie d'avoir fait votre connaissance. Au revoir!

Thank you, Mathéo. It was nice meeting you. Bye.

MATHÉO: Au revoir et à bientôt.

Bye and see you soon.

Camélia sort un cahier de son sac à main et commence à dessiner une fleur.

Camélia takes a notebook out of her bag and starts to draw a flower.

 **IRL** When referring to an email, a friend may ask you to send **un email**, sometimes spelled **un e-mail**, but most commonly **un mail.** In writing, or in a formal setting, **un courriel** is often used. It is a combination of **courrier** et **électronique**, a word coined in Quebec. (The contraction, **mél**, looked too strange to find many followers.) If you are interested, the online magazine Le Figaro.fr offers some advice in an article called "Dix formules à éviter dans **un mail.**"

EXERCISES

EXERCISE 7.1

Conjugate the following reflexive verbs using the present tense.

1. Nous (se laver) _____ les mains.

2. Il (se couper) _____ les cheveux lui-même.

3. Je (se baigner) _____ dans un lac.

4. Tu (se peigner) _____ avec une brosse.

5. Vous (se coucher) _____toujours trop tard.

6. Nous (se balader) _____ le long de la Seine.

7. Elles (se préparer) _____ pour la réunion.

8. Je (se maquiller) _____ avant de sortir.

9. On (s'amuser) _____ dans un parc d'attractions.

10. Ils (se brosser) _____ les dents avant de se coucher.

EXERCISE 7.2

Put the following sentences in the negative form.

1. Jérémie se promène dans le parc avec son chien.

2. Caroline se coupe les cheveux elle-même.

3. Je me détends en regardant des films d'horreur.

4. Nous nous asseyons dans l'herbe.

5. Ils s'amusent à Euro Disney.

6. Vous vous baladez au bord de la mer.

7. Il s'habille formellement pour la réunion.

8. Tu te réveilles à cinq heures le matin.

9. Amanda se baigne dans l'océan Atlantique.

10. Je m'entraîne pour le match à Roland-Garros.

EXERCISE 7.3

Turn the following sentences into questions using inversion.

1. Elle se brosse les dents après le petit déjeuner.

2. Tu te reposes avant l'examen.

3. Vous vous brossez les cheveux avec un peigne.

4. Il se couche toujours à minuit.

5. Vous vous amusez dans les arcades de jeux.

6. Nous nous chargeons encore de tous les détails.

7. Il se douche avant de se coucher.

8. Tu te maquilles pour jouer Aïda.

9. Vous vous occupez de ce communiqué de presse.

10. Elle se prépare pour l'entretien.

EXERCISE 7.4

Conjugate the following reciprocal verbs using the present tense.

1. Camille et Jade (se voir) _____ tous les jeudis au cours de danse.

2. Nous (se disputer) _____ trop souvent.

3. Est-ce qu'ils (s'aimer)_____ toujours?

4. Louise et Léa (se dire)_____ leurs secrets.

5. Pourquoi est-ce que vous (se détester) _____?

6. Elles (se quittent) _____ sur le quai de la gare.

7. Inès et Alexis (se croiser) _____ souvent dans la rue.

8. Nous (se rencontrer) _____ parfois au Forum des Halles.

9. Lina et Sébastien (se connaître) _____depuis dix ans.

10. Les amoureux (s'embrasser) _____ sur le Pont-Neuf.

EXERCISE 7.5

Match the items in the two columns. Choose the most logical answer.

1. Je me souviens   a. de ses dossiers inutiles.

2. Elle se repose   b. dans le hamac.

3. Rose se débarrasse   c. d'un nouvel ordinateur.

4. Nous nous servons   d. de mes amis d'enfance.

5. Ils ne se rendent pas compte   e. des conséquences graves.

EXERCISE 7.6

Match the items in the two columns. Choose the most logical answer.

1. Ils se promènent dans le parc   a. parce qu'ils veulent gagner le match.

2. Ils s'attendent à une catastrophe   b. parce qu'ils sont de bons amis.

3. Ils se téléphonent chaque jour   c. parce qu'ils aiment la nature.

4. Ils s'entraînent   d. parce qu'ils ont peur de tout.

5. Ils se plaignent   e. parce que leurs voisins font trop de bruit.

EXERCISE 7.7

Translate the following sentences using pronominal verbs. When asking questions, use the inversion form.

1. I never make fun of my friends.

2. Margaux is getting dressed for a ceremony.

3. Bathing in a public fountain; this is not done.

4. Who is taking care of the children today?

5. We are walking on the Champs-Élysées.

6. They call each other on Sundays.

7. Are they getting married in June?

8. Quentin trusts his intuition.

9. How is it said in Japanese?

10. Do you realize the importance of this decision?

EXERCISE 7.8

*Rewite the sentence stressing the subject pronouns in bold with a disjunctive pronoun using the expression **c'est... qui.***

1. **Je** m'occupe du verger.

2. **Ils** portent des vêtements en fibres végétales.

3. **Tu** dessines les feuilles de l'abricotier.

4. **Il** anime l'atelier sur l'origine des plantes.

5. **Vous** expliquez la germination des graines.

6. **Elle** nous apprend à reconnaître les arbres.

7. **Tu** vas nous informer sur la protection des espèces végétales.

8. **Elle** a gagné le concours de « À Fleur de Ville » de Tours.

9. **Tu** vas partager tes expériences avec nous.

10. **Ils** vont nous faire découvrir les plantes indispensables aux animaux et aux humains.

EXERCISE 7.9

Translate the following sentences using disjunctive pronouns, and stress the pronouns in bold.

1. —Who is the gardener who works for them? —I don't know.

2. **He** does not have a green thumb.

3. Marc is taller than me.

4. **She** is always late.

5. Milo does not like to share his tools with us.

6. **You** and **your** friend are so lucky.

7. I am going to draw this tree for you. (*tu*)

8. —You like red roses. —So do I. (*tu*)

9. Iza always picks flowers for us.

10. —You don't like lentils. —Neither do I. (*vous*)

LE COIN DES CRÉATEURS

LA CARTE POSTALE

Write a postcard to a friend or family member. Tell them about the weather, the landscape, the food, and any pleasant or funny experience. Make sure to use as many pronominal verbs as possible. Here's an example:

Je suis dans les gorges du Verdon avec Vincent.
On se baigne tous les jours et on fait du kayak.
On ne s'aperçoit pas du temps qui passe.
On s'amuse et on pense à vous...
Salut!
Bastien et Vincent

À votre tour!

NOTE CULTURELLE

BREST

The city of Brest, home to the Jardin du Conservatoire botanique national, is a port city in the Finistère department in Brittany. Located in a sheltered bay, the *rade de Brest*, it is an important harbor and the second most important French military port after Toulon. Located on the western edge of continental Europe, it is the third-largest city in Brittany, behind Nantes and Rennes. It was heavily bombed during the Battle for Brest in 1944, and much of the old city was destroyed at that time. However, two vestiges of old Brest remain: the Château de Brest, the castle, and the Tour Tanguy, the medieval tower.

The castle is the oldest structure in Brest. With origins dating back to Roman times, the site has over 1,700 years of history. For most of those years, it was primarily used as a military fortress due to its strategic location. It has the distinction of being the oldest castle in the world still in use, and has been classified as a French historic monument since 1923. Recently renovated, it now houses the National Naval Museum (musée national de la Marine de Brest), which recounts seventeen centuries of history about the Brest shipyard and oceangoing fleets through its large collection of model ships, paintings, sculptures, a pocket submarine, and descriptions of old Brest. It is also the home of a world-famous aquarium, the Océanopolis marine center. Its three-themed exhibition buildings are each devoted to a different ecosystem: polar, tropical, and temperate, and the content is constantly updated by a team of scientists (60 percent of French oceanographers and related research scientists work in Brest).

The Tanguy Tower, probably built in the fourteenth century, faces the castle. Used for military purposes, it fell into private hands after the French Revolution. In 1862, it was bought by an architect who used it as his private residence. Its last occupant and private owner abandoned it after it caught fire during the bombardment of 1944. The town of Brest acquired it in 1954 and had it restored in 1962, when it reopened as the Museum of Old Brest. Its collection of dioramas depict the city as it used to be, on the eve of World War II.

In the period following World War II, Brest worked hard to rebuild itself, with a focus on the future. The city's many postwar buildings were built in a utilitarian style that emphasizes granite and concrete. However, some of its newer structures are notable. There is the Recouvrance Bridge, which, when it was built in 1954, was the largest vertical-lift bridge in France. Then there is the Iroise, a cable-stayed bridge that crosses the Elorn River. Opened in 1994, it is an impressive architectural achievement. Parallel to this is the Plougastel or Albert Louppe Bridge, an older structure rebuilt after the war. Now used only by pedestrians and cyclists, it offers a different view of the city and the rade de Brest, a sheltered area of the sea big enough for great ships to lie at anchor. The French naval base now houses the Brest Naval Training Centre and, in 1972, the French Navy opened its nuclear weapon–submarine (deterrence) base in the rade de Brest. This continues to be an important base for the French nuclear-armed ballistic missile submarines.

Brest, le vieux château et la rade, 1911.
Source: Gallica.

8 Talking About the Past

MUST ⚡ KNOW

⚡ In the **passé composé**, the negation surrounds **être** or **avoir**.

⚡ Beware of irregular past participles!

⚡ Verbs that use **être** in the **passé composé** agree in gender and number with the subject.

⚡ Six common verbs change meaning when used with **être** or **avoir**: **sortir, rentrer, monter, descendre, passer,** and **retourner.**

Throughout our journey thus far, we have talked in the present and the future; now it's time for us to cross over into the past. You can think of the **passé composé** as a two-part tense, containing an auxiliary verb and a past participle. With this, you'll finally be able to tell your friends what you did over the holiday

Everyday Chores

Doing chores, taxing though it may be, is unavoidable. It keeps us going and help us to stay organized throughout the day, even if it's boring at times. Still, let's tackle this chore and learn about everyday tasks in French.

partager les tâches ménagères	to share the domestic chores
faire la cuisine	to cook
faire la vaisselle	to do the dishes
faire la lessive	to do the laundry
trier les vêtements	to sort out clothing
nettoyer la table	to clean the table
mettre la table	to set the table
essuyer la vaisselle	to wipe the dishes
allumer les bougies	to light candles
débarrasser la table	to clear the table
vider le lave-vaisselle	to empty the dishwasher
nettoyer le four et le four à micro-ondes	to clean the oven and the microwave
nettoyer les plaques de cuisson	to clean the cooktop
nettoyer le réfrigérateur/le frigo	to clean the fridge
dégivrer le congélateur	to defrost the freezer
nettoyer le comptoir	to clean the counter

ranger le linge dans le placard	*to put away the linen in the closet*
repasser le linge	*to iron the linen*
changer les draps	*to change the sheets*
faire le lit	*to make the bed*
secouer les oreillers	*to shake the pillows*
ranger les affaires	*to tidy up your stuff*
aérer la chambre	*to air the room*
épousseter	*to dust*
passer l'aspirateur	*to vacuum*
nettoyer la douche et la baignoire	*to clean the shower and the tub*
nettoyer les vitres et les miroirs	*to clean the windows and the mirrors*
vider/sortir la poubelle	*to empty/take out the trash*
cirer les chaussures	*to polish your shoes*
porter les chaussures chez le cordonnier	*to take your shoes to the shoemaker*
faire du bricolage	*to do handiwork*
jardiner	*to garden*
arroser les fleurs	*to water the flowers*
ramasser les feuilles mortes	*to pick up leaves*
laver la voiture	*to wash the car*
vérifier que tout est prêt pour le lendemain	*to check that everything is ready for the next day*
changer la litière du chat	*to change the cat's litter*
sortir le chien	*to walk the dog*

The *Passé Composé*

There are several tenses that are used in French when referring to the past. For now, we will focus on the **passé composé**, the most commonly used past tense. It refers to a single action in the past, and it is composed of two parts: an auxiliary verb (**avoir** or **être**) and a past participle.

This past participle is formed by adding an ending to the stem of the verb. Regular past participles are paired with the following endings:

- **-er** verbs take **–é**: **regarder** (*to watch*) → **regardé** (*watched*)

- **-ir** verbs take **–i**: **dormir** (*to sleep*) → **dormi** (*slept*)

- **-re** verbs take **–u**: **attendre** (*to wait*) → **attendu** (*waited*)

The *Passé Composé* of *-er* Verbs Using *Avoir*

Most verbs in the **passé composé** are conjugated with **avoir**. Let's first review the verb.

avoir:

j'ai	*I have*	nous avons	*we have*
tu as	*you have*	vous avez	*you have*
il/elle/on a	*he/she/one has*	ils/elles ont	*they have*

Generally, when **avoir** is used with the **passé composé**, the past participle agrees neither in gender nor in number with the verb's subject. Let's take a look at the **passé composé** of **commencer** using **avoir**.

commencer *to start/begin*

j'ai commencé	*I started*	nous avons commencé	*we started*
tu as commencé	*you started*	vous avez commencé	*you started*
il/elle/on a commencé	*he/she/one*	ils/elles ont commencé	*they started*

Elle a commencé à travailler lundi.	*She started working on Monday.*
J'ai préparé le repas.	*I prepared the meal.*
Nous avons regardé la télé.	*We watched television.*

Elle a apporté un bouquet de fleurs.	*She brought a bouquet of flowers.*
	She has brought a bouquet of flowers.
	She did bring a bouquet of flowers.

When using the **passé composé** in the negative form, the **ne** and **pas** *directly* surround the auxiliary verb (**avoir** or **être**).

Elle a noté la date et l'heure du rendez-vous.	*She wrote the date and time of the appointment.*
Elle **n'**a **pas** regardé le film.	*She did not watch the film.*

Ils ont vendu leur maison.	*They had sold their house.*
Ils **n'**ont **pas** vendu leur maison.	*They did not sell their house.*

Similar to questions in the present tense, there are three ways to form a question using the **passé composé**.

Vous avez rencontré Éric?	*Did you meet Éric?*
Avez-vous rencontré Éric?	*Did you meet Éric?*
Est-ce que vous avez rencontré Éric?	*Did you meet Éric?*

Using inversion in the third person with the **passé composé** might seem daunting, though it, too, follows these rules.

A-t-il gagné le match?	*Did he win the match?*
A-t-elle demandé une augmentation?	*Did she ask for a raise?*
Ont-elles nagé dans l'océan?	*Did they swim in the ocean?*

The *Passé Composé* of *-ir* and *-re* Verbs Using *Avoir*

Similarly, the past participle of regular **-ir** and **-re** verbs is formed by attaching the appropriate endings.

finir	*to finish*	fini	*finished*
choisir	*to choose*	choisi	*chosen*
vendre	*to sell*	vendu	*sold*
perdre	*to lose*	perdu	*lost*

Il a choisi une chaise ergonomique.	*He chose an ergonomic chair.*
Elle a perdu son portefeuille.	*She lost her wallet.*

Note that when **avoir** is used, the past participle agrees with the direct object only when it precedes the verb.

Elle a pris les photos.	*She took the pictures.*
Elle les a pris**es**.	*She took them.*

Il a lavé les assiettes.	*He washed the plates.*
Il les a lavé**es**.	*He washed them.*

In the negative form, the **ne** is placed in front of **avoir** or **être** and the **pas** after **avoir** or **être**.

Elle a suivi deux cours en ligne.	*She took two online courses.*
Elle n'a pas suivi deux cours en ligne.	*She did not take two online courses.*

J'ai fait des heures supplémentaires.	*I worked overtime.*
Je n'ai pas fait d'heures supplémentaires.	*I did not work overtime.*

Like in the present tense, there are three ways to make a question.

Vous avez rencontré Marie?	*Did you meet Marie?*
Avez-vous rencontré Marie?	*Did you meet Marie?*
Est-ce que vous avez rencontré Marie?	*Did you meet Marie?*

Irregular Past Participles

Many verbs conjugated with **avoir** in the **passé composé** have irregular past participles that you simply have to learn by heart.

Il a appris à coder.	*He learned coding.*
J'ai bu un verre d'eau.	*I drank a glass of water.*

Here is a list of common irregular past participles:

acquérir	*to acquire*	acquis	*acquired*
apprendre	*to learn*	appris	*learned*
avoir	*to have*	eu	*had*
boire	*to drink*	bu	*drunk*
comprendre	*to understand*	compris	*understood*
conduire	*to drive*	conduit	*driven*
craindre	*to fear*	craint	*feared*
devoir	*must*	dû	*had to*
dire	*to say*	dit	*said*
écrire	*to write*	écrit	*written*
être	*to be*	été	*been*
faire	*to do, to make*	fait	*done, made*
falloir	*to have to*	fallu	*had to*
lire	*to read*	lu	*read*

mettre	*to put*	mis	*put*
mourir	*to die*	mort	*dead*
naître	*to be born*	né	*born*
offrir	*to offer*	offert	*offered*
ouvrir	*to open*	ouvert	*opened*
peindre	*to paint*	peint	*painted*
plaire	*to please*	plu	*pleased*
pleuvoir	*to rain*	plu	*rained*
pouvoir	*can, to be able to*	pu	*could*
prendre	*to take*	pris	*taken*
recevoir	*to receive*	reçu	*received*
rire	*to laugh*	ri	*laughed*
savoir	*to know*	su	*known*
suivre	*to follow*	suivi	*followed*
vivre	*to live*	vécu	*lived*
voir	*to see*	vu	*seen*
vouloir	*to want*	voulu	*wanted*

Aimé Césaire est né en Martinique en 1913.

Il a vécu à Paris pendant des années.

La pièce de théâtre nous a plu.

Il a écrit « Une tempête ».

Aimé Césaire was born in Martinique in 1913.

He lived in Paris for years.

We enjoyed the play.

He wrote A Tempest.

The *Passé Composé* with *Être*

Some verbs use **être** instead of **avoir** in the **passé composé**. Most importantly, you should memorize the list of verbs that are arbitrarily conjugated using **être**. But thankfully, all the pronominal verbs (see Chapter 7) are conjugated with **être**.

The past participle of the verb conjugated with **être** agrees in gender and number with the subject.

Il est all**é** en France.	*He went to France.*
Elle est all**ée** en France.	*She went to France.*
Ils sont arriv**és** ensemble.	*They arrived together.*
Elles sont arriv**ées** ensemble.	*They arrived together.*

Here are some verbs conjugated with **être** in the **passé composé**:

aller	*to go*
arriver	*to arrive*
descendre	*to go down*
devenir	*to become*
entrer	*to enter*
intervenir	*to intervene*
monter	*to go up*
mourir	*to die*
naître	*to be born*
partir	*to leave*
rentrer	*to return*
rester	*to stay*
retourner	*to return*
revenir	*to come back*
sortir	*to go out*
survenir	*to occur/to arise*
tomber	*to fall*
venir	*to arrive*

J'ai lu le journal puis je suis sorti(e).	*I read the paper and I left.*
Où êtes-vous né(e)?	*Where were you born?*

Il est rentré du travail totalement épuisé.	*He came back from work totally exhausted.*
Nous sommes monté(e)s jusqu'au sommet de la montagne.	*We went to the top of the mountain.*

BTW

There is no such thing as a "motion verb rule"! **Courir** *(to run),* **parcourir** *(to wander, to browse),* **sauter** *(to jump),* **voyager** *(to travel),* **circuler** *(to circulate, to move),* **sillonner** *(to scour, to travel),* **voler** *(to fly),* **s'envoler** *(to fly away),* **s'enfuir** *(to flee),* **errer** *(to wander), and many other verbs are conjugated with* **avoir!**

Conseil d'amie: *just memorize the list of verbs using être; you'll be sure not to make these too-common mistakes.*

Using Adverbs with the *Passé Composé*

In the **passé composé**, adverbs of quantity, quality, and frequency are placed *between* **avoir** or **être** and the past participle.

bien	*well*
mal	*badly*
mieux	*better*
beaucoup	*a lot*
trop	*too much*
assez	*enough*
peu	*little*
tant/tellement	*so much*
souvent	*often*
encore	*still/yet*
déjà	*already*

When using this grammar construction in the negative, the adverb is placed between **ne** and **pas**.

Il a **déjà** fini son rapport.	*He already finished his report.*
Je n'ai pas **encore** fini mon rapport.	*I have not yet finished my report.*
Elle a **beaucoup** travaillé.	*She worked a lot.*
Nous avons **bien** dormi.	*We slept well.*
J'ai **souven**t rêvé de lancer une startup.	*I often dreamed of launching a startup.*

To express time with the **passé composé**, **pendant** (*for, during*) is commonly used, although it can be omitted. The golden rule to remember is that **pour** (*for*) is never used in the past. Let's take a look at some sentences that carry the same meaning.

J'ai travaillé cinq ans à Toulouse.	*I worked five years in Toulouse.*
J'ai travaillé **pendant** cinq ans à Toulouse.	*I worked five years in Toulouse.*
Nous avons marché une heure dans la forêt.	*We walked for one hour in the woods.*
Nous avons marché **pendant** une heure dans la forêt.	*We walked for one hour in the woods.*

Pronominal Verbs in the *Passé Composé*

As we mentioned earlier, all pronominal verbs are conjugated with **être**. In this case, the reflexive pronoun precedes the auxiliary verb. And most of the time, the past participle agrees in gender and number with the subject.

se lever (*to get up*)

je me suis levé(e)	*I got up*	nous nous sommes levé(e)s	*we got up*
tu t'es levé(e)	*you got up*	vous vous êtes levé(e)(s)	*you got up*
il/elle s'est levé(e)	*he/she got up*	ils/elles se sont levé(e)s	*they got up*

Elle s'est assis**e** dans son fauteuil.   *She sat in her armchair.*

Ils se sont bien amus**és** à la fête.   *They had a great time at the party.*

Nous sommes promené(**e**)s le long de la   *We walked along the Seine.*
Seine.

In the negative, the negation is placed around the auxiliary verb **être**.

Il **ne** s'est **pas** habitué au télétravail.   *He did not get used to woking from home.*

Elles **ne** se sont **pas** reposées cet   *They did not rest this afternoon.*
après-midi.

In the interrogative form, the reflexive pronoun is placed before **être**.

S'est-elle lavé les mains avant de s'asseoir à table?   *Did she wash her hands before sitting at the table?*

T'es-tu souvenu de l'anniversaire de Marie?   *Did you remember Marie's birthday?*

Vous êtes-vous promenés dans le parc?   *Did you take a walk in the park?*

> **BTW**
>
> *Note that the past participle does not agree with the subject pronoun when the reflexive verb is followed by a direct object or by another verb.*

Elles se sont donné trois mois pour créer une application.   *They gave themselves three months to create an application.*

Elle s'est offert une console de jeux vidéo.   *She treated herself to a video game console.*

When reciprocal verbs take a direct object, the past participle agrees.

Ils se sont aperçus dans le théâtre.	*They caught a glimpse of each other in the theater.*
Ils se sont enlacés tendrement.	*They hugged each other tenderly.*

When reciprocal verbs take an indirect object, the past participle does not agree.

Marie et Clara se sont dit au revoir.	*Marie and Clara said good-bye to each other.*
George Sand et Alfred de Musset se sont écrit de longues lettres d'amour.	*George Sand and Alfred de Musset wrote each other long love letters.*

Versatile Verbs

Six versatile verbs can use either **avoir** or **être** in the **passé composé**: **sortir**, **rentrer**, **monter**, **descendre**, **passer**, and **retourner**. As we will see, depending on whether **avoir** or **être** is used, the meaning changes.

Elle **est** sortie du bureau à 18 heures.	*She left the office at 6 pm.*
Elle **a** sorti le chien ce matin à l'aube.	*She took the dog out at dawn.*

 IRL   For your own fun, memorize the lyrics for "Enfants du désert" by Diam's, where she sings: **Je suis sortie de ma bulle** (*I got out of my bubble*).

Elle **est rentrée** très tard.	*She came back home late.*
Elle **a rentré** les meubles de jardin dans le garage.	*She brought the garden furniture into the garage.*

Note here that **les meubles** is the direct object, so **avoir** is used.

Nous **sommes passés** par Bruxelles pour aller à Berlin.	*We drove through Brussels to go to Berlin.*
Nous **avons passé** la journée au Salon numérique.	*We spent the day at the Digital Fair.*

Note here that **la journée** is the direct object, so **avoir** is used.

Tu **es monté** en haut de la colline.	*You walked to the top of the hill.*
Tu **as monté** une armoire en vingt minutes.	*You assembled an armoire in twenty minutes.*

Note here that **une armoire** is the direct object, so **avoir** is used.

Je **suis descendue** dans la grotte de Chauvet.	*I went down the Chauvet grotto.*
J'**ai descendu** les marches prudemment.	*I went down the steps carefully.*

Note here that **les marches** is the direct object, so **avoir** is used.

Ils **sont retournés** à Bora Bora pour leur lune de miel.	*They went back to Bora Bora for their honeymoon.*
J'**ai retourné** la crêpe dans la poêle.	*I flipped the pancake in the pan.*

Note that **la crêpe** is the direct object so **avoir** is used.

Parts of the Home

Let's take a tour of the house.

l'entrée	entrance/foyer
le couloir	hallway
la cuisine	kitchen
la salle à manger	dining room

le salon	*living room*
la chambre	*bedroom*
l'escalier	*staircase*
le bureau	*office*
la salle de bain	*bathroom*
les toilettes	*restroom*
le placard	*closet*
le balcon	*balcony*
la terrasse	*terrace*
la cave	*cellar*
le grenier	*attic*
le sous-sol	*basement*
le garage	*garage*

Since, For, and Ago

Like in English, when talking about time, we often use to these complex grammar constructions: since, for, and ago. Because it's easy to conflate them, proceed with caution!

Since

The word *since* can be translated as **depuis** in French. In its simplest form, it can refer to an ongoing condition from a specific day, month, or year. While in English we use the word *since* with the past tense, in French it is used with the present tense.

Nous sommes fiancés **depuis** mai.   *We have been engaged since May.*
Elle enseigne le français **depuis** 2010.   *She has been teaching French*
                                              since 2010.

When expressing how a specific *event* changes an ongoing state of affairs, the **depuis que** and **depuis quand** are used.

Marie est en meilleure santé **depuis qu**'elle a commencé à travailler à la maison.	*Marie has been in better health since she started working at home.*
Elle est aux anges **depuis qu**'elle a été acceptée à Sciences Po.	*She has been over the moon ever since she got accepted to Sciences Po.*
Depuis quand connais-tu Clara?	*Since when have you known Clara?*
Depuis quand fais-tu partie de cette équipe?	*Since when have you been part of this team?*

For

When expressing the *duration* of an ongoing action, you have several options: **depuis, depuis combien de temps, il y a... que**, and **cela (ça) fait... que**. Note that all of these options use a length of time to modify the ongoing action. Most importantly, French uses the present tense, whereas English uses the past tense.

Let's begin with **depuis**. To ask a question about the duration of an action, use **depuis quand** (*since when*) or **depuis combien de temps** (*how long*). The grammar construction is different, but the meaning is the same.

Elle travaille chez elle **depuis** deux ans.	*She has been working at home for two years.*
Il y a deux ans **qu**'elle travaille chez elle.	*She has been working at home for two years.*
Cela fait deux ans **qu**'elle travaille chez elle.	*She has been working at home for two years.*

Il suit un cours en ligne **depuis** trois mois.	*He has been taking an online course for three months.*
Il y a que trois mois **qu**'il suit un cours en ligne.	*He has been taking an online course for three months.*
Cela fait trois mois **qu**'il suit un cours en ligne.	*He has been taking an online course for three months.*

Still, there is an important exception with negative sentences, where the **passé composé** is used instead of the present. Let's take a look.

Je n'ai pas vu Léa **depuis** un mois.	*I haven't seen Léa for a month.*
Il y a un mois **que** je n'ai pas vu Léa.	*I haven't seen Léa for a month.*
Cela fait un mois **que** je n'ai pas vu Léa.	*I haven't seen Léa for a month.*

Il n'est pas allé en Sicile **depuis** trois ans.	*He has not been to Sicily for three years.*
Il y a trois ans **qu**'il n'est pas allé en Sicile.	*He has not been to Sicily for three years.*
Cela fait trois ans **qu**'il n'est pas allé en Sicile.	*He has not been to Sicily for three years.*

Ago

To specify how long ago something was done, use **il y a** followed by a length of time.

Milo a créé son site web **il y a** un an.	*Milo created his website a year ago.*
Ils ont fait construire leur maison **il y a** dix ans.	*They had their house built ten years ago.*

DIALOGUE *Télétravailler et coder en ligne* Teleworking and coding online

Marie tells her friend Clara she is now working from home, juggling work and domestic chores while enjoying her online coding course.

IRL **Télétravail** has become more and more prevalent among professsionals. It allows workers to reduce their carbon footprint and cut down on the costs of commuting while allowing employers to more consistently rely on their workers regardless of weather conditions. Since 2012, the French government has been regulating **télétravail** to protect the rights of employees.

CLARA: Allô, Marie? C'est Clara. Comment vas-tu?

Hello, Marie? It's Clara. How are you doing?

MARIE: Ça va. Très occupée. Vraiment débordée!

I'm okay. Very busy. Truly overwhelmed!

CLARA: Je te dérange?

Am I bothering you?

MARIE: Pas du tout! J'ai eu une journée d'enfer. Contente de faire une pause.

Not at all! I had a hellish day. Happy to take a break.

CLARA: Qu'est-ce que tu as fait aujourd'hui?

What did you do today?

MARIE: Je ne sais pas si tu es au courant, mais j'ai commencé à télétravailler il y a deux mois.

I don't know if you are aware, but I started to work from home two months ago.

CLARA: Tu as changé d'emploi?

Did you change jobs?

MARIE: Non, mais depuis mon accident, la fatigue et les trajets dans les embouteillages avaient un impact négatif sur mon état de santé.

No, but since my accident, fatigue and commuting in traffic jams have had a negative impact on my health.

CLARA: Tu te sens mieux?

Do you feel better?

MARIE: Oui, mais j'ai eu raison d'accepter l'offre de mon employeur.

Yes, but I was right to accept my employer's offer.

CLARA: Qu'est-ce qu'il t'a proposé?

What did he offer you?

MARIE: Il a fait installer une station de travail ergonomique dans notre chambre d'amis, et il m'a offert un ordinateur.

He had an ergonomic work station installed in our guest room, and he gave me a computer.

CLARA: Mon patron n'est pas si généreux.

My boss isn't so generous.

MARIE: C'est tout à son avantage. Je ne peux jamais être en retard, je fais des heures supplémentaires et je libère un bureau dans l'entreprise.

It's all to his benefit. I can never be late, I work overtime, and I free up a desk in the company.

CLARA: Et tu évites la poussière, la pollution, et les potins des collègues.

And you avoid dust, pollution, and office gossip.

MARIE: Pas vraiment. Nous avons des vidéoconférences chaque semaine, potins compris.

Not really. We have video conferences each week, gossip included.

CLARA: Mais ce n'est pas difficile d'organiser sa journée? Il y a tant de choses à faire à la maison!

But is it not difficult to organize one's day? There are so many things to do at home!

MARIE: Très tôt ce matin, j'ai fait la lessive et j'ai passé l'aspirateur. Après, je me suis mise en mode télétravail.

Very early this morning, I did laundry and I vacuumed. After that, I put myself into work mode.

CLARA: Quelle discipline!

What discipline!

MARIE: J'ai appris à être autonome, à respecter le rythme, et à séparer le privé du professionnel.

I learned to be independent, to respect the work rhythm, and to separate the personal from the professional.

CLARA: Le monde a beaucoup changé, il faut s'adapter.

The world has changed a lot, we have to adapt.

MARIE: C'est vrai! Aussi, je me suis inscrite à une formation en ligne à La Capsule Academy pour apprendre à coder.

That's true! Also, I signed up for an online training at La Capsule Academy to learn coding.

CLARA: Tu vas passer encore plus de temps le soir devant ton écran?

Are you going to spend even more time at night in front of your screen?

MARIE: Oui, mais c'est génial et il y a beaucoup d'interaction avec des geeks super cool!

Yes, but it's awesome, and there is a lot of interaction with supercool geeks!

CLARA: Alors tu ne t'ennuies pas.

So you are not bored.

MARIE: Pas du tout! Et je suis en train d'apprendre à créer des sites web et des applications mobiles.

Not at all! And I am in the process of creating websites and mobile apps.

CLARA: Tu vas lancer une startup?

Are you going to launch a startup?

MARIE: J'ai toujours pensé qu'il n'y avait pas assez d'applications au service des personnes handicapées. Je pense à une application du genre Lpliz avec d'autres outils.

I always thought that there weren't enough apps for the handicapped. I am thinking of an app like Lpliz with other tools.

CLARA: Ouah! C'est fantastique! Bon courage et n'oublie pas de faire la cuisine ce soir. On ne code pas l'estomac vide. Au revoir.

Wow! That's fantastic! Good luck and don't forget to cook tonight. You don't code on an empty stomach.

MARIE: On se parle bientôt. Ciao, ciao.

We'll talk soon. Bye bye.

 IRL **Ciao** is an informal greeting borrowed from Italian to say good-bye. Here are some other words borrowed from Italian, many of which are used in music: **piano, adagio, a capella, maestro, carnaval, Mama Mia, al dente, charlatan, macaroon,** and many others. Thanks, Italy!

EXERCISES

EXERCISE 8.1

*Conjugate the following -er verbs using the **passé composé**.*

1. Il (passer) _____ l'aspirateur dans la chambre.

2. Nous (nettoyer) _____ la table du salon.

3. Elle (repasser) _____ sa robe blanche.

4. Vous (ranger) _____ les livres de cuisine.

5. Tu (débarrasser) _____ la table.

6. Il (vider) _____ la poubelle.

7. Je (cirer) _____ mes chaussures.

8. Il (demander) _____ une augmentation.

9. Nous (arroser) _____ les fleurs du jardin.

10. Elles (vérifier) _____ le thermostat.

EXERCISE 8.2

*Conjugate the following verbs in the **passé composé**.*

1. Ils (investir) _____ en Europe.

2. Nous (attendre) _____ André sur le quai de la gare.

3. Elle (choisir) _____ de télétravailler.

4. L'autobus (ralentir) _____ au croisement.

5. Vous (réussir) _____ à l'examen.

6. Nous (applaudir) _____ l'acrobate.

7. Je (perdre) _____ une boucle d'oreille.

8. Tu (agrandir) la photo de tes vacances.

9. Je (sentir) _____ une présence étrange.

10. Elles (faire) _____ la vaisselle.

EXERCISE 8.3

*Translate the following sentences using the **tu** form when applicable. When asking a question, use the **est-ce que** form.*

1. Did you cook last night?

2. He ironed his shirt and polished his shoes.

3. We did the laundry on Sunday morning.

4. Who emptied the dishwasher?

5. He cleaned the refrigerator.

6. I sorted out my summer clothes.

7. We did not do the dishes last night.

8. You did not wipe all the tables.

9. Did you vacuum the bedroom?

10. She set the table and lit the candles.

EXERCISE 8.4

Conjugate the following verbs in the **passé composé.**

1. Il (voir) _____ la liste des corvées domestiques et il (paniquer) _____.

2. Nous (suivre) _____ une formation informatique en ligne.

3. Tu (lire) _____ l'ordonnance « Macron » sur le télétravail.

4. L'employeur (mettre) _____ en place un bon système de télétravail.

5. Il (falloir) _____ s'ajuster à ce nouveau rythme de travail.

6. Il (recevoir) _____ un équipement adapté à son handicap.

7. Nous (vivre) _____ une expérience extraordinaire.

8. Vous (acquérir) _____ des compétences en informatique.

9. Il (repeindre) _____ son bureau en bleu.

10. Je lui (offrir) _____ un disque dur externe.

EXERCISE 8.5

Match the items in the two columns. Choose the most logical answer.

1. J'ai suivi   a. la vaisselle après le dîner.

2. Tu as repeint   b. une formation en ligne.

3. Il a plu   c. en 1850.

4. J'ai fait   d. toute la journée.

5. Balzac est mort   e. les murs d'une couleur différente.

EXERCISE 8.6

Conjugate the following verbs in the **passé composé.**

1. Diane, dans quelle ville _____ -vous (naître) _____?

2. L'enfant (tomber) _____ dans la cour de récréation.

3. Je (partir) _____ de chez moi à huit heures ce matin.

4. Toi et tes amis, vous (rentrer) _____ très tard.

5. Elles (rester) _____ une heure de plus.

6. Il (descendre) _____ du train.

7. Elle (devenir) _____ codeuse pour un studio d'animation.

8. Lise (monter) _____ dans l'avion.

9. Quel personnage de la série (mourir) _____ en premier?

10. Jeanne et moi, nous (aller) _____ au Salon des métiers du numérique à Lille.

EXERCISE 8.7

Rewrite the following sentences using the **passé composé.** *Be careful with the position of the adverb.*

1. L'enfant timide parle peu.

2. Nous dormons bien.

3. Elle téléphone souvent à sa collègue Patrice.

4. Vous ne mangez pas assez.

5. Ils dépensent trop dans le magasin d'électronique.

6. Il écrit bien le scénario.

7. Je m'exprime mal.

8. Il ment toujours.

9. Nous vivons mal cette expérience.

10. Je vais souvent au Bénin.

EXERCISE 8.8

*Translate the following sentences using the **tu** form when applicable. When asking a question, use **the est-ce que** form.*

1. He got off the train and he saw his parents on the platform.

2. I walked for an hour, then I drank two glasses of water.

3. René, did you go out this weekend?

4. She went to the animation studio.

5. We took the train from Paris to Lille.

6. Marie received a new computer.

7. They spent a lot of money during their vacation.

8. Sophie, at what time did you come back last night?

9. I already washed the dishes!

10. He waited for an hour, then he left.

EXERCISE 8.9

*Conjugate the following verbs in the **passé composé**. Watch out for the agreement of the past participle.*

1. Marie (se promener) _____ dans le jardin botanique.

2. Ils (ne pas s'écrire) _____ pendant des années.

3. Marie (se faire) _____ faire une nouvelle robe pour les fiançailles de Clara.

4. Marie et Carla (se rencontrer) _____ dans leur entreprise.

5. Mona (s'asseoir) _____ dans une chaise ergonomique.

6. Paul (ne pas se souvenir) _____ de l'heure du rendez-vous.

7. Ils (s'embrasser) _____ dans le parc.

8. Nora et Fiona (ne pas s'habituer) _____ au rythme de travail.

9. Est-ce qu'elles (se parler) _____ ce matin?

10. Elle (s'offrir) _____ une moto.

EXERCISE 8.10

*Conjugate the following verbs in the **passé composé**.*

1. Le crêpier (retourner) _____ les crêpes avec beaucoup d'agilité.

2. Marie (passer) _____ un examen pour obtenir son certificat.

3. Ashley (monter) _____ en haut de la tour Eiffel.

4. Pourquoi est-ce qu'elle (retourner) _____ en Alaska sans Victor?

5. Nous (passer) _____ devant le Panthéon.

6. Est-ce que tu (rentrer) _____ la voiture? Il va neiger.

7. Édouard (sortir) _____ de chez lui en courant.

8. Raoul (monter) _____ par l'escalier. Moi, j'ai pris l'ascenseur.

9. Je (descendre) _____ les poubelles dans la rue. Quelle corvée!

10. Qui (sortir) _____ le chien ce matin?

EXERCISE 8.11

Match the items in the two columns. Choose the most logical answer.

1. Nous sommes passés   a. la crypte.

2. J'ai monté   b. des vacances en Croatie.

3. Je suis descendu dans   c. un spectacle avec mes amis.

4. J'ai passé   d. sa plus belle robe de l'armoire.

5. Elle a sorti   e. devant les Galeries Lafayette.

EXERCISE 8.12

*Translate the following sentences using the **tu** form when applicable. When asking a question, use inversion.*

1. We went to Henri's on Friday night.

2. Jonathan remembered his appointment with Mr. Rufin.

3. She did not get used to her new job in Paris.

4. Did you bring the bicycle in?

5. They had a house built in Sicily.

6. Yves did not rest before his exam.

7. They called each other almost every day.

8. Benoît and Alexandra, where did you meet?

9. She passed by Lyon to go to Menton.

10. Why didn't you take the dog out this morning?

EXERCISE 8.13

Match the items in the two columns. Choose the most logical answer.

1. On range nos vêtements   a. dans la cuisine.

2. On prépare le dîner   b. dans la salle à manger.

3. On prend une douche   c. dans le placard.

4. On dort   d. dans la salle de bain.

5. On déjeune   e. dans la chambre.

EXERCISE 8.14

Translate the phrases in parentheses.

1. (*Since when*) _____ connais-tu Pierre? —Je connais Pierre depuis 2015.

2. (*How long*) _____ est-ce que tu travailles pour eux? —Depuis quatre ans.

3. (*Since when*) _____ sont-elles amies? —Elles sont amies depuis leur enfance.

4. (*Since when*) _____ est-ce qu'il repasse ses chemises? —Depuis qu'il travaille chez Airbus.

5. (*How long*) _____ est-ce qu'elle arrose les fleurs? —Depuis vingt minutes.

6. (*How long*) _____ est-ce que Balzac est mort? —Depuis plus d'un siècle et demi.

7. (*Since when*) _____ habitent-ils à Reims? —Ils habitent à Reims depuis qu'ils sont mariés.

8. (*How long*) _____ avez-vous pris votre retraite? —Depuis huit mois.

9. (*How long*) _____ Mathéo anime-t-il ses ateliers? —Il anime ses ateliers depuis trois ans.

10. (*Since when*) _____ Camélia est-elle la principale? —Depuis 2017.

EXERCISE 8.15

Rewrite the following sentences using **Cela fait... que** *instead of* **depuis**.

1. Il pleut sans cesse depuis deux heures.

2. J'ai cette chaise ergonomique depuis un mois.

3. Ils sont autonomes depuis plusieurs années.

4. La repasseuse repasse le linge depuis une heure.

5. Elle écrit ses mémoires depuis des années.

6. Clara et Marie se parlent depuis une heure et demie.

7. Nous conduisons sur l'A7 depuis des heures.

8. On boit du thé vert depuis un certain temps.

9. Vous suivez un cours en ligne depuis trois ans.

10. Il fait du judo depuis un an.

EXERCISE 8.16

Following the model, reconstruct the following sentences.

Charles/regarder la série/trente minutes. → <u>**Charles regarde la série depuis trente minutes.**</u>

1. Nous/connaître Marie/longtemps.

2. Il/lire ce livre de science-fiction/deux heures.

3. Vous/chercher un appartement/des mois.

4. Elle/dessiner/une demi-heure.

5. Ils/porter des vêtements vintage/les années 1980.

6. Nous/randonner dans la forêt/des heures.

7. Il/être amoureux de Sara/trois ans.

8. Elle/organiser ces fêtes/des années.

9. Il/ être le petit ami de Claire/un mois.

10. Tu/conduire malgré la tempête de neige/une heure.

EXERCISE 8.17

*Translate the following sentences using the **vous** form when applicable. When asking a question, use inversion.*

1. Since what year have you been working in this company?

2. They have been living in the 15th arrondissement forever.

3. I have not gone to Paris for three years.

4. How long have you been living in this apartment?

5. We have not seen our parents since December.

6. How long have you known Roland?

7. I have been waiting for you for half an hour!

8. Since when have you been eating quinoa?

9. She had been playing Phaedra for two months.

10. I have been studying Mandarin for two years.

LE COIN DES CRÉATEURS

LES LIEUX DU SOMMEIL

Imagine you spent the night in an unusual place. Describe the place and how you felt during the night, using as many **passé composé** constructions as possible.

Check these places you might consider in your dictionary: dans un train, sur un bateau, dans un arbre, dans un igloo, dans un champ, dans un monastère, sur une île, dans une maison sur pilotis, dans une caravane, sous la tente, dans une jarre, dans un musée, sur une gondole, etc. Select a place and write a short paragraph, following the example below:

La nuit dernière, **j'ai dormi** dans un hamac. **J'ai trouvé** ce hamac accroché à deux arbres au bord de la mer, et **j'ai décidé** de me reposer. **Je me suis installé** et **j'ai commencé** à rêver. Tout à coup **j'ai entendu...**

NOTE CULTURELLE

THE NEW WORK SPACE

Historically, "going to work" meant leaving the house and traveling to a specific location, a workplace or work site, where a job was performed for a specified time period. Once done with the day's work, the employee left the workplace, only to return the next scheduled working day to repeat the process. While many people are still on a "9 to 5" work schedule, advances in technology and telecommunications have made it possible for many jobs to be performed elsewhere, either at home, during business travel, or in shared workplaces like WeWork. The new workplace is not always what it used to be. People working under these new arrangements are "teleworkers" (*télétravailleurs*), performing "telework" or "teleworking" (*télétravail*).

Teleworking is a worldwide phenomenon, and it has become increasingly popular in France. According to a study conducted in 2018 by the Institut Français d'Opinion Publique (IFOP), an international polling and market research firm, approximately 25 percent of French employees make use of teleworking. However, only 6 percent of those do so based on an employment contract. In order to provide legal structure and protection for all teleworkers and their employers, the French government has enacted legislation defining what it is and listing the obligations of both teleworking employees and their employers.

In France, Article L1222-9 of the Labor Code defines teleworking as "any manner of arranging work in which a job that could also be performed in the employer's premises is done by an employee outside of those premises, on a voluntary basis, using information communications technologies." This law was amended by a presidential order, known as an *ordonnance*, to cover teleworking done on a regular basis, as well as occasional or situational telework made necessary due to inclement weather, natural disaster, or special work assignments.

Both the order and the law emphasize the voluntary aspect of teleworking and the need for an agreement between the employee and employer authorizing it. Such an agreement may be made when an employee is hired, or introduced later. The location where the work is to be performed is not specified: it may be at home, at a remote location, while in transit, at a business center, or elsewhere. These agreements may be part of a collective bargaining agreement negotiated by a union or directly with the employer, or privately negotiated. However, teleworking is not an absolute right for an employee, and an employer can reject a request for such an arrangement provided it is based on solid legal grounds. And, with the exception of certain cases such as a health epidemic or natural disaster, when the employer's premises cannot be accessed, an employee cannot be required to telework. It is important to remember that the teleworker has the same rights as the employee who performs his duties on the company's premises.

The flexibility teleworking provides is definitely one of its major advantages. This can be particularly appealing for employees with disabilities who may have difficulty in accessing the employer's premises. It allows them to adapt their working hours to accommodate their physical requirements and to schedule regular medical or rehabilitative treatments otherwise impossible during the "normal" workday. For those with mobility problems, it also reduces or even eliminates travel time and the stress and fatigue that often accompany a daily commute. If adaptation of the disabled employee's work premises is needed, it is the responsibility of the employer. However, funds are available to assist both public- and private-sector employers in covering the cost. The law also applies to temporary teleworking, enabling employees with temporary disabilities to adjust their work schedules according to their physical condition.

Teleworking has many advantages for employees and employers alike, and for the most part, it is a win-win concept, but it is not perfect. For the employer, there is the missed opportunity of constant interaction with staff. There is also a need to be mindful at all times of the laws governing teleworking, so that the rights of teleworkers are not violated and they are treated the same way as regular employees.

For the teleworker, working off-site requires discipline, particularly when it is at home. Schedules must be respected, and the amount of work produced and the number of working hours must be the same as if on the employer's premises. Vigilance is also needed to maintain the separation between private and professional life. Finally, there is the issue of isolation and loneliness. An employee who works alone often misses out on the face-to-face interaction with colleagues that is so important for job satisfaction and success.

Teleworking is not "one-size-fits-all" and may not be for everyone, but the concept is appealing and is sure to become more widespread over time.

To Know and How to Use Object Pronouns

MUST KNOW

 Connaître is never followed by a dependent clause.

 Use **savoir** to say you know something by heart.

 Le, la, and **les** are direct and **lui** and **leur** are indirect object pronouns.

 Je lui parle can refer to either *him* or *her*.

kepticism is very French. As Montaigne said, **"Que sais-je?"** To be able to dissect this profound question, you'll need to understand the differences between **savoir** and **connaître,** which both mean *to know.* But to say "I know it," you'll also need to learn about direct and indirect object pronouns. This will be a challenge, but once you get a grip on the ordering of object pronouns, you'll finally get to say "I know it!"

Savoir vs. Connaître

Both **savoir** and **connaître** mean *to know*, though they are used differently.

Savoir

Savoir means to know a fact or to know how to do something from memory. This is how it is conjugated in the present tense:

je sais	*I know*	nous savons	*we know*
tu sais	*you know*	vous savez	*you know*
il/elle/on sait	*he/she/one knows*	ils/elles savent	*they know*

Here are some sample sentences:

Elles savent cette chanson.	*They know this song (by heart).*
Il sait tout.	*He knows everything.*
Je sais compter.	*I know how to count.*
Est-ce que tu sais coudre?	*Can you sew?*
Savez-vous nager?	*Can you swim?*

> **BTW**
> **Savoir** *will sometimes be translated as* can.

Savoir is also used before before an infinitive or before a dependent clause.

Elle sait écrire un discours émouvant.	*She knows how to write a moving speech.*
Savez-vous combien coûte l'essence en France?	*Do you know how much gas costs in France?*

Je sais **qui il** est.   *I know who he is.*

Nous savons qu'il étudie le portugais.   *We know that he studies Portugese.*

Connaître

Connaître means *to know*, *to be acquainted with*, or *to be familiar with*. It also means *to enjoy* or *experience*. It is always followed by a direct object, never by a dependent clause.

je connais	*I know*	nous connaissons	*we know*
tu connais	*you know*	vous connaissez	*you know*
il/elle/on connaît	*he/she/one knows*	ils/elles connaissent	*they know*

Here are some sample sentences:

Connaissez-vous cet acteur anglais?	*Do you know this English actor?*
Elle connaît un bon restaurant mexicain.	*She knows a good Mexican restaurant.*
Ce nouvel opéra connaît un grand succès.	*This new opera is enjoying a great success.*

Direct and Indirect Object Pronouns

Because object pronouns replace a noun that is being acted on, shared knowledge of the topic is presumed when using it. In this way, they help us to avoid repetition and be more concise. There are two types of object pronouns: direct and indirect.

The Direct Object Pronoun

In English there are seven direct object pronouns: *me*, *you*, *him*, *her*, *it*, *us*, and *them*. Because of the distinction between **tu** and **vous**, in French there are eight direct object pronouns instead of seven. While in English there is a distinction between a direct object pronoun that replaces a person (*him*, *her*, or *them*) and a thing (*it* or *them*), in French **le**, **la**, and **les** can replace both people and things.

singular		plural	
me	*me*	nous	*us*
te	*you* (familiar)	vous	*you* (plural or formal)
le	*him* or *it* (masc.)	les	*them* (masc. and fem.)
la	*her* or *it* (fem.)		

An object is called direct if it immediately follows the verb without a preposition. The direct object pronoun replaces the direct object noun. In French, the direct object pronoun must agree in gender and in number with the noun it replaces. And it precedes the main verb of the sentence.

Note that when there are compound verbs, the placement of the direct object pronoun may change. But for now, keep it directly before the main verb. Here are some examples of how they are used in the third person:

Nicolas regarde le film.	*Nicolas is watching the movie.*
Nicolas **le** regarde.	*Nicolas is watching it.*
Sabine prend la photo.	*Sabine is taking the picture.*
Sabine **la** prend.	*Sabine is taking it.*
Il aime le thé noir.	*He likes black tea.*
Il **l'**aime.	*He likes it.*
Nous comprenons les questions.	*We understand the questions.*
Nous **les** comprenons.	*We understand them.*

When used in a negative sentence, the direct object pronoun comes immediately before the conjugated verb.

Je ne connais pas Madame Duvernay.	*I don't know Madame Duvernay.*
Je ne **la** connais pas.	*I don't know her.*
Nolan ne connaît pas les élèves du lycée Claude Monet.	*Nolan does not know the students at Claude Monet High School.*
Nolan ne **les** connaît pas.	*Nolan does not know them.*

When used in a question, the direct object pronoun also comes before the conjugated verb.

Tu vois la bibliothèque?	*Do you see the library?*
Tu **la** vois?	*Do you see it?*

Est-ce que Clémence connaît les secrets de Nolan?	*Does Clémence know Nolan's secrets?*
Est-ce que Clémence **les** connaît?	*Does Clémence know them?*

> **BTW**
> When using inversion to ask a question, the direct object pronoun begins the sentence.

Tu sais le poème par cœur?	*Do you know the poem by heart?*
Le sais-tu par cœur?	*Do you know it by heart?*

Elle prend ses photos avec un iPhone?	*Does she take her pictures with an iPhone?*
Les prend-elle avec un iPhone?	*Does she take them with an iPhone?*

Remember that direct object pronouns can also be used in the first person and second person, both singular and plural. And it follows the same rules as **le**, **la**, and **les**.

Il me contacte par email.	*He contacts me by email.*
Nous vous croyons.	*We believe you.*
Je t'aime.	*I love you.*
Et toi, est-ce que tu m'aimes?	*And you, do you love me?*
Vous ne nous écoutez pas!	*You are not listening to us!*
Je vous remercie de votre générosité.	*Thank you for your generosity.*

Indirect Object Pronouns

In English, there are seven indirect object pronouns: *me, you, him, her, it, us, them*. As always, French distinguishes between an informal *you* (**tu**) and a formal and/or plural *you* (**vous**). But the French indirect object pronouns do not specify gender. **Lui** and **leur** replace all nouns, both masculine and feminine. Furthermore, inanimate ideas and things are replaced with the indrect object pronouns **y** and **en**, which will be mentioned later in the chapter.

singular		plural	
me (m')	*me*	nous	*us*
te (t')	*you* (familiar)	vous	*you* (plural or formal)
lui	*him*, *her*	leur	*them* (masc. and fem.)

The object is labeled *indirect* when the verb is controlled by a preposition (**parler à**, **écrire à**, etc.), and the indirect object pronoun is placed before the conjugated verb. And in cases where there are compound verbs, it goes before **avoir**. Finally, remember to distinguish between **leur**, the indirect object pronoun, and **leur(s)**, the possessive adjective. Here are some sentences using indirect object pronouns in the third-person singular and plural:

Elle téléphone **à** son neveu.	*She calls her nephew.*
Elle **lui** téléphone.	*She calls him.*
Il parle **à** sa nièce.	*He talks to his niece.*
Il **lui** parle.	*He talks to her.*
Je prête mon appartement **à** mes copains.	*I am lending my apartment to my friends.*
Je **leur** prête mon appartement.	*I am lending them my apartment.*
Nous souhaitons un joyeux anniversaire **aux** sœurs jumelles.	*We are wishing the twin sisters a happy birthday.*
Nous **leur** souhaitons un joyeux anniversaire.	*We are wishing them a happy birthday.*

Now let's add the indirect object pronouns **me**, **te**, **nous**, and **vous** into the mix.

Je te dis la vérité.	*I am telling you the truth.*
Il ne me répond jamais.	*He never responds to me.*
Qu'est-ce que tu nous racontes?	*What are you telling us?*
Elle vous pose des questions difficiles.	*She asks you difficult questions.*

Remember that when object pronouns precede a verb beginning with a vowel, **me** and **te** become **m'** and **t'**.

Elle **m'**envoie des fleurs pour mon anniversaire.	*She sends me flowers for my birthday.*

The Order of Object Pronouns

When a direct and indirect object pronoun are combined in the same sentence, the indirect object pronoun comes first, unless the direct and indirect pronouns are in the third person. In this case, the direct object pronoun comes first.

The first-person and the second-person pronouns are:

indirect object	direct object
me (m')	
te (t')	+ le, la, l', les
nous	
vous	

Je t'envoie une réponse demain.	*I will send you an answer tomorrow.*
Je **te l'**envoie demain.	*I will send it to you tomorrow.*

Il me donne les clés.	*He gives me the keys.*
Il **me les** donne.	*He gives me them.*

Elle ne va pas te prêter sa moto!	*She is not going to lend you her motorcycle!*
Elle ne va pas **te la** prêter!	*She is not going to lend you it!*

The third-person pronouns are:

direct object   **indirect object**

le (l')
la (l')   + lui, leur
les

Nous lui racontons la fin du film.   *We are telling him the end of the movie.*
Nous **la lui** racontons.   *We are telling it to him.*

Est-ce que tu leur vends ton voilier?   *Are you selling them your sailboat?*
Est-ce que tu **le leur** vends?   *Are you selling it to them?*

Je ne lui pardonnerai jamais son   *I will never forgive him for his behavior!*
comportement.
Je ne **le lui** pardonnerai jamais!   *I will never forgive him for it!*

Restrictions on the Use of Object Pronouns

Some verbs followed by the preposition **à** or **de** do not follow the aforementioned rule. Instead of an indirect object pronoun, a stressed pronoun (**moi, toi, lui, elle, nous, vous, eux**) comes after the verb. And depending on the preposition, the meaning of the verb may change; it is just a matter of memorizing.

Je pense à Philippe.   *I am thinking about Philippe.*
Je pense à lui.   *I am thinking about him.*

Que penses-tu de la nouvelle   *What do you think of the new president?*
présidente?
Que penses-tu d'elle?   *What do you think of her?*

Ils parlent des joueuses de foot.   *They are talking about the soccer players.*
Ils parlent d'elles.   *They are talking about them.*

Nous avons besoin de nos assistants.	*We need our assistants.*
Nous avons besoin d'eux.	*We need them.*
Est-ce que tu as peur de ton patron?	*Are you afraid of your boss?*
Est-ce que tu as peur de lui?	*Are you afraid of him?*
Le moniteur s'occupe des surfeurs.	*The monitor takes care of the surfers.*
Le moniteur s'occupe d'eux.	*The monitor takes care of them.*
Nous ne nous souvenons pas de l'ancien entraîneur.	*We do not remember the former trainer.*
Nous ne nous souvenons pas de lui.	*We do not remember him.*
Je ne me fie pas à cet avocat.	*I don't trust this lawyer.*
Je ne me fie pas à lui.	*I don't trust him.*
L'agent s'intéresse à cette nouvelle actrice.	*The agent is interested in this new actress.*
L'agent s'intéresse à elle.	*The agent is interested in her.*
Vous ne vous plaignez jamais de vos voisins.	*You never complain about your neighbors.*
Vous ne vous plaignez jamais d'eux.	*You never complain about them.*

En and y

Here's a simple trick: **y** goes with **à**, and **de** goes with **en**. You can think of them as grammatical shortcuts for not repeating objects.

The Pronoun *en*

En is an indirect object pronoun that precedes the verb. It usually replaces an inanimate object (thing or idea) preceded by **de**. The pronoun **en** immediatelty precedes the verb, except in affirmative imperative commands. In this case, **en** follows the verb and is connected with a hyphen. And with pronominal verbs, the **en** goes right after the reflexive pronoun.

Les journaux parlent du championnat de surf.	*The newspapers are talking about the surf championship.*
Les journaux en parlent.	*The newspapers are talking about it.*
L'association s'occupe de tous les détails.	*The association is dealing with all the details.*
L'association s'en occupe.	*The association is dealing with all of it.*
Emmanuelle a besoin d'une combinaison de plongée.	*Emmanuelle needs a wet suit.*
Emmanuelle en a besoin.	*Emmanuelle needs it.*
Henri et moi nous n'avons pas peur des grosses vagues.	*Henri and I are not afraid of big waves.*
Henri et moi nous n'en avons pas peur.	*Henri and I are not afraid of them.*
Je m'approche du bateau.	*I am getting close to the boat.*
Je m'en approche.	*I am getting close to it.*
Manon a envie de faire de la plongée en Australie.	*Manon feels like going diving in Australia.*
Manon en a envie.	*Manon feels like it.*
On veut se débarrasser de tous ces trucs inutiles.	*We want to get rid of all this useless stuff.*
On veut s'en débarrasser.	*We want to get rid of it.*
Tu te plains toujours du bruit.	*You always complain about the noise.*
Tu t'en plains toujours.	*You always complain about it.*
Michel se sert d'une lampe de plongée.	*Michel is using a diving lamp.*
Michel s'en sert.	*Michel is using it.*
Te souviens-tu des paroles de la chanson?	*Do you remember the song lyrics?*
T'en souviens-tu?	*Do you remember them?*

The Pronoun *y*

Y is also an indirect object pronoun that precedes the verb. It usually replaces an inanimate object (thing or idea). The object replaced by **y** is considered indirect because it is preceded by a preposition, usually **à**. And it follows the same gramatical rules as **en**.

On s'habitue facilement **au** climat de Biarritz.	*We easily adjust to the Biarritz climate.*
On s'y habitue facilement.	*We easily adjust to it.*
Nous nous inscrivons **à** un cours de plongée.	*We are signing up for a diving class.*
Nous nous y inscrivons.	*We are signing up for it.*
Pourquoi est-ce que tu ne réponds pas **à** mes textos?	*Why are you not responding to my texts?*
Pourquoi est-ce que tu n'y réponds pas?	*Why are you not responding to them?*
Je ne m'intéresse pas **à** tous ces potins.	*I am not interested in all this gossip.*
Je ne m'y intéresse pas.	*I am not interested in it.*
Florentin réfléchit **à** son passé.	*Florentin is reflecting about his past.*
Florentin y réfléchit.	*Florentin is reflecting about it.*
Fabrice tient **à** sa Clio IV.	*Fabrice is attached to his Clio IV.*
Fabrice y tient.	*Fabrice is attached to it.*
Tu veux goûter **à** cette sauce épicée?	*Do you want to taste this spicy sauce?*
Tu veux y goûter?	*Do you want to taste it?*
Vous ne prêtez jamais attention **à** ce qu'elle dit.	*You never pay attention to what she says.*
Vous n'y prêtez jamais attention.	*You never pay attention to it.*
La sorcière croit **à** la magie.	*The witch believes in magic.*
La sorcière y croit.	*The witch believes in it.*

On obéit **aux** règlements.   *We obey the rules.*
On y obéit.   *We obey them.*

Object Pronouns with Compound Tenses

Now it's time to mix and match what we just learned with the **passé composé**. The two most important items to remember are the placement and order of the object pronouns, as well as possible agreements with **avoir**.

Direct Object Pronouns

In the **passé composé** and other compound tenses, the direct object pronoun is placed before the auxiliary verb. The past participle agrees in number and gender with the direct object when the direct object precedes the verb.

As-tu lu ce roman de Laurent   *Have you read this Laurent*
Mauvignier?   *Mauvignier novel?*
L'as-tu **lu**?   *Have you read it?*

Il a remercié Madame Legrand.   *He thanked Madame Legrand.*
Il l'a remerci**ée**.   *He thanked her.*

L'agent immobilier n'a pas   *The real estate agent did not contact*
contacté ses clients.   *his clients.*
L'agent immobilier ne les a pas   *The real estate agent did not*
contact**és**.   *contact them.*

Amélie a pris les photos d'anniversaire.   *Amélie took the birthday pictures.*
Amélie les a pris**es**.   *Amélie took them.*

Indirect Object Pronouns

Like direct object pronouns, when indirect object pronouns are combined with compound tenses, they are placed right before the auxiliary verb. But unlike direct object pronouns, the participle is not modified to make it agree.

Fabien a prêté sa voiture à Paul.	*Fabien lent his car to Paul.*
Fabien lui a prêté sa voiture.	*Fabien lent him his car.*

When direct and indirect object pronouns are combined with compound tenses, the participle is modified to agree with the direct object pronoun, and it follows the order rules found in the chart above.

Rémi a rendu le stylo à sa camarade de classe.	*Rémi returned the pen to his classmate.*
Rémi le lui a rend**u**.	*Rémi returned it to her.*
Le professeur a expliqué la leçon aux élèves.	*The teacher explained the lesson to the students.*
Le professeur la leur a expliqu**ée**.	*The teacher explained it to them.*
On n'a pas envoyé les documents aux stagiaires.	*We didn't send the interns their documents.*
On ne les leur a pas envoy**és**.	*We didn't send them to them.*

And remember that the order changes when dealing with the first person and second person, both singular and plural.

Il m'a décrit l'incident.	*He described the incident to me.*
Il me l'a décri**t**.	*He described it to me.*
Nous t'avons envoyé l'invitation.	*We sent you the invitation.*
Nous te l'avons envoy**ée**.	*We sent it to you.*

When **en** is combined with an indirect object pronoun, it is always in the second position. The past participle agrees neither in number nor gender with **en** (nor does it agree with any other indirect object pronoun).

Angèle lui a apporté deux billets pour le concert.	*Angèle brought her two tickets to the concert.*
Angèle lui en a apporté deux.	*Angèle brought her two of them.*

Je leur ai parlé du nouveau film de Louis Garrel.	*I talked to them about the new Louis Garrel film.*
Je leur en ai parlé.	*I talked to them about it.*

 ### DIALOGUE *Après-midi de bavardages!* ## Some Afternoon Small Talk!

Maëlys and Nolan are talking in front of their school, the lycée Gabriel Fauré in the 13th arrondissement. Nolan is surprised that Maëlys' brother Loïc is not around. Time for gossip.

NOLAN: Ton frère n'est pas là?   *Is your brother not here?*

MAËLYS: Euh... non. Loïc est à Hossegor avec Émilie.   *Uh...no. Loïc is in Hossegor with Émilie.*

NOLAN: Émilie? C'est qui?   *Émilie? Who is she?*

MAËLYS: C'est la voisine de Julien.   *She is Julien's neighbor.*

NOLAN: C'est incroyable, tu sais toujours tout sur tout le monde!   *It is unbelievable, you always know everything about everybody!*

MAËLYS: Julien, c'est mon frère, non?   *Julien is my brother, isn't he?*

BTW

In the sentence **C'est mon frère, non?**, *the* **non** *is the equivalent of "isn't he?":* **Il est heureux, non?** *(He is happy, isn't he?) It is more common in modern language to use* **non?** *than* **n'est-ce pas**, *which often sounds affected. Otherwise,* **non** *means no, like* **Si je dis non, c'est non!** *(If I say no, I mean no!) With* **Bien sûr que non!** *(Of course not!), you'll have everybody's attention!*

NOLAN: Hossegor? Dans les Landes?   *Hossegor? In the Landes department?*

MAËLYS: Oui, Hossegor, près de Biarritz. C'est pour le championnat du monde de longboard.   *Yes, Hossegor, near Biarritz. It's for the longboard surfing world championship.*

NOLAN: Il s'intéresse au surf maintenant? Et toi, tu la connais cette Émilie?

Is he interested in surfing now? And you, do you know that Émilie?

MAËLYS: Non, je ne la connais pas. Mais je sais qu'elle va au lycée Claude Monet dans le 13ᵉ.

No, I don't know her. But I know she goes to Claude Monet high school in the 13th arrondissement.

NOLAN: Claude Monet? C'est le lycée de ma cousine Claire!

Claude Monet? That's my cousin Claire's high school!

MAËLYS: Le monde est petit!

It is a small world!

NOLAN: Je ne sais pas pourquoi Loïc ne m'a rien dit.

I don't know why Loïc didn't tell me anything.

MAËLYS: Tu sais, Loïc a beaucoup de secrets...

You know, Loïc has lots of secrets...

NOLAN: Ouais, mais c'est un de mes meilleurs copains. Il est amoureux?

Yeah, but he is one of my best friends. Is he in love?

BTW

The word **ouais** is an informal way to say **oui**. But when you're talking to your teacher or your boss, just use **oui**. Otherwise, it might come across as disrespectful.

MAËLYS: Je ne sais pas. Il ne me dit pas tout. Il te le dira peut-être.

I don't know. He does not tell me everything. Maybe he will tell you.

NOLAN: Je vais appeler Claire. Elle connaît probablement Émilie.

I am going to call Claire. She probably knows Émilie.

MAËLYS: Tu rêves? Il y a plus de 2000 élèves dans cette boîte.

Are you dreaming? There are more than 2,000 students in that school.

BTW

*The word **boîte** carries many meanings. It can refer to a box, a dance club, a company, or, as we saw in the dialogue, a school (**lycée, collège**). Don't forget the **accent circonflexe** on the î; otherwise, you might indicate that you twisted your ankle or you are limping: **je boite**. Evidently, the word **boîte** can open up **une boîte de Pandore** (Pandora's box) of meanings!*

NOLAN: De toute façon, ce n'est pas parce que Loïc fait du surf que la terre va cesser de tourner.

Anyway, it is not because of Loïc's surfing that the earth is going to stop spinning.

MAËLYS: C'est vrai et j'ai un essai à écrire pour mon cours de français.

True, and I have an essay to write for my French class.

NOLAN: Tu veux venir avec moi à la bibliothèque François Mitterrand?

Do you want to come with me to the François Mitterrand library?

MAËLYS: Non, je n'ai pas le temps. Qu'est-ce que tu cherches?

No, I don't have time. What are you looking for?

NOLAN: J'ai besoin de lire un texte publié dans *Le Monde* en 1950.

I need to read an article published in Le Monde in 1950.

MAËLYS: Je ne peux pas écrire dans une bibliothèque. Trop de distractions.

I cannot write in a library. Too many distractions.

NOLAN: Pas du tout! C'est un lieu très calme pour étudier.

Not at all! It is such a quiet place to study.

MAËLYS: (ironique) C'est aussi un bon endroit pour rencontrer des gens...

(with a touch of irony) It is also a great place to meet people...

NOLAN: Ce n'est pas faux...

It is quite true...

MAËLYS: Amuse-toi bien. Salut!

Have fun. Bye!

NOLAN: Bye, Maëlys! À la prochaine!

Bye, Maëlys! See you next time!

BTW

When someone is rebutting a negative question or statement, the word si *is used instead of* oui. *This comes in especially handy when trying to correct someone:*

—Nolan, tu n'aimes pas le surf? —Mais si! J'adore le surf.

—Rémi, tu n'as pas fait tes devoirs! —Si, je les ai faits!

Talking about negative... Like in English, a negative statement may imply a positive idea. When Nolan says « ce n'est pas faux », he really means it is quite true. If your friend tells you « Ce film n'est pas mal », it most probably implies that the film is quite good. L'art de la litote *is an art you will master as you progress in your French studies.*

 IRL When saying **un ami** or **une amie** (*friend*), you might be implying different meanings. It can mean a good friend or a special friend, or even a boyfriend or girlfriend. The word **copain/copine** (*pal/buddy*) is a less formal way to introduce your friend, but, again, it can also mean your boyfriend or girlfriend when used with a possessive adjective (**C'est mon copain/c'est ma copine**). You'll have to pay attention to the context to discern the nature of the relationship. Finally, if you want to refer more specifically to a romantic partner, use the word **compagnon/compagne: c'est mon compagnon/c'est ma compagne.**

EXERCISES

EXERCISE 9.1

*Conjugate **savoir** and **connaître** in the present tense.*

1. Je (connaître) _____ bien ce comédien.

2. Je (ne pas savoir) _____ où ils habitent.

3. Manon (savoir) _____ ce poème.

4. Est-ce que vous (connaître) _____ ce nouveau logiciel?

5. Joséphine (savoir) _____ le nom de la capitale du Kirghizistan.

6. Luc (ne pas connaître) _____ l'histoire du Kirghizistan.

7. Gaël et moi, nous (connaître) _____ une très bonne auberge en Dordogne.

8. Est-ce que tu (connaître) _____ Christophe Lambert?

9. Vous (savoir) _____ combien ça coûte?

10. Ils (savoir) _____ de quoi ils parlent.

EXERCISE 9.2

*Complete the sentences with **savoir** or **connaître** in the present tense.*

1. Théo _____ Roland depuis trois mois.

2. Est-ce que vous _____ pourquoi il est en retard?

3. Noah _____ parler le russe couramment.

4. Cette pièce de théâtre _____ un grand succès.

5. Je _____ la mère de Véronique.

6. Lucy et Hélène _____ une excellente brasserie dans le sixième arrondissement.

7. Est-ce que tu _____ compter jusqu'à mille en français?

8. Nous _____ jouer du saxophone.

9. _____ -vous un coiffeur dans ce quartier?

10. Je _____ qu'Audric a un excellent professeur d'informatique.

EXERCISE 9.3

Translate the following sentences. When asking questions, use the **est-ce que** *form.*

1. Do you know Arthur? (*tu*)

2. Claire and Gaspard can speak Japanese.

3. Simon knows all the songs by Dalida by heart.

4. They don't know if this village is in Provence.

5. How do you know Liam's sister? (*tu*)

6. The new film by Louis-Julien Petit is enjoying a great success.

7. We know where the best Chinese restaurant in the 13th arrondissement is located.

8. I do not know if Oscar knows how to swim.

9. We know a software that can translate documents into ancient Greek.

10. Do you know the poem by Baudelaire called *L'invitation au voyage*? (*vous*)

EXERCISE 9.4

*Rewrite the following sentences and replace the words in bold with direct object pronouns in the third person (**le, la, les**).*

1. Les élèves comprennent **l'explication du professeur d'anthropologie**.

2. Suivez-vous **le cours d'anglais de Madame Atherton**?

3. Nolan ne porte pas **la planche de surf d'Émilie**.

4. Il regarde **le championnat du monde de surf** à la télé.

5. Le professeur apporte **tous les documents** pour la présentation.

6. Prenez-vous **le train** à la gare Montparnasse ou à la gare d'Austerlitz?

7. La famille Thominet n'invite pas **le directeur du lycée** à leur soirée.

8. Lola et Isabelle racontent **leurs aventures en Patagonie**.

9. Nous n'aimons pas **les examens de géométrie**.

10. Est-ce que tu appelles **la nouvelle élève** Angélique ou Angie?

EXERCISE 9.5

*Translate the following sentences. When translating questions, use the **est-ce que** form.*

1. I believe you. (*tu*)

2. Do we invite him? (*on*)

3. He takes it with sugar.

4. She thanks me.

5. They do not understand us. (*elles*)

6. We respect them.

7. He does not know them.

8. Do you see me? (*vous*)

9. They call me every day.

10. Why do you do it? (*tu*)

EXERCISE 9.6

*Rewrite the following sentences and replace the words in bold with indirect object pronouns in the third person (**lui, leur**).*

1. Il écrit **à sa tante**.

2. Le guide montre les sculptures de Nikki de Saint Phalle **aux touristes**.

3. Cette planche de surf appartient **au moniteur**.

4. L'employée explique **aux clients** comment remplir les formulaires.

5. Sylvain raconte l'histoire de « Réparer les vivants » **à sa mère**.

6. Pourquoi est-ce que tu donnes ton argent de poche **à ton frère aîné**?

7. Nous faisons souvent des cadeaux **à nos arrière-grands-parents**.

8. Xavier téléphone **à sa copine Odile**.

9. Hugo rend le roman de Maylis de Kerangal **à son professeur**.

10. Je ne sais pas comment répondre **à Félix**. C'est trop compliqué!

EXERCISE 9.7

*Rewrite the following sentences and replace the words in bold with **y** or **en**.*

1. Clara s'occupe **des réservations d'hôtel**.

2. Est-ce que tu as envie **d'aller en Normandie**?

3. Son copain s'intéresse **aux films de science-fiction**.

4. Nous pensons **à nos examens**.

5. Noémie ne se souvient pas **de l'adresse du club nautique**.

6. Pierre renonce **à sa candidature**.

7. Elles ne s'habituent pas **à leur nouvel emploi**.

8. Pensez-vous **à vos prochaines vacances**?

9. J'ai peur **des fantômes**.

10. Delphine tient **à ses bijoux**.

EXERCISE 9.8

Rewrite the following sentences and replace the words in bold with the appropriate object pronouns. Watch out for agreement.

1. Clément a prêté **sa lampe de plongée à Yanis**.

2. J'ai emprunté **le dictionnaire des synonymes français à Gilles**.

3. Avez-vous recommandé **ce candidat au directeur des ressources humaines**.

4. Sophia m'a envoyé **sa lettre de motivation**.

5. Ils t'ont promis **une augmentation**.

6. Vous avez encore fait **les mêmes erreurs**!

7. Alexandra a vendu **son appartement à Rita et Hisham**.

8. J'ai donné **mon mot de passe à mon petit frère et son copain**.

9. Pourquoi est-ce que Adam ne nous a pas encore servi **les desserts**?

10. On a mis **les assiettes sales** dans le lave-vaisselle.

EXERCISE 9.9

Translate the following sentences. When asking questions, use inversion.

1. Agathe knows this French song by heart.

2. Is he afraid of it?

3. Lise did not thank us.

4. We got rid of it. (*on*)

5. I don't know if you remember me. (*tu*)

6. Romane is thinking about him.

7. The divers don't need it.

8. Do you know Alicia's neighbors? (*vous*)

9. I never got used to it.

10. Do you know who sent them to me? (*tu*)

LE COIN DES CRÉATEURS

BIOGRAPHÈME

Re-create fragments (real or imaginary) of the life of a writer you know, following the example below. Mark Twain, Toni Morrison, Annie Proulx, Ernest Hemingway? Choose any writer, whatever the century or the nationality.

Marguerite Duras

Marguerite Duras passe des heures sur son balcon à Trouville.
Je me souviens du jour où Duras m'a raconté sa vie en Indochine.
Duras aimait traverser le Mékong tôt le matin.
Elle se promenait dans les rues de la ville.
Elle...

À votre tour!

NOTE CULTURELLE

THE FRENCH PRESS: YOU ARE WHAT YOU READ, SERIOUSLY!

Much as it has throughout the world, the serious press in France has lost ground to more popular tabloids and magazines that focus on personalities and gossip rather than hard news. *La presse people* is the French version of *People* magazine–style journalism, and it has its fans. Who doesn't love some celebrity gossip every now and then? However, let us not forget the serious press and the important role it still plays, both in paper and online.

In France, it used to be that if you saw someone reading a newspaper, you would immediately know a lot about them. In recent years, the printed press has gradually been ceding its place to digital formats, so it is not always possible to do this now, but it is still an interesting exercise in observation. What would you know? You would know something about their politics (left, right or center), whether they were interested in serious "hard" news as provided by the quality newspapers, also known as newspapers of record, or in "softer" stories of local or human interest (and gossip, of course!) as provided by the more popular papers and tabloids. If they are reading a regional newspaper but are not in that region, you might guess that it is due to nostalgia and a desire to maintain a connection with the place they come from (or, perhaps, are relocating to). You might also get an idea of their attention span, based on whether they prefer in-depth reporting and analyses or brief, more anecdotal news. However, it is probably best not to be too carried away because they may have simply picked up the paper left behind by the previous occupier of the adjacent seat on the Metro and are reading it because there is nothing else available!

Newspapers have played an important part in French history and culture. Almost all have digital editions online, making them more accessible to foreign students of French. Here are some of the names that you should know.

Le Monde is France's most important national daily "hard news" newspaper. It was founded by Hubert Beuve-Méry on December 19, 1944, shortly after the liberation of Paris, at the request of Charles de Gaulle and has published continuously since its first issue. In its early years, the paper focused on analysis and opinion more than on news reporting, but that has changed, and it is now one of France's newspapers of record, much like the *New York Times* in the United States and the London *Times* in the U.K. Politically, it often reflects establishment views and is considered center-left. *Le Monde* is the preferred daily of French intellectuals, civil servants, and academics. It provides the most detailed coverage of world events and politics, and is a major forum for political and intellectual debate and discussion. Foreign students of French often know *Le Monde* because, in pre-digital days, it was the French newspaper most readily available abroad. There is also *Le Monde diplomatique*, a monthly newspaper offering analysis and opinion on politics, culture, and current affairs. It is owned by a subsidiary company of *Le Monde* but has been given complete autonomy by the publisher. It is published in French but is also available in English and twenty-five other languages.

Le Figaro is a national daily newspaper published in Paris. It was founded as a satirical weekly in 1826 and takes its name from the main character in the 1778 play by Beaumarchais, *The Marriage of Figaro*. The editor considered it an appropriate choice since the paper, like the play, pokes fun at privilege. It became a daily newspaper in 1866. With its center-right editorial perspective, it is the most conservative of the quality newspapers of record and the one with the highest circulation.

Libération, or *Libé* as it is popularly known, is the third of France's newspapers of record. A national daily, it was founded in 1973 by Jean-Paul Sartre, Serge July, and other left-wing intellectuals following the protest movement of May 1968. Initially a newspaper of the far-left, it never identified with a specific political party. According to Serge July, "the equation of *Libération* consisted in combining counter-culture and political radicalism." At first, it did not accept any advertising, enabling the paper to freely express opinions. However, this was not a good financial model, and the idea was ultimately abandoned as the paper dealt with several financial crises. It also mellowed as its readership grew older, becoming a more center-left newspaper. *Libé* has the distinction of being the first of the major dailies to go digital with an online version.

Some Other Titles to Know

Le Parisien is a daily Parisian newspaper that covers international and national news, as well as local news of Paris and its suburbs. A national edition, *Aujourd'hui en France* (Today in France), covers the rest of France. Combined, they have the highest circulation among the country's national papers. The paper was established as *Le Parisien libéré* (*The Free Parisian*) by Émilien Amaury in 1944 and was published for the first time on August 22, 1944. It was originally a paper of the French underground during the German occupation. It is not a paper of record, but rather a mid-market tabloid, similar to *USA Today* in the United States.

L'Humanité was founded in 1904 by the French socialist leader Jean Jaurès. From 1920 to 1999, it was first the unofficial, then the official newspaper of the French Communist Party. It has been editorially independent since 1999, but for the most part is still written, produced, and promoted by French Communist Party members or supporters.

Les Échos is France's equivalent of the *Wall Street Journal*. Established in 1906 as a monthly publication under the name of *Les Échos de l'Exportation* by brothers Robert and Émile Servan-Schreiber, it became a daily in 1928, shortening its name to *Les Échos*. Originally focused on economic and financial news and analysis, since 2010 its coverage has been expanded to cover other topics, such as innovations in science, technologies, green growth, medicine and health, and skills concerning marketing and advertising, management, education, strategy and leadership, law and finance, and high tech and media. It is considered liberal in its outlook.

L'Équipe, is a national daily newspaper devoted almost exclusively to sports. In a country that loves sports, perhaps it is not surprising that it has the highest circulation of any of France's daily newspapers. It covers all sports but is particularly noted for its coverage of soccer, rugby, motor sports, and cycling.

Discussing the Future and Making Plans

MUST ⚡ KNOW

⚡ The French are keen on balancing tenses—especially when it comes to the future.

⚡ **Puis-je** is the formal way to say **Est-ce que je peux**.

⚡ **En** is general. **Dans** is specific.

⚡ Going straight ahead? **Tout droit**. Turning left? **À gauche**. Turning right? **À droite**.

⚡ Prepositions and definite articles often contract in French.

e can never know for sure what the future will hold. But **heureusement,** the future tense in French, is quite predictable. Still, you'll have to memorize the stems for irregular verbs, and, as the French often say: **Vouloir c'est pouvoir**. While this expression literally translates to "Willing is to be able to," it carries nearly the same meaning as the expression *Where there's a will, there's a way*. Keep this expression in mind as you learn in this chapter about verbs such as **vouloir**, **pouvoir**, and **devoir**.

The Simple Future

French has two main future tenses: the **futur simple** and the **futur antérieur**. For most verbs, to form the futur simple, use the infinitive as the stem and add the appropriate endings (**-ai, -as, -a, -ons, -ez,** or **-ont**). For **-re** verbs, remember to first drop the **e** from the infinitive and then add the appropriate ending.

Here are a few examples:

parler   *to speak*

je parler**ai**	*I'll speak*	nous parler**ons**	*we'll speak*
tu parler**as**	*you'll speak*	vous parler**ez**	*you'll speak*
il/elle/on parler**a**	*he/she/one'll speak*	ils/elles parler**ont**	*they'll speak*

finir   *to finish*

je finir**ai**	*I'll finish*	nous finir**ons**	*we'll finish*
tu finir**as**	*you'll finish*	vous finir**ez**	*you'll finish*
il/elle/on finir**a**	*he/she/one'll finish*	ils/elles finir**ont**	*they'll finish*

répondre   *to answer*

je répondr**ai**	*I'll answer*	nous répondr**ons**	*we'll answer*
tu répondr**as**	*you'll answer*	vous répondr**ez**	*you'll answer*
il/elle/on répondr**a**	*he/she/one'll answer*	ils/elles répondr**ont**	*they'll answer*

Ce soir nous regarderons un film à la télé.

Tonight we'll watch a movie on TV.

Il finira son projet d'ici le 30 juin.

He'll finish his project by June 30.

Je répondrai à votre lettre dès que possible.

I'll respond to your letter as soon as possible.

Irregular Future Verbs

The endings of the **futur simple** are the same for all verbs, yet many verbs have irregular stems. You'll have to pay extra attention to these!

aller	*to go*	j'irai	*I'll go*
apercevoir	*to notice*	j'apercevrai	*I'll notice*
avoir	*to have*	j'aurai	*I'll have*
courir	*to run*	je courrai	*I'll run*
devenir	*to become*	je deviendrai	*I'll become*
devoir	*must*	je devrai	*I'll have to*
envoyer	*to send*	j'enverrai	*I'll send*
être	*to be*	je serai	*I'll be*
faire	*to do*	je ferai	*I'll do*
falloir	*to have to*	il faudra	*one will have to*
mourir	*to die*	je mourrai	*I'll die*
pleuvoir	*to rain*	il pleuvra	*it'll rain*
pouvoir	*can, to be able to*	je pourrai	*I'll be able to*
recevoir	*to receive*	je recevrai	*I'll receive*
revenir	*to return*	je reviendrai	*I'll return*
savoir	*to know*	je saurai	*I'll know*
tenir	*to hold*	je tiendrai	*I'll hold*
valoir	*to be worth*	il vaudra	*it will be worth*
venir	*to come*	je viendrai	*I'll come*
voir	*to see*	je verrai	*I'll see*
vouloir	*to want*	je voudrai	*I'll want*

Elle enverra le formulaire au service des objets trouvés.		*She will send the form to the Lost and Found Department.*	
Elle pourra récupérer sa tablette au Service des objets trouvés.		*She will be able to pick up her tablet at the Lost and Found Department.*	

And with some verbs, the spelling changes when conjugated in the future tense.

acheter	*to buy*	j'achèterai	*I'll buy*
amener	*to bring*	j'amènerai	*I'll bring*
appeler	*to call*	j'appellerai	*I'll call*
balayer	*to sweep*	je balaierai	*I'll sweep*
employer	*to hire*	j'emploierai	*I'll hire*
essuyer	*to wipe*	j'essuierai	*I'll wipe*
jeter	*to throw*	je jetterai	*I'll throw*
nettoyer	*to clean*	je nettoierai	*I'll clean*

Tu essuieras la vaisselle.		*You'll wipe the dishes.*
Ton frère balaiera le sol.		*Your brother will sweep the floor.*
J'achèterai des éponges et du savon de Marseille.		*I'll buy some sponges and Marseille soap.*
Tu jetteras les ordures dans la poubelle.		*You'll throw the trash in the garbage can.*

 IRL In 1884, Eugène Poubelle, the prefect of the Seine (the chief administrator of Paris), promulgated an ordinance stating that all building owners in Paris should provide garbage cans for their tenants. The garbage can (**la poubelle**) still bears his name. And today, you'll see **Les hommes verts** (*green men*), sweeping the streets of the capital with a broom or with state-of-the-art cleaning equipment.

Temporal Conjunctions

Similar to English, the future tense is used to describe upcoming events, like **Elle ira à Paris en mai** (*She'll go in May*). In a compound sentence, if the main clause is in the future, the dependent clause introduced by a conjunction will also be in the future. This is a stark contrast with English, where the dependent clause is put in the present tense.

quand	*when*
lorsque	*when*
pendant que	*while*
dès que	*as soon as*
aussitôt que	*as soon as*
tant que	*as long as*

Elle nous **rendra** visite quand elle **aura** le temps.   *She'll visit us when she has time.*

Quand il **sera** à Paris, Jérôme **prendra** le métro.   *When he is in Paris, Jérôme will take the subway.*

The Future Perfect Tense

The **futur antérieur** (*future perfect*) describes an action that will take place and be completed before another future action. To form the compound tense, use the future tense of **avoir** or **être** and the past participle of the main verb. Agreement rules are the same as for the **passé composé**. Although it is rarely used in English, it must be used in French under certain circumstances.

finir   *to finish*

j'aurai fini	*I'll have finished*	nous aurons fini	*we'll have finished*
tu auras fini	*you'll have finished*	vous aurez fini	*you'll have finished*
il/elle/on aura fini	*he/she/one'll have finished*	ils/elles auront fini	*they'll have finished*

arriver   *to arrive*

je serai arrivé(e)	*I'll have arrived*
tu seras arrivé(e)	*you'll have arrived*
il/elle/on sera arrivé(e)	*he/she/one'll have arrived*
nous serons arrivé(e)s	*we'll have arrived*
vous serez arrivé(e)(s)	*you'll have arrived*
ils/elles seront arrivé(e)s	*they'll have arrived*

Il enverra son discours au directeur aussitôt qu'il l'aura fini.	*He'll send his speech to the director as soon as he finishes.*
Je ferai le tour du monde quand j'aurai fini d'écrire mon roman.	*I'll travel around the world when I finish writing my novel.*

The Verbs *Vouloir, Pouvoir,* and *Devoir*

Vouloir, **pouvoir**, and **devoir** are three of the most useful verbs with the suffix **-oir**.

Vouloir

The verb **vouloir** means *to want*, allowing you to express wishes and desires. Let's take a look at how it is conjugated in the present tense.

je veux	*I want*	nous voulons	*we want*
tu veux	*you want*	vous voulez	*you want*
il/elle/on veut	*he/she/one wants*	ils/elles veulent	*they want*

Est-ce que tu veux un café?	*Do you want a coffee?*
Nous ne voulons pas trop de devoirs pendant les vacances.	*We don't want too much homework during vacation.*
Voulez-vous une tasse de thé?	*Do you want a cup of tea?*
Ils ne veulent pas se lever à l'aube.	*They don't want to get up at dawn.*

Pouvoir

The verb **pouvoir** means *can* or *to be able to*.

je peux	*I can*	nous pouvons	*we can*
tu peux	*you can*	vous pouvez	*you can*
il/elle/on peut	*he/she/one can*	ils/elles peuvent	*they can*

Peux-tu me déposer à la gare?	*Can you drop me off at the train station?*
Elle ne peut pas assister au cours de danse aujourd'hui.	*She can't attend dance class today.*
Nous pouvons être à la gare à midi.	*We can be at the station at noon.*
Pouvez-vous me prêter votre chargeur?	*Can you lend me your charger?*

In a formal context, when using **pouvoir** to ask permission with inversion, the first-person singular of **pouvoir** takes a different form.

Puis-je vous aider?	*May I help you?*
Puis-je vous déposer à l'aéroport?	*Can I drop you off at the airport?*

Another formal way to ask a question is to use the conditional form.

Pourriez-vous me dire où se trouve la poste?	*Could you tell me where the post office is?*
Pourrais-tu m'envoyer les photos que tu as prises?	*Could you send me the photos you took?*

BTW

*Your intuition might tell you to use the verb **pouvoir** when expressing a person's abilities. If you want to refer to skills like "I can swim" or "She can speak four languages," the verb **savoir** is used, as we recall from Chapter 9. Let's take a look at how these verbs differ: **Patrick ne sait pas nager** means that Patrick never learned how to swim. **Patrick ne peut pas nager** implies that Patrick is temporarily unable to swim. Perhaps he does not have time or is feeling under the weather.*

Devoir

The verb **devoir** (*must*, *to have to*, *to be supposed to*, *to owe*) is an irregular verb with several meanings.

je dois	*I must*	nous devons	*we must*
tu dois	*you must*	vous devez	*you must*
il/elle/on doit	*he/she/one must*	ils/elles doivent	*they must*

Let's start with the notion of *debt* in both a literal and figurative sense.

- **Devoir** as *debt*

Combien est-ce que je vous dois?	*How much do I owe you?*
Il nous doit 500 €.	*He owes us 500 euros.*
Elle ne vous doit rien.	*She doesn't owe you anything.*
Il doit sa vie à son chirurgien.	*He owes his life to his surgeon.*

- **Devoir** as *obligation*

Vous devez récupérer votre valise avant 30 septembre.	*You must pick up your suitcase by September 30.*
Tu dois acheter un carnet de tickets métro.	*You have to buy a book of subway tickets.*
Je dois m'entraîner pour le match.	*I have to train for the match.*
Nous devons les contacter immédiatement.	*We have to contact them immediately.*

- Devoir as *probability*

L'avion doit décoller à 20h30.	*The plane is supposed to take off at 8:30 pm.*
Son nouveau film doit sortir le 15 décembre.	*Her new film is supposed to premiere December 15.*
Il a dû perdre ses clés dans le sable.	*He probably lost his keys in the sand.*
Mathieu doit nous rendre visite ce weekend.	*Mathieu is supposed to visit us this weekend.*

> ## BTW
>
> *Evidently, **devoir** carries many nuances. The voice intonation often determines if **devoir** implies an obligation or a probability. For example, **elle doit venir nous aider** may mean she is supposed to come and help us, or she must come and help us. The voice intonation and gestures will help you determine the precise meaning.*

- **Devoir** as *warning* or *suggestion*   When using in the conditional or the past conditional, **devoir** takes on the meaning of *should* or *should have*. Again, this will be explored further in Chapter 12.

Vous devriez confirmer votre vol.	*You should confirm your flight.*
Tu devrais laisser ton passeport dans le coffre-fort.	*You should leave your passport in the safe.*

Main Prepositions

Prepositions connect two elements in a sentence. Note than when using some prepositions like **à** and **de**, there are contractions with certain articles:

$$à + le \rightarrow au$$
$$à + les \rightarrow aux$$
$$de + le \rightarrow du$$
$$de + les \rightarrow des$$

à	*to/in*	contre	*against*
de	*of/from*	sans	*without*
chez	*at*	entre	*between*
en	*in*	devant	*in front of*
dans	*in*	derrière	*behind*
sur	*on*	à côté de	*next to*
sous	*under*	jusque	*until*
avant	*before*	vers	*towards/about*
après	*after*	près de	*near*

par	by	loin de	far from
pour	for	autour de	around
avec	with	en face de	opposite from
parmi	among	pendant	during

Il t'attend devant le magasin.

He is waiting for you in front of the store.

Ne pars pas sans moi!

Don't leave without me!

J'arriverai vers midi.

I'll arrive around noon.

Je suis loin de toi, mais je pense à toi.

I am far from you, but I am thinking about you.

 IRL | Listen to Florent Pagny's song, "Loin de toi" on YouTube and memorize the lyrics.

BTW

*In some instances, the preposition **à** will denote nature, function, or purpose:*

une machine à laver	washing machine
un moulin à poivre	pepper mill

*While **à** denotes function and purpose, **de** denotes content and composition:*

un verre à eau	water glass
un verre d'eau	glass of water
une tasse à thé	teacup
une tasse de thé	cup of tea

*With some prepositions like **chez**, its translation can change with context:*

Nous sommes allés chez Henri.	We went to Henri's house.
Nous avons fait une réservation pour dîner chez Julien.	We made a dinner reservation at Julien's.
On trouve d'excellents thés chez Fauchon.	We find excellent tea at the Fauchon Store.
Chez Balzac, tout est précision.	With Balzac, everything comes down to detail.
Chez les préadolescents, on distingue des pathologies liées à leur surconsommation de la technologie.	With preteens, many pathologies are linked to their overconsumption of technology.
Il va chez le médecin mardi.	He is going to the doctor's on Tuesday.

En versus *dans*

While both **en** and **dans** often mean similar things, each is used differently. **En** is used directly before a noun, whereas **dans** can be followed by an article, possessive adjective, or demonstrative adjective. Additionally, **en** carries a more general sense, while **dans** is more specific.

Sarah circule toujours **en** autobus.	*Sarah always travels by bus.*
Bertrand finit ses devoirs **dans** l'autobus.	*Bertrand finishes his homework on the bus.*
Odile aime voyager **en** avion.	*Odile loves to travel by plane.*
Dans cet avion, les sièges sont toujours confortables.	*In this plane, the seats are always comfortable.*
Les élèves ne doivent pas dormir **en** classe.	*Students must not sleep in class.*
Dans la classe, il n'y a pas de wifi.	*There is no WiFi in the classroom.*
Vaishali habite **en** Inde.	*Vaishali lives in India.*
La vie était plus paisible **dans** l'Inde de sa grand-mère.	*Life was more peaceful in her grandmother's India.*
Il peut traduire le document **en** trois jours.	*He can translate the document in three days.*
Je vous enverrai le document traduit **dans** trois jours.	*I'll send you the translated document in three days.*

Speaking About Directions

You'll want to learn the points of the compass:

nord	*north*
sud	*south*

est	*east*
ouest	*west*

Notre chambre est orientée à l'ouest.	*Our room faces the west.*
Nous avons roulé vers le sud pendant cinq heures.	*We drove south for five hours.*
Ils ont parcouru le pays d'est en ouest.	*They traveled the country from east to west.*

BTW

When simply referring to cardinal directions, the word remains in lowercase. But when the direction includes a proper noun like **l'Amérique du Nord**, *it becomes uppercase.*

Elle a visité plusieurs pays d'Amérique du Sud.	She visited several countries in South America.
Ils vont prendre leur retraite dans le Sud.	They are going to retire in the South of France.
Le train pour Berlin part de la gare de l'Est.	The train for Berlin leaves from Gare de l'Est (*Station of the East*).

When you include the word *left* or *right* as a modifier, you may have to change the preposition. Let's a look at the following examples:

Elle écrit toujours ses lettres de remerciements **à** la main.	*She always writes her thank-you letters by hand.*
Les résultats des examens sont retranscrits **à** la main.	*The test results are transcribed by hand.*
Le président écrit **de** la main gauche.	*The president writes left-handed.*
Il tient la fourchette **de** la main gauche et le couteau **de** la main droite.	*He holds the fork with his left hand and the knife with his right.*

Asking for and Giving Directions

Help! **Où se trouve la gare?** In order to find a destination, knowing how to ask for and follow directions really comes in handy. Here are some helpful expressions:

tourner à gauche	to turn left
tourner à droite	to turn right
aller tout droit	to go straight ahead
au bout de la rue	at the end of the street
au coin de la rue	at the street corner
suivre	to follow
traverser la rue	to cross the street
traverser le pont	to cross the bridge

Mathieu, who works at La Défense, takes the afternoon off to see an exhibit at the musée Yves Saint-Laurent, 5 avenue Marceau. When he is about to leave the museum, he suddenly runs into an American tourist looking for the Eiffel Tower. Let's look at a **plan de Paris** and follow the directions:

Vous sortez du musée et vous tournez à droite.

↓

Vous suivez l'avenue Marceau jusqu'à l'avenue de Président Wilson.

↓

Vous tournez à gauche et vous vous dirigez vers le pont de l'Alma.

↓

Vous traversez le pont de l'Alma et ensuite vous tournez à droite sur le quai Branly.

↓

Vous allez tout droit et vous trouverez la tour Eiffel et le célèbre Champ-de-Mars.

Phone Etiquette

The following lines represent different situations that might arise during a phone call; it will help you get an idea of the flow of French exchanges over the phone.

Call 1

Allô, c'est bien le bureau de Madame Duroy?	*Hello, is this Madame Duroy's office?*
C'est Madame Deschamps.	*It's Madame Deschamps speaking.*
Pourrais-je parler à Madame Duroy?	*Could I speak to Madame Duroy?*
Pourriez-vous me passer son assistant?	*Could you pass me over to her assistant?*
Veuillez patienter/ne quittez pas.	*Please wait one moment.*
Un moment/un instant, s'il vous plaît.	*One moment, please.*
Je vous le passe.	*I am passing you to him.*
Est-ce que Monsieur Blondel est là?	*Is Monsieur Blondel there?*
Je voudrais parler au responsable du Service des objets trouvés.	*I would like to talk to the person in charge of the Lost and Found.*
C'est bien Monsieur Blondel?	*Is this Monsieur Blondel?*
C'est à quel sujet?	*What are you calling about?*
C'est personnel.	*It's personal.*
Voulez-vous laisser un message sur sa boîte vocale?	*Do you want to leave a voicemail message?*

Call 2

Allô, j'aimerais parler à Maître Rahimi.	*Hello, I would like to speak to Maître Rahimi.*
Qui est à l'appareil?	*Who's on the phone?*
Je suis sa cliente américaine, Madame Winston.	*I am his American client, Mrs Winston.*
Comment?	*Sorry?*
Je n'ai pas compris ce que vous avez dit.	*I didn't catch what you said.*
Je ne parle pas très bien le français.	*I don't speak French too well.*
Pourriez-vous répéter plus lentement, s'il vous plaît?	*Could you please repeat that more slowly, please?*
Pouvez-vous le rappeler demain?	*Can you call him back tomorrow?*
Non, c'est urgent.	*No, it's urgent.*
Pouvez-vous l'appeler sur son pager? Ou lui envoyer un texto?	*Can you page him? Or send him a text?*
Il est au tribunal. Je ne peux pas le déranger maintenant.	*He is at the courthouse. I cannot disturb him right now.*
Laissez-moi vos coordonnées.	*Leave me your contact information.*

Call 3

Qui est à l'appareil?	*Who's on the phone?*
C'est de la part de qui?	*Whom am I speaking with?*
Elle est occupée.	*Sbe's busy.*
Elle est en ligne.	*She's on the phone.*
Elle est en réunion.	*She's in a meeting.*
Elle n'est pas disponible.	*She's not available.*
Voulez-vous laisser un message?	*Do you want to leave a message?*
Veuillez rappeler plus tard?	*Would you kindly call back later?*

Call 4

Allô, je voudrais parler à Monsieur Jardin.	*Hello, I would like to speak to Mr. Jardin.*
Qui dois-je annoncer?	*Who should I tell him is calling?*
Merci de rester en ligne.	*Thank you for holding.*
Merci de patienter.	*Thank you for waiting.*
Monsieur Jardin est en entretien.	*Mr. Jardin is interviewing right now.*
Et son associé?	*What about his partner?*
Il est en extérieur.	*He's out of the office.*
Ils sont vraiment difficiles à joindre!	*They're really difficult to track down!*
Voulez-vous laisser un message?	*Do you want to leave a message?*
C'est noté. Au revoir, monsieur.	*It's been noted. Good-bye, sir.*

Call 5

Allô, c'est Élisabeth?	*Hello, is that Élisabeth?*
Vous vous êtes trompé de numéro.	*You got the wrong number.*
Il n'y a pas d'Élisabeth dans ce bureau.	*There's no Élisabeth in this office.*
Ce n'est pas possible!	*That's not possible!*
Monsieur, vous faites erreur. Vérifiez le numéro.	*Sir, you made a mistake. Check the number.*
Oh non! Ce n'est pas possible!	*Oh no! It's not possible!*

DIALOGUE *Service des objets trouvés*
Lost and Found Department

Mathieu lives in Nogent-sur-Marne and works at La Défense. The RER A from Grande-Arche-La-Défense makes seven stops and takes about 23 minutes to reach Mathieu's home. Célia is reading a graphic novel based on *La délicatesse* written by best-selling author, David Foenkinos.

 **IRL** The term RER is an acronym for *Réseau Express Régional,* or "Regional Express Network." It is a rapid transit system serving Paris and its many suburbs. Currently, the RER runs five lines, the RER A, RER B, RER C, RER D, and RER E. These five lines connect to the **metro** at several stations and run with fewer stops. Riding east to west, from Vincennes to La Défense, will take only about twenty minutes!

Mathieu: Allô? Bonjour, c'est bien le Service des objets trouvés?	*Hello? Good morning, is this the Lost and Found Department?*
Employé 1: Oui, monsieur. Que puis-je faire pour vous?	*Yes, sir. What can I help you with?*
Mathieu: J'ai laissé mon sac à dos dans le RER A vers 8h30 ce matin.	*I left my backpack in the RER A around 8:30 this morning.*
Employé 1: Le RER A? Attendez un instant, je transfère votre appel. Ne quittez pas!	*The RER A? Wait one moment, I am going to transfer your call. Hold on!*
Employé 2: Bonjour! Vous avez oublié votre sac à dos? *Pourriez-vous me le décrire?*	*Hello! You forgot your backpack? Could you describe it to me?*
Mathieu: Oui, c'est un petit sac à dos Augur gris.	*Yes, it's a small gray Augur backpack.*

Employé 2: Un Augur gris? Pas d'autre détail? On récupère tant de choses tous les jours!

A gray Augur? Any other details? We get so many things every day!

Mathieu: C'est vrai?

Is that so?

Employé 2: Sacs, portefeuilles, clés, lunettes, téléphones, liseuses, gants, écharpes, bonnets, parapluies, bijoux, et même des ours en peluche!

Bags, wallets, keys, glasses, phones, tablets, gloves, scarves, hats, umbrellas, jewelry, and even teddy bears!

Mathieu: Pas d'ours en peluche, mais sur mon sac à dos, il y a un petit patch en cuir marron avec mes initiales M.D.

No teddy bears, but on my backpack there is a small brown leather patch with my initials M.D.

Employé 2: Ça pourra servir.

That may be helpful.

Mathieu: Il y a le patch et dans le sac, ma carte de membre du club de forme Nogent Tonic.

There is the patch and, in the bag, my Nogent Tonic gym membership card.

Employé 2: Très bien. Je vous tiendrai au courant. Quel est votre nom?

Good. I'll keep you posted. What's your name?

Mathieu: Mathieu Deschamps. D.E.S.C.H.A.M.P.S.

Mathieu Deschamps. D.E.S.C.H.A.M.P.S.

Employé 2: C'est bon. Mais je vous rappelle que le sac ne vous sera restitué que si vous présentez une pièce d'identité.

It's OK. But I want to remind you that the bag will be returned to you only if you show an ID.

Mathieu: Pas de problème, merci.

No problem, thank you.

Trois heures plus tard.

Three hours later.

Célia: Allô? Puis-je parler à Mathieu Deschamps?

Hello? May I speak to Mathieu Deschamps?

Mathieu: Oui, c'est moi. Qui est à l'appareil?

Yes, that's me. Who is calling?

Célia: Célia Gauthier. Étiez-vous dans le RER A ce matin?

Célia Gauthier. Were you in the RER A this morning?

Mathieu: Euh... oui.

Uh... yes.

Célia: Connaissez-vous la version de *La délicatesse* en roman graphique?

Do you know the graphic adaptation of Delicacy?

Mathieu: Oui, j'adore les BD et cette adaptation est super. Et ce matin...

Yes, I love comic books and that adaptation is great. And this morning...

Célia: Ce matin vous avez fait un commentaire sur le livre que je lisais.

This morning you made a comment about the book I was reading.

Mathieu: Vous êtes...

And you are...

Célia: Oui, c'est moi. Vous aviez plusieurs sacs et vous avez oublié votre petit sac à dos sous le siège!

Yes, it's me. You had several bags and you forgot your small backpack under the seat!

Mathieu: Vous l'avez?

Do you have it?

Célia: Oui!

Yes, I do!

Mathieu: Oh, je ne sais pas comment vous remercier!

Oh, I don't know how to thank you!

Célia: J'ai essayé... mais les portières se sont refermées et c'était trop tard, vous étiez parti.

I tried... but the doors closed, and it was too late, you were gone.

Mathieu: C'est incroyable! C'est la faute à Voltaire? Ou c'est la faute à Rousseau?

That's unbelievable! Is it the fault to Voltaire? Or is it the fault to Rousseau?

 IRL This dialogue makes references to Victor Hugo's *Les Misérables*, particularly to the character Gavroche. When Mathieu from the dialogue says **C'est la faute à Voltaire? C'est la faute à Rousseau?**, he alludes to a famous song that Gavroche sings. Feel free to listen to it online!

Célia: C'est la faute à Foenkinos!

It is Foenkinos' fault!

Mathieu: Vous avez fini de lire le roman?

Did you finish reading the novel?

Célia: Oui. C'était triste au début puis on découvre une belle histoire d'amour.

Yes. It was sad at the beginning but little by little you discover a beautiful love story.

Mathieu: Hum... Au fait, comment puis-je récupérer mon sac?

Hmm... By the way, how can I get my bag back?

Célia: Je suis à La Varenne, à cinq arrêts de Nogent.

I am in La Varenne, five stops from Nogent.

Mathieu: J'ai vraiment de la chance!

I am so lucky!

Célia: Pouvez-vous me retrouver demain à 8h devant mon club de forme?	*Can you meet me tomorrow at 8am in front of my gym?*
Mathieu: Bien sûr.	*Of course.*
Célia: Demain à 8h devant L'Orange bleue.	*Tomorrow at 8am in front of the L'Orange bleue.*
Mathieu: Je serai à L'Orange bleue à 8h pile. Mille mercis. À demain!	*I'll be at L'Orange bleue at 8am sharp. Many thanks. See you tomorrow!*
Célia: À demain!	*See you tomorrow!*

BTW

The French alphabet, like the English, is based on the Latin alphabet. It has six vowels: **a, e, i, o, u,** *and* **y.** *In addition, French uses several accents:* **l'accent aigu** *(acute accent):* **é; l'accent grave** *(grave accent):* **à, è, ù; l'accent circonflexe** *(circumflex accent):* **â, ê, î, û;** *and* **le tréma** *(dieresis):* **ë, ï, ü.** *You have already encountered the* **oe** *in* **soeur** *and* **coeur** *and the* **ç** *in* **ça va** *and* **nous commençons.** *Practice spelling your* **prénom** *(first name) and* **nom de famille** *(family name).*

EXERCISES

EXERCISE 10.1

Conjugate the following verbs in the future.

1. Je (suivre) _____ un cours d'espagnol l'été prochain.

2. Nous (chercher) _____ un appartement dans le 20e arrondissement.

3. Ils (écouter) _____ un concert à l'Olympia.

4. Tu (rester) _____ en France toute l'année?

5. J'espère que Mathieu (ne pas perdre) _____ son sac à dos dans le métro.

6. Elle (choisir) _____ un beau cadeau pour sa camarade de classe.

7. Est-ce que vous (sortir) _____ demain soir avec nous?

8. On (dîner) _____ tous ensemble samedi.

9. Je (ne pas travailler) _____ le 14 juillet.

10. On (remplacer) _____ toutes les chaises de bureau avant la fin de l'année.

EXERCISE 10.2

Conjugate the following verbs in the future.

1. Je pense qu'il (pleuvoir) _____ ce soir.

2. Je (venir) _____ te chercher à la sortie du RER.

3. Nicole (s'apercevoir) _____ qu'elle a perdu ses lunettes.

4. Nous (aller) _____ à Nogent-sur-Marne ce weekend.

5. Est-ce que tu (être) _____ disponible demain après-midi?

6. Les cours (avoir) _____ lieu dans l'amphithéâtre.

7. (faire) _____ -vous un stage chez Saint-Gobain?

8. Jean (recevoir) _____ son diplôme en juin.

9. Combien de temps est-ce qu'il te (falloir) _____ pour terminer le projet?

10. Dans cinquante ans, cet investissement (ne rien valoir) _____.

EXERCISE 10.3

Conjugate the following verbs in the future tense.

1 Je vous (prévenir) _____ dès que je (savoir) _____ la date du pique-nique.

2. Tu me (envoyer) _____ un mail dès que tu (pouvoir) _____.

3. Nous (prendre) _____ une décision lorsque nous (avoir) _____ plus d'information.

4. Dès qu'Annabelle (revenir) _____ chez elle, elle (commencer) _____ ses devoirs.

5. Tant qu'il (faire) _____ beau, nous (dîner) _____ dans le jardin.

6. Aussitôt que je (arriver) _____ à Roissy, je vous (téléphoner) _____.

7. Je (acheter) _____ une nouvelle robe quand il (se marier) _____.

8. Il (devoir) _____ payer ses impôts quand il (travailler) _____.

9. Qu'est-ce que tu (faire) _____ quand tu (être) _____ grand?

10. Tant qu'elles (être) _____ performantes, elles (jouer) _____ dans cette équipe.

EXERCISE 10.4

Conjugate the following verbs in the future perfect.

1. D'ici la fin de la semaine je (apprendre) _____ le poème par cœur.

2. Christian (déménager) _____ à La Rochelle avant la fin de l'année.

3. Quand tu (apprendre) _____ à nager, tu pourras aller à la plage.

4. Dès que les candidats (présenter) _____ leur programme, nous en discuterons ensemble.

5. D'ici la rentrée, nous (visiter) _____ cinq pays africains.

6. Aussitôt que vous (lire) _____ ce recueil de nouvelles, vous m'en ferez un résumé.

7. Quand tu (essuyer) _____ la vaisselle, tu la rangeras dans le placard.

8. Dès que le printemps (arriver) _____, nous irons cueillir des fleurs sauvages.

9. Dès que Lise (changer) _____ le pneu, nous reprendrons la route.

10. D'ici la fin du semestre, les élèves (écrire) _____ quatre essais.

EXERCISE 10.5

Translate the following sentences. When asking a question, use the est-ce que form.

1. She'll call you as soon as she's ready. (*vous*)

2. I hope it won't rain tomorrow.

3. By the end of the week, they'll have resolved the problem.

4. As long as there are men, there will be wars.

5. By the end of the month, the director will have signed Xavier's contract.

6. Will you remember your sister's birthday? (*tu*)

7. I am sure you won't die of hunger in France. (*tu*)

8. As soon as I am finished preparing dinner, I'll set the table.

9. We will never know who took Mathieu's backpack.

10. As long as we love each other, we'll be happy. (*on*)

EXERCISE 10.6

Conjugate the following verbs in the present tense.

1. Est-ce que tu (pouvoir) _____ m'apporter une bouteille d'eau?

2. Je (ne pas pouvoir) _____ lui rendre visite aujourd'hui.

3. Nous (vouloir) _____ les inviter à la fête.

4. Tu (vouloir) _____ nous rejoindre au jardin zoologique?

5. Elles (pouvoir) _____ y aller en voiture.

6. Je (ne pas vouloir) _____ vous déranger.

7. Il (vouloir) _____ vérifier que l'objet n'est pas chez lui.

8. Vous (pouvoir) _____ prendre contact avec le service en composant le 3246.

9. Nous (vouloir) _____ récupérer les clés de l'appartement.

10. (pouvoir) _____-je vous aider à porter les bagages?

EXERCISE 10.7

Conjugate the verb devoir in the present tense.

1. Tu (devoir) _____ laisser ton sac à dos au vestiaire.

2. Vous lui (devoir) _____ 1000 €.

3. Je (devoir) _____ fermer toutes les fenêtres avant de partir.

4. L'avion (devoir) _____ atterrir à 16h20.

5. On (ne pas devoir) _____ parler trop fort au téléphone dans les transports publics.

6. Ils (devoir) _____ tenir leur promesse.

7. Nous (devoir) _____ passer nos vacances avec nos amis au Portugal.

8. Vous (devoir) _____ signaler un objet perdu sur les réseaux sociaux.

9. Je (devoir) _____ arriver à Bordeaux vers 19h00.

10. Elle (ne pas devoir) _____ sa réussite qu'à elle-même.

EXERCISE 10.8

Translate the following sentences using the **vous** *form when necessary. When asking a question, use inversion.*

1. I can't remember the password.

2. We want to spend our vacation in Mexico.

3. She owes us an apology.

4. Can you drop me off at the movie theater?

5. They want to take time to reflect.

6. You must always tell the truth.

7. It's supposed to rain this weekend.

8. Can I help you choose a dress for the wedding?

9. Are we supposed to learn these verbs by heart?

10. They want to meet the new history teacher.

EXERCISE 10.9

Match the items in the two columns. Choose the most logical answer.

1. Elles se promènent   a. vers la plage.

2. Il va passer le week-end   b. chez ses parents.

3. Veux-tu aller   c. avec moi au cinéma?

4. Nous nous dirigeons   d. par la fenêtre.

5. Je regarde les nuages   e. dans la rue.

EXERCISE 10.10

*Translate the following sentences using the **vous** form when necessary. When asking a question, use inversion.*

1. I'll call you in three days.

2. He placed his backpack under the seat.

3. Do you want to sit next to us?

4. Do you have to go to the bank today?

5. Between us, I think that Julien likes my cousin Claire a lot.

6. Can I park my car in front of your house?

7. We'll go to welcome them upon their arrival to Havana.

8. She is able to write a speech in less than 24 hours.

9. You are with us or against us.

10. He probably left without them.

LE COIN DES CRÉATEURS

L'expansion is a fun activity where you can fluff up an idea and a sentence. Take the example:

Le président est assis.
Le président est assis bien droit.
Le président est assis bien droit derrière son bureau.
Le président est assis bien droit derrière son bureau en chêne massif.
Le président est assis bien droit derrière son bureau en chêne massif. Il décroche le téléphone.
…
…
…

Write at least six more sentences, using the future, starting the sentence with:

La princesse ira en Islande…
…
…

NOTE CULTURELLE

TAKE A CHANCE, TAKE THE TRAIN!

Take the train, not the plane. Many people in France are now opting to do just that. The digital version of the daily newspaper *Le Figaro* recently conducted a poll asking users to indicate their preference and received more than 40,000 responses. The surprising result: 59 percent of those responding prefer to take trains rather than planes, even if it means abandoning their dreams of long-distance travel in favor of locations closer to home. Even more surprising is their reason: to preserve the environment and lower individual carbon dioxide (CO_2) emissions. According to the European Environment Agency, a passenger in a plane emits 285 grams of CO_2 per kilometer, versus 158 grams in a car and only 14 grams in a train. It is obvious that opting for the train can have a significant impact on the environment if enough people do so.

Although saving the planet is an admirable objective, it is just one reason to take the train. Travel by train is quick, easy, and economical. The opportunity to jump-start your vacation by seeing some beautiful scenery en route to your destination is an extra advantage you typically do not have in a plane at 35,000 feet. If you are traveling from Paris, you can go almost anywhere in Europe by train. And, if you don't want to go too far, there are many day trips that you can take, leave early in the morning and be back in Paris by evening. So why not take a chance and take the train?

There are seven major train stations in Paris for trains that go beyond the Ile de France region. Before taking the train, stop and admire their architecture and décor. In some cases, it is worth a trip to the station even if you not traveling!

The Gare du Nord, officially Paris-Nord, is the busiest railway station in Europe and the hub for Eurostar trains arriving and departing Paris. Eurostar is an international high-speed railway service connecting London with Paris, Amsterdam, Avignon, Brussels, Bourg-Saint-Maurice, Disneyland Paris, Lille, Fréthun, Lyon, Marseille, and Rotterdam. Gare du Nord is also the stop for Thalys trains. Thalys is a French-Belgian high-speed train operator originally built around the LGV Nord high-speed line between Paris and Brussels. This track is shared with Eurostar trains and with French domestic TGV trains. Along with the local and national train lines, this station is always a bustling beehive of activity with trains running to Northern France and the northern suburbs of Paris.

The Gare de l'Est, officially Paris-Est, is located a short ten-minute walk from Gare du Nord (you can also take the bus or metro—it connects to the Magenta metro stop). It is the terminus of an important railway network extending towards the eastern part of France, and in the past, it saw large mobilizations of French troops, most notably in 1914, at the beginning of the First World War. In the main-line train hall, a monumental painting by Albert Herter, *Le Départ des poilus, August 1914*, dating from 1926, illustrates the departure of these soldiers for the Western Front. The SNCF began LGV East European services from the Gare de l'Est in June 2007, with TGV and ICE services to northeastern France, Luxembourg, southern Germany, and Switzerland. Trains to the eastern suburbs of Paris also depart from this station.

The Gare d'Austerlitz, officially Paris-Austerlitz, is located on the left bank of the Seine in the southeastern part of the city. It is the starting point of the Paris–Bordeaux railway, and the line to Toulouse is also connected to this line. Some 30 million passengers use the station annually, about half the number passing through Montparnasse. Trains from the Gare d'Austerlitz go to central France, Toulouse, and the Pyrenees. It is also the station for Elipsos high-speed trains to and from Barcelona.

The Gare de Bercy is a modern station that occupies the site of a large former freight station, once famous as the main arrival point and distribution center for wine in Paris. The renovated station was designed for sleeper trains, allowing passengers to travel with their car in the same train. This is not possible at any of the other Parisian terminal stations, as they have never been adapted for auto-train service. Between 2002 and 2011, it was the terminus for overnight trains to Italy. These now depart from the Gare de Lyon. The station has been renamed the Paris Gare de

Bercy Bourgogne Pays d'Auvergne Train Station and is used primarily as a terminus for medium-distance domestic train service.

The Gare de Lyon, officially Paris-Gare-de-Lyon, is the third busiest train station in France and one of the busiest in Europe, handling about 90,000,000 passengers every year. It was built for the World Exposition of 1900 and is considered a classic example of the architecture of its time. Of particular note is the large clock tower atop one corner of the station, similar in style to London's Big Ben. The station houses the *Le Train Bleu* restaurant, which has served drinks and meals to travelers and other guests since 1901 in an ornately decorated setting that is a destination on its own. The Gare de Lyon is the northern terminus of the Paris-Marseille railway. It is named after the city of Lyon, a stop for many long-distance trains departing here, most en route to the south of France. It is served by high-speed TGV trains to south and eastern France, Switzerland, Germany, Italy, and Spain. The station also hosts regional trains, the RER, and the Gare de Lyon metro station.

The Gare Montparnasse, officially Paris-Montparnasse, is located in the 14th and 15th arrondissements of Paris. The station opened in 1840, was rebuilt in 1852, and was relocated in 1969 to a new station just south of the original location—where subsequently the Montparnasse Tower, the tallest skyscraper in France until 2011, was constructed. The station serves intercity TGV trains to the west and southwest of France, including Tours, Bordeaux, Rennes, and Nantes, and suburban and regional services on the Transilien Paris–Montparnasse routes. There is also a major metro stop at the station. It is worth noting that the Gare Montparnasse is the only mainline terminus in Paris that is not directly connected to the RER system.

The Gare Saint-Lazare, officially Paris-Saint-Lazare, is the station serving Normandy, northwest of Paris, along the Paris–Le Havre railway. It is the second-busiest station in Paris, after the Gare du Nord, but most of today's buildings, including the façade, date from 1889. The station was renovated in 1936 and again in 2012, when the three-level shopping mall was created. The Gare Saint-Lazare has been represented in a number of artworks. It attracted artists during the Impressionist period, and many of them lived very close to the Gare Saint-Lazare during the 1870s and 1880s. The station is the subject of paintings by Édouard Manet, Gustave Caillebotte, and Claude Monet, and also plays a role in literary works by Émile Zola (*La bête humaine*) and Raymond Queneau (*Exercises in Style*).

Claude Monet: La Gare Saint-Lazare, le train de Normandie (*Arrival of the Normandy Train, Gare Saint-Lazare*), 1877. Collection of the Art Institute of Chicago.

In Search of Lost Time... with French Past Tenses

MUST KNOW

⚡ A verb in the **passé composé** can "interrupt" an ongoing **imparfait**.

⚡ With **-cer** and **-ger** verbs, don't forget the tricky spelling!

⚡ If you miss someone, say **Tu me manques**.

⚡ The **passé simple** is all about drama.

re you feeling nostalgic yet? Let's take a trip down memory lane. The **imparfait** will allow you to express how things used to be or what you were doing yesterday. In this chapter, you'll also learn about the literary **passé simple**, which translates equivalently to the **passé composé**.

The *Imparfait*

The **imparfait** (*imperfect*) is one of the most challenging tenses to master in French. Remember that the **passé composé** is used to talk about a past action that has taken place at a specific point in time. While the **imparfait** also refers to past actions, it carries more nuances; it is used to describe a state of both mind and being in addition to continuous or habitual past actions.

To form the imperfect, take the **nous** form of the present tense and remove the **-ons** ending; this will leave just the stem of the **imparfait**. Then add to the stem the **imparfait** endings (**-ais**, **-ais**, **-ait**, **-ions**, **-iez**, **-aient**).

lire   *to read*

nous lisons → lis-

je lisais	*I read*	nous lisions	*we read*
tu lisais	*you read*	vous lisiez	*you read*
il/elle/on lisait	*he/she/one reads*	ils/elles lisaient	*they read*

Note that the **-ais**, **-ait**, and **-aient** endings are pronounced the same. But verbs with spelling changes in the present tense of the **nous** form, such as **nager** and **commencer** (see Chapter 2), retain the spelling change only for the **je**, **tu**, **il**, **elle**, **ils**, and **elles** pronouns. Likewise, with the **nous** and **vous** form of the **imparfait**, the extra **e** or **ç** is not needed.

je mangeais	I ate
tu changeais	you changed
elle corrigeait	she ran
nous partagions	we shared
vous exigiez	you demanded
ils annonçaient	they announced
nous étudiions	we studied
vous oubliiez	you forgot
nous remerciions	we thanked

BTW
What about verbs ending in -ier? While it may seem counterintuitive, two consecutive is *are used in the* **nous** *and* **vous** *forms of -ier verbs, like* **oublier, étudier,** *or* **remercier** *in the imperfect.*

Depending on the context, the **imparfait** can be the equivalent to several tenses in English.

Elle parlait…   *She was speaking…*
                                 She used to speak…
                                 She did speak…
                                 She would speak…

Note that the verb **être** is an irregular verb in the **imparfait**.

j'étais	*I was*	nous étions	*we were*
tu étais	*you were*	vous étiez	*you were*
il/elle/on était	*he/she/one was*	ils/elles étaient	*they were*

Let's look at the different ways in which the **imparfait** is used. First, it is used in establishing backgrounds and describing past events.

Le musée était fermé.	*The museum was closed.*
Il pleuvait à verse.	*It was pouring rain.*
Nous avions très faim.	*We were very hungry.*
Ils étaient fatigués.	*They were tired.*
Je ne savais pas quoi faire.	*I didn't know what to do.*

Another use of the **imparfait** is to describe past habitual, repetitive action. Depending on context, this use of the **imparfait** can be translated as *used to* or *would*.

Nous allions au jardin botanique le jeudi.	*We used to go to the botanical garden on Thursdays.*
À cette époque-là, elle vivait dans le Midi.	*At the time, she lived in the South of France.*
Je rendais visite à mes grands-parents tous les étés.	*I would visit my grandparents every summer.*

Expressions of time or repeated action are often used with the **imparfait**:

toujours	*always*
souvent	*often*
parfois	*sometimes*
rarement	*rarely*
le mercredi	*on Wednesdays*
le dimanche	*on Sundays*
chaque jour	*every day*
tous les jours	*everyday*
chaque semaine	*every week*
chaque mois	*every month*
chaque année	*every year*
d'ordinaire	*ordinarily*
d'habitude	*usually*
normalement	*normally*
en général/généralement	*generally*
habituellement	*usually*
régulièrement	*regularly*
autrefois	*formerly*
jadis	*in times past*

Imparfait vs. Passé Composé

The **imparfait** and the **passé composé** can sometimes be used together. For instance, when a past continuous action is interreputed by another action, both tenses are invoked. The continuous actions takes the **imparfait**, whereas the interrupting action takes the **passé composé**.

Je regardais le film quand ma sœur est entrée.	*I was watching the movie when my sister walked in.*
Nous nous promenions quand soudain il a commencé à pleuvoir.	*We were walking when it suddenly started to rain.*
Elle dormait quand, soudain, elle a entendu un bruit bizarre venant de la cuisine.	*She was sleeping when suddenly she heard a strange noise from the kitchen.*

Verbs Commonly Used in the Imperfect

Some verbs appear more often in the **imparfait** than they do in the **passé composé**, largely because they express a mental or physical state. These verbs include **être** (*to be*), **avoir** (*to have*), **penser** (*to think*), **croire** (*to believe*), **savoir** (*to know*), **espérer** (*to hope*), **sembler** (*to seem*), and **paraître** (*to appear*). But when these verbs are used in the **passé composé**, they may take on a different meaning. Compare the examples below:

Hier elle était malade.	*Yesterday she was sick.*
Elle a mangé un morceau de poulet et tout de suite elle a été malade.	*She ate a piece of chicken and she got sick right away.*
On savait qu'il était coupable.	*We knew he was guilty.*
On l'a écouté et immédiatement on a su qu'il était coupable.	*We listened to him and immediately we knew that he was guilty.*
J'attendais l'autobus quand j'ai aperçu un taxi.	*I was waiting for the bus when I saw a taxi.*
Je suis sorti de la maison, j'ai couru vers l'arrêt d'autobus et j'ai attendu vingt minutes.	*I left home, ran to the bus stop, and waited for twenty minutes.*

The Conjunctions *Quand*, *Lorsque*, *Pendant que*, *Alors que*, and *Tandis que*

All of these conjunctions can relate two or more conditions in a temporal sense, but each has different nuances. And note that each of the conjunctions are followed by verbs in the indicative.

Quand/**lorsque** can be translated as *when*.

Il prononçait un discours **quand** il s'est mis à pleuvoir.	*He was giving a speech when it started to rain.*
Lorsqu'il était jeune, il écrivait des poèmes.	*When he was young, he used to write poems.*

Pendant que can be translated as "while" and indicates that two actions are simultaneous.

La chorale chantait **pendant que** deux enfants allumaient des bougies commémoratives.	*The choir was singing while two children were lighting memorial candles.*

Alors que also indicates that two actions are simultaneous but is used to draw a contrast or contradiction between them.

Le premier ministre jouait au tennis **alors que** des hectares de forêt brûlaient.	*The prime minister was playing tennis while acres of forest were burning.*

Tandis que can be translated as "while" or "whereas," and it draws the starkest contrast or tension between two actions.

Elle faisait la grasse matinée **tandis que**, moi, je faisais la lessive!

She was sleeping in, whereas I was doing laundry!

The Pluperfect Tense

The **plus-que-parfait** (*pluperfect*) indicates an action that happened before another past action has begun. It is like a "past" past tense, so to speak. And it is often combined with a dependent clause stating this anteriority.

To form the **plus-que-parfait**, the imperfect of **avoir** or **être** is used in conjunction with the past participle of the main verb. And remember to have the past participle agree with the subject when using **être**!

To start, let's review the auxiliary verbs **être** and **avoir**.

être   *to be*

j'étais	*I was*	nous étions	*we were*
tu étais	*you were*	vous étiez	*you were*
il/elle/on était	*he/she/one was*	ils/elles étaient	*they were*

avoir   *to have*

j'avais	*I had*	nous avions	*we had*
tu avais	*you had*	vous aviez	*you had*
il/elle/on avait	*he/she/one had*	ils/elles avaient	*they had*

Ils avaient invité tous les membres de la famille.

They had invited all the members of the family.

Elle n'était pas revenue sur les lieux de son enfance.

She had not been back to the places of her childhood.

Il ne s'était pas souvenu du prénom de sa cousine éloignée.

He hadn't remembered the name of his distant cousin.

—Avaient-ils déjà visité Honfleur?	—*Had they already visited Honfleur?*
—Non, jamais.	—*No, never.*

Zoé a fait traduire les documents qu'on lui avait donnés.	*Zoé had the documents that we gave (had given) her translated.*
Alain a partagé l'information qu'il avait découverte.	*Alain shared the information that he (had) discovered.*

Making a Suggestion with *si + on + imparfait*

With a **si + on** construction, the **imparfait** is used to make a suggestion, to invite someone to do something. The informal **on** refers to two or more people and is conjugated in the third person singular.

Si on allait à Menton?	*What about going to Menton?*
Si on triait toutes ces photos?	*What about sorting out all these pictures?*
Si on chantait une chanson de Johnny?	*What about singing a song by Johnny?*
Si on téléphonait à Tante Marie?	*What about calling Aunt Marie?*

You will encounter the **imparfait** and **plus-que-parfait** in other idiomatic constructions, for instance, to express a wish or a regret.

Si seulement elle n'habitait pas si loin!	*If only she did not live so far away!*
Si seulement vous pouviez trouver ces documents!	*If only you could find these documents!*

Si seulement elle était à l'heure!	*If only she were on time!*
Si seulement tu avais rencontré ton arrière-grand-père!	*If only you had met your great-grandfather!*
Si seulement vous aviez résolu le mystère!	*If only you had resolved the mystery!*

Using *Depuis* with the Imperfect

As you recall from Chapter 8, we have seen **depuis** used with the present tense and the **passé composé**. **Depuis** can be used in the **imparfait** when it refers to a continuous action. Note that in this case, English uses the pluperfect while French uses the **imparfait**.

First, let's review the continuous action that requires the present tense:

Mon neveu habite à Marseille depuis cinq ans.	*My nephew has been living in Marseille for five years.*

And the past:

Mon neveu habitait à Marseille depuis cinq ans quand il a décidé de s'installer à Berlin.	*My nephew had been living in Marseille for five years when he decided to settle down in Berlin.*
Nora fait des recherches depuis trois mois.	*Nora has been doing research for three months.*
Nora faisait des fouilles depuis trois mois quand soudain elle a trouvé une amphore du huitième siècle.	*Nora had been digging for three months when suddenly she found an amphora from the eighth century.*

Be sure to review *since*, *for*, and *ago*, and practice the different usages of the tenses.

The *Passé Simple*

The **passé simple** (*simple past*) is a tense used mainly in written French, although it may be heard during a formal speech. It is the equivalent of the **passé composé**, relating to a specific action in the past. When relating events, quality newspapers use the **passé simple**. Scandal sheets will often use it to convey a sense of drama. When reading French literature of all periods, you need to identify the **passé simple** to get a full appreciation of the text. Twenty-first-century writers write in the **passé simple**! It is considered one of the most beautiful tenses of the French language.

The **passé simple** of regular **-er** verbs like **penser** (*to think*) is formed by adding the endings **-ai**, **-as**, **-a**, **-âmes**, **âtes**, and **-èrent** to the infinitive stem.

parler   (*to speak*)

je parl**ai**	*I spoke*	nous parl**âmes**	*we spoke*
tu parl**as**	*you spoke*	vous parl**âtes**	*you spoke*
il/elle/on parl**a**	*he/she/one spoke*	ils/elles parl**èrent**	*they spoke*

The same rules apply to verbs ending in **-cer** and **-ger**, adding a cedilla or an extra **e**.

Il commen**ç**a à lire son essai.	*He started reading his essay.*
J'annon**ç**ai la nouvelle.	*I announced the news.*
Il mélang**e**a les dates.	*He got the dates mixed.*
Elle partag**e**a ses opinions.	*She shared her views.*

The **passé simple** of regular **-ir** and **-re** verbs, like **partir** (*to leave*) and **répondre** (*to answer*), is formed by adding the endings **-is**, **-is**, **-it**, **-îmes**, **-îtes**, and **-irent** to the infinitive stem.

partir   *to leave*

je partis	*I left*	nous partîmes	*we left*
tu partis	*you left*	vous partîtes	*you left*
il/elle/on partit	*he/she/one left*	ils/elles partirent	*they left*

Avoir (*to have*) and **être** (*to be*) have an irregular conjugation in the **passé simple**.

j'eus	*I had*	nous eûmes	*we had*
tu eus	*you had*	vous eûtes	*you had*
il/elle/on eut	*he/she/one had*	ils/elles eurent	*they had*

je fus	*I was*	nous fûmes	*we were*
tu fus	*you were*	vous fûtes	*you were*
il/elle/on fut	*he/she/one was*	ils/elles furent	*they were*

Napoléon envoya une lettre à Joséphine de Beauharnais.	*Napoléon sent a letter to Joséphine de Beauharnais.*
Elle lui répondit un mois plus tard.	*She replied to him a month later.*
Il fut surpris par son message.	*He was surprised by her message.*
Il lui rapporta un châle en cachemire.	*He brought her a cashmere shawl.*
Joséphine lança la mode à la cour.	*Joséphine started a craze at the court.*

Here are some of the verbs in the **passé simple** that have an irregular stem. You should start memorizing these in order to identify them when you read a newspaper or a novel. Since the **passé simple** is mostly found in narration, the third person singular and plural subjects (*il, elle, ils, elles*) are most often used. Here are some examples in the masculine and the feminine forms:

boire (*to drink*)	il but	*he drank*	ils burent	*they drank*
connaître (*to know*)	il connut	*he knew*	ils connurent	*they knew*
courir (*to run*)	il courut	*he ran*	ils coururent	*they ran*
écrire (*to write*)	il écrivit	*he wrote*	ils écrivirent	*they wrote*
faire (*to do*)	il fit	*he did*	ils firent	*they did*
lire (*to read*)	elle lut	*she read*	elles lurent	*they read*

mettre (*to put*)	elle mit	*she put*	elles mirent	*they put*
mourir (*to die*)	elle mourut	*she died*	elles moururent	*they died*
pleuvoir (*to rain*)	il plut	*it rained*		
pouvoir (*can*)	elle put	*she could*	elles purent	*they could*
rire (*to laugh*)	elle rit	*she laughed*	elles rirent	*they laughed*
savoir (*to know*)	elle sut	*she knew*	elles surent	*they knew*
tenir (*to hold*)	il tint	*he held*	elles tinrent	*they held*
venir (*to come*)	il vint	*he came*	ils vinrent	*they came*
vivre (*to live*)	il vécut	*he lived*	ils vécurent	*they lived*

The Verb *Manquer*

What do you miss most from your childhood? The verb **manquer** carries many different meanings.

- **Manquer** expresses a failure to participate in, attend, or catch something or someone:

  J'ai manqué le début du film.   *I missed the start of the movie.*
  Hier elle a manqué le cours de yoga.   *Yesterday she missed yoga class.*

Note that this version of **manquer** is not followed by a preposition.

- **Manquer de** expresses an insufficient amount:

  Il manque d'imagination.   *He lacks imagination.*
  Cette ratatouille manque de thym.   *This ratatouille is missing thyme.*

- **Manquer** is also used in impersonal expressions indicating an insufficient amount:

Il me manque deux euros.	*I'm short two euros.*
Il lui manque du fromage pour faire ce soufflé.	*He/she is short on cheese to make the soufflé.*
Il leur manque des preuves pour lui faire un procès.	*They are missing proof to sue him.*

- **Manquer à** expresses a failure to meet expectations or requirements:

Tu as manqué à tes obligations.	*You failed to meet your obligations.*
Ils ont manqué à leur promesse.	*They neglected their promise.*

- **Manquer** also expresses nostalgia or a longing for someone or something:

Mon ancien quartier me manque.	*I miss my old neighborhood.*
Tu me manques.	*I miss you.*
Je lui manque.	*He/she misses me.*
Nous leur manquons.	*They miss us.*
Vous me manquez.	*I miss you.*
Ils leur manquent.	*They miss them.*

BTW

As we just saw, one meaning of **manquer** is to fail to catch something (**J'ai manqué le train de 7h36**). But there are other informal ways to express the same idea, using the verb **rater** or **louper**: **nous avons loupé le bus** (we missed the bus) and **elle a raté son vol** (she missed her flight).

DIALOGUE *Souvenir, souvenirs...*
Memories, memories...

Julien is spending the weekend with Céleste, his grandmother, aka Mamie, who was a history teacher. She has decided to leave her Norman town, Bayeux, to settle in Menton on the French Riviera. Julien is helping sort out some items before the big move. While going through photo albums, she is trying to decide what furniture to take to Menton.

IRL Bayeux is in the Calvados department of Normandy. It is best known for the eponymous tapestry that depicts the 11th-century Norman conquest. Menton, **la perle de France**, is in the Alpes-Maritimes, close to the Italian border. Its microclimate makes it famous for its lemons. If you are in Menton in February, do not miss the **Fête du citron**, the Lemon Festival!

JULIEN: Mamie, cette belle photo, où est-ce qu'elle a été prise?

Nana, where was this beautiful picture taken?

CÉLESTE: C'était à Fécamp. J'avais sept ou huit ans. Mon père voulait reproduire la scène du tableau de Berthe Morisot *Sur la plage.*

It was in Fécamp. I was seven or eight. My brother wanted to reproduce Berthe Morisot's Sur la plage.

IRL Like Honfleur and the cliffs and arches in Étretat, Fécamp attracted the impressionist painters like Édouard Manet, Pierre-Auguste Renoir, Claude Monet, Camille Pissaro, and Edgar Degas. Berthe Morisot, one of the first women impressionists, defied the social norms of her time to join the French avant-garde. Morisot's work is exhibited in Paris and in major museums in the United States.

JULIEN: Tu étais si mignonne avec ton maillot de bain à volants rouge et blanc. Vous habitiez à Fécamp?

You were so cute with your red and white ruffle bathing suit. Did you live near Fécamp?

CÉLESTE: Non, nous habitions près de Honfleur, puis nous avons déménagé à Bayeux.

No, we lived near Honfleur, then we moved to Bayeux.

JULIEN: Et ce monsieur? Qui est-ce?

And this gentleman? Who is he?

CÉLESTE: C'est Monsieur Ollagnier, mon professeur de français. C'était un professeur exceptionnel. Sans lui, j'aurais raté le bac!

It's Mr. Ollagnier, my French teacher. He was an excellent teacher. Without him I would have failed the bac!

 IRL The **bac**, instituted by Napoleon in 1808, is a national exam that represents successful completion of secondary education and enables students to go to college or pursue other forms of higher education. It is a rite of passage. Students study extremely hard in the months leading up to the bac, stressing themselves and their parents.

JULIEN: Mamie! Toi, rater le bac? C'est impossible!

Nana! You, failing the bac? *It is impossible!*

CÉLESTE: J'étais timide. Monsieur Ollagnier m'encourageait. Il me donnait des devoirs supplémentaires tous les jours. C'est lui qui m'a redonné confiance en moi. Et j'ai eu le bac avec mention très bien!

I was shy. Mr. Ollagnier used to encourage me. He would give me extra homework every day. It was he who restored my confidence. I passed the bac *with the highest honor.*

JULIEN: Mamie, arrête de frimer… (rires) Bon, il faut trier ces photos. Il y en a beaucoup trop!

Nana, stop showing off… (laughter) Well, we need to sort out these pictures. There are too many of them!

CÉLESTE: Tu as raison. J'aimerais en garder quelques-unes quand même.

You're right. I'd like to keep a few, though.

JULIEN: Choisis une trentaine de photos. Les autres, je vais les numériser.

Pick about thirty pictures. I'll digitize the others.

BTW

*To express "about twenty," the French say **une vingtaine**: **une trentaine** (about thirty), **une quarantaine** (about forty), **une cinquantaine** (about fifty), **une centaine** (about a hundred). "Ten to twelve" is expressed by **une dizaine** when "dozen" is used in English. You invite **une dizaine de personnes**, you go on vacation **une dizaine de jours**, you read **une dizaine de livres**. However, French uses **douzaine** when buying roses, eggs, or oysters; you buy **une douzaine de roses**, **une douzaine d'oeufs**, or **une douzaine d'huîtres**.*

CÉLESTE: Merci, Julien. Comme c'est gentil! Est-ce que tu pourrais aussi numériser tous ces meubles?

Thank you, Julien. How nice of you! Could you also digitize all this furniture?

JULIEN: Je ne suis pas magicien.

I am not a magician.

CÉLESTE: Je ne sais pas quels meubles je vais emporter à Menton. L'appartement est au bord de la mer, mais il n'est pas très grand.

I don't know which pieces of furniture to take to Menton. The apartment is by the sea, but it is not that large.

BTW

*Do you need some furniture? Go to the flea market, **le marché aux puces**, where you might find something to your liking, such as: **une chaise** (chair), **un fauteuil** (armchair), **un tabouret** (stool), **une table basse** (coffee table), **un lit** (bed), **une lampe de chevet** (bedside lamp), **une commode** (chest of drawers), **un coffre** (chest), **une bibliothèque** (bookcase), **une étagère** (shelf), or **un tapis** (rug).*

BTW

*Remember that you bring a dozen roses (**vous apportez une douzaine de roses**), but you take three suitcases on vacation (**vous emportez trois valises**). You bring a friend to Nana's house (**vous amenez un ami chez Mamie**), and you take Nana to the movies (**vous emmenez Mamie au cinéma**).*

JULIEN: À qui appartenait cette armoire?

Whose armoire was it?

CÉLESTE: Elle appartenait à ma grand-mère. C'est une armoire normande en merisier du 19ᵉ siècle. Elle l'avait reçue en cadeau de mariage. Je dois l'emporter!

It belonged to my grandmother. It is a cherrywood 19th-century Normandy armoire. She had received it as a wedding gift. I must take it with me!

BTW

You pick cherries from a **cerisier**, but furniture is made out of a wild cherry tree called a **merisier**. Furniture comes in oak (**chêne**), solid oak (**chêne massif**), pine (**pin**), walnut (**noyer**), beech (**hêtre**), chestnut (**châtaignier**), poplar (**peuplier**), or ash (**frêne**). These trees, like most trees in French, are masculine. Here are a few more examples: a coconut tree (**un cocotier**), a weeping willow (**un saule pleureur**), a maple tree (**un érable**), and a cedar tree (**un cèdre**).

JULIEN: Et le secrétaire avec ses tiroirs secrets? Tu l'emportes aussi?

What about the secretary desk with its secret drawers? Are you taking it, too?

CÉLESTE: Il te plaît?

Do you like it?

JULIEN: Euh… Oui, mais…

Uh… Yes, but…

CÉLESTE: C'était le secrétaire de ton grand-père. Il l'avait hérité de son père. C'est là qu'il faisait son courrier. Nous n'avions pas internet à cette époque-là.

It was your grandfather's desk. He had inherited it from his father. That's where he used to write his mail. We didn't have internet at that time.

BTW

JULIEN: Oui, mais maintenant c'est là où tu poses ton ordinateur.

Yes, but now that's where you place your computer.

CÉLESTE: Il est en chêne massif. Il est lourd et trop encombrant. Cela me ferait plaisir de te l'offrir.

It is in solid oak. It is heavy and takes too much space. I would love to give it to you.

JULIEN: Merci Mamie. C'est le père de Papy qui est... Je crois me souvenir...

Thank you, Nana. It is Grandpa's father who is... I think I remember...

CÉLESTE: Oui, mon petit Julien, le père de Papy est mort en 1917. La bataille du Chemin des Dames fut un véritable carnage. Victorine, la maman de Papy, a dû élever seule trois enfants.

Yes, my dear Julien, Grandpa's father died in 1917. The battle of the Chemin des Dames was a pure slaughter. Victorine, Grandpa's mother, had to raise her three children alone.

JULIEN: Est-ce que Victorine s'est remariée?

Did Victorine marry again?

CÉLESTE: Il y avait tant de veuves en 1917! Elle était si triste et la vie était dure.

There were so many widows in 1917! She was sad and life was tough.

JULIEN: Est-ce qu'elle travaillait?

Was she working?

CÉLESTE: Elle a trouvé un emploi de vendeuse dans une chapellerie à Rouen.

She found a job as a saleswoman in a hat store in Rouen.

JULIEN: La chapellerie où Madame Bovary faisait ses courses avec Léon…?

The hat store where Madame Bovary was shopping with Léon…?

CÉLESTE: Ah, ah… Au moins, tu connais tes classiques! Victorine a travaillé quelques années, puis elle s'est remariée vers 1925 et son mari a adopté ses trois enfants. Tant de souvenirs qui remontent à la surface.

Ah, ah… At least you know your classics! Victorine worked for a few years, then she remarried in 1925 and her husband adopted her three children. It brings back so many memories.

IRL Gustave Flaubert published *Madame Bovary* in 1856. Emma Bovary is a doctor's wife who lives beyond her means in order to escape provincial life and pursue passionate love. The novel, considered Flaubert's masterpiece of realism, had a major influence on literature.

BTW

*You come back from vacation with great memories (**de bons souvenirs**). If you remember all these memories, you have a good memory (**une bonne mémoire**), maybe even **une mémoire d'éléphant**. If you want to finish your master's, you have to write a thesis (**un mémoire**). And later, when you're famous, you will be writing your memoirs (**mémoires**), like Simone de Beauvoir's Memoirs of a Dutiful Daughter (**Les mémoires d'une jeune fille rangée**). And you'll be able to quote from memory (**citer de mémoire**) the first French woman **académicienne** Marguerite de Yourcenar's **Les mémoires d'Hadrien**. Note that the word **mémoire** takes on different meanings in the masculine, feminine, or plural.*

JULIEN: Nostalgie, nostalgie... Tu veux continuer?

Nostalgia, nostalgia... Do you want to keep going?

CÉLESTE: Je suis fatiguée. Faisons une pause. Tu sais, Papy me manque. Je me sens seule.

I am tired. Let's take a break. You know, I miss Grandpa. I feel lonely.

JULIEN: Je sais, Mamie, mais on ira te voir à Menton. Je ferai une photo de toi en m'inspirant de *Sur la plage* de Berthe Morisot!

I know, Nana, but we'll go and see you in Menton. I'll take a picture of you with Berthe Morisot's painting Sur la plage *in mind.*

CÉLESTE: Dans cinquante ans, si on te demande comment elle était ta Mamie, qu'est-ce que tu diras?

In fifty years from now, if one asks you how your Nana was, what will you say?

JULIEN: Ma Mamie, elle était prof d'histoire à Bayeux; elle aimait l'opéra et la peinture; elle était géniale; et elle faisait les meilleures tartes normandes!

My Nana, she was a history teacher in Bayeux; she liked opera and painting; she was awesome; and she used to make the best Norman tarts!

CÉLESTE: Ah, ah... Et bientôt les tartes au citron!

Ah, ah... And soon, lemon tarts!

Julien commence à chanter «Souvenirs, souvenirs» de Johnny Hallyday et Mamie essaie de se souvenir des paroles.

Julien starts to sing "Memories, Memories" by Johnny Hallyday and Nana tries to remember the lyrics.

CÉLESTE: La, la, la…. (elle commence à danser) *Et vous faites refleurir tous les rêves de bonheur….*

La, la, la…. (she starts to dance) And again you rekindle all my dreams of happiness….

 IRL Inspired by Elvis Presley, Johnny Hallyday brought rock and roll to France. He was a singer, an actor, and a legend who transcended generations for nearly sixty years. He inspired countless singers and had a great impact on the French musical landscape. «**Souvenirs, souvenirs**» was one of the songs that launched his long career in 1960. Memorize the lyrics of his song and rock, rock, rock.

EXERCISES

EXERCISE 11.1

Conjugate the following verbs in the imperfect tense.

1. Il (faire) _____ beau.

2. Ils (marcher) _____ rapidement.

3. Les élèvent (avoir) _____ tous un nouveau sac à dos.

4. Nous (suivre) _____ des cours de danse.

5. Notre professeur (s'appeler) _____ Monsieur Gallatin.

6. Mon père (être) _____ passionné de musique baroque.

7. Vous (réfléchir) _____ à la situation.

8. L'institutrice (avoir) _____ mal à la gorge.

9. Mon frère et moi, nous (partager) _____ une chambre.

10. Elle (s'habiller) _____ en bleu et blanc.

EXERCISE 11.2

Conjugate the following verbs in the imperfect tense.

1. Je (jouer) _____ au tennis tous les jeudis.

2 Ma grand-mère nous (faire) _____ de la très bonne cuisine cajun.

3. Il (paraître) _____ épuisé.

4. Est-ce que tu (aller) _____ souvent à la plage?

5. Quand je (être) _____ enfant, je (craindre) _____ l'obscurité.

6. On (déménager) _____ tous les cinq ans.

7. Madame Berger (remplacer) _____ souvent sa collègue quand elle était malade.

8. Nous (avoir) _____ un jardin potager.

9. Elles (partager) _____ un studio dans le 20ᵉ arrondissement.

10. Claude Monet (peindre) _____ en plein air sur la côte d'Albâtre.

11. Vous (boire) _____ du thé noir tous les matins.

12. Ils (se voir) _____ chaque weekend.

13. Je (voyager) _____ toujours avec ma meilleure amie.

14. Elle (ne jamais effacer) _____ le tableau!

15. Adolescent, il (faire) _____ du judo.

16. Elles (s'habiller) _____ en noir et blanc.

17. Autrefois, ils (savoir) _____ toutes les chansons de Georges Moustaki.

18. Il (changer) _____ de baskets tous les mois.

19. C'est toi qui (choisir) _____ les joueurs de l'équipe.

20. Le directeur (exiger) _____ notre ponctualité.

EXERCISE 11.3

Conjugate the following verbs in the **imparfait** *and the* **passé composé.**

1. Tu (faire) _____ le ménage quand l'aspirateur (tomber) _____ en panne.

2. Ils (marcher) _____ dans le parc quand tout à coup ils (voir) _____ Fanny Ardant.

3. Leïla (venir) _____ de finir son roman quand un éditeur la (appeler) _____.

4. Je (lire) _____ le journal quand on (frapper) _____ à la porte.

5. Hamed (conduire) _____ quand l'orage (éclater) _____ .

6. On (venir) _____ de finir les rénovations quand on (trouver) _____ un nid d'abeilles.

7. Nous (se reposer) _____ quand ma sœur (sonner) _____ .

8. Le présentateur (parler) _____ quand soudain l'image (disparaître) _____ .

9. Mes parents nous (montrer) _____ des vidéos quand soudain ma tante (se mettre) _____ à pleurer.

10. Je (regarder) _____ l'album de photos quand je (reconnaître) _____ mon arrière-grand-père.

EXERCISE 11.4

*Translate the following sentences. When asking a question, use the **est-ce que** form.*

1. I was thinking about you when you entered the room. (*tu*)

2. Would you wear a uniform to school? (*tu*)

3. They were watching a movie when the cat jumped on the table.

4. We used to play basketball when we were in high school.

5. Aisha was walking along the Seine when she noticed a restaurant on a barge.

6. When my aunt cooked, she always used a lot of spices.

7. Diego was writing a letter to his grandmother when she called.

8. There was not a cloud in the sky when I arrived at the library.

9. I was doing research at the library when I found the article I needed.

10. Did you take a picture of the article when you found it? (*tu*)

EXERCISE 11.5

Using the sentence for context, conjugate each verb in either the **passé composé** *or the* **imparfait.**

1. Je (ne pas savoir) _____ où aller en vacances, et tout à coup je (avoir) _____ l'idée brillante d'aller à Bora Bora.

2. Hier je (penser) _____ à toi quand je (être) _____ à la plage.

3. Je (avoir) _____ 20 ans quand je (se fiancer) _____.

4. Après ma longue explication, il (soudain) (sembler) _____ comprendre.

5. Il (ne pas espérer) _____ plus la revoir, et soudain elle (apparaître) _____.

EXERCISE 11.6

Connect the two fragments of sentences with the conjunction suggested, using the **imparfait.**

1. Je (tondre) la pelouse / mon neveu (lire) un roman policier. (tandis que)
   _____

2. Elle (écouter) de la musique / elle (se promener) avec son chien. (pendant que) _____

3. Il (vouloir) manger des pâtes / nous (vouloir) partager une pizza. (alors que) _____

4. Il (rire) aux éclats / leur collègue (pleurer) à chaudes larmes. Pas gentil! (tandis que) _____

5. Elle (se plaire) sur cette île isolée au Japon / alors qu'elle (ne pas parler) un mot de japonais. (alors que) _____

EXERCISE 11.7

Conjugate the following verbs in the **plus-que-parfait.**

1. Julien (espérer) _____ retrouver les traces de ses ancêtres.

2. Nous (établir) _____ la généalogie de cet enfant abandonné.

3. Je (se promener) _____ dans le cimetière du Père-Lachaise.

4. Ils (effectuer) _____ des recherches dans quinze départements.

5. Est-ce que vous (mettre) _____ des fleurs sur la tombe d'Isadora Duncan.

6. Isabelle (se souvenir) _____ de l'emplacement de la tombe de Proust.

7. On (ne pas réussir) _____ à trouver son livret militaire.

8. Je (interroger) _____ plusieurs membres de ma famille.

9. Elles (ne jamais se rencontrer) _____.

10. Il (recueillir) _____ tous les documents nécessaires.

EXERCISE 11.8

Match the items in the two columns. Choose the most logical answers.

1. Elle était furieuse	a. quand elle aura pris contact avec la mairie.
2. L'historienne voulait savoir	b. à effacer ces souvenirs de sa mémoire.
3. Elle ne se souvenait plus	c. car elle ne pouvait pas retrouver son acte de naissance.

4. Elle ira à Orléans   d. de sa date de naissance.

5. Elle n'a pas réussi   e. si la grand-mère avait gardé le livret de famille.

EXERCISE 11.9

*Translate the following sentences using the **tu** form when necessary.*

1. What about taking a picture on the beach?

2. What about ordering a pizza?

3. If only you knew!

4. What about digitizing all these pictures?

5. What about choosing a film?

6. If only he had arrived on time!

7. What about buying a dozen white roses?

8. If only you knew how to make an apple tart!

9. What about calling Julie?

10. If only you had kept Grandpa's hat!

EXERCISE 11.10

*Conjugate the following verbs in the **passé simple**.*

1. Il parlait et soudain il (se souvenir) _____ de son professeur de philosophie.

2. Les photos de l'album (raviver) _____ les souvenirs de Mamie.

3. Il (perdre) _____ la mémoire pendant trois mois puis il la (recouvrir) _____ .

4. Vite, ils (effacer) _____ ces souvenirs de leur esprit.

5. Elle (feuilleter) _____ l'album et (reconnaître) _____ son arrière-grand-mère.

6. Tout à coup, en l'entendant, je (éprouver) _____ un sentiment étrange.

7. Le conférencier (évoquer) _____ l'engagement des intellectuels.

8. Ils (conserver) _____ des traces de la mémoire collective.

9. Ces souvenirs les (rendre) _____ nostalgiques.

10. Lors de la conversation, des souvenirs leur (venir) _____ à l'esprit.

EXERCISE 11.11

Identify the verbs in the **passé simple** *and the* **imparfait** *in this excerpt from André Gide's* **Isabelle.**

Gérard Lacase, chez qui nous nous retrouvâmes au mois d'août 189., nous mena, Francis Jammes et moi, visiter le château de la Quartfourche dont il ne restera bientôt plus que des ruines, et son grand parc délaissé où l'été fastueux s'éployait à l'aventure. Rien plus n'en défendait l'entrée: le fossé à demi comblé, la haie crevée, ni la grille descellée qui céda de travers à notre premier coup d'épaule. Plus d'allées; sur les pelouses débordées quelques vaches pâturaient librement l'herbe surabondante et folle: d'autres cherchaient le frais au creux des massifs éventrés; à peine distinguait-on de-ci de-là, parmi la profusion sauvage, quelque fleur ou quelque feuillage insolite, patient reste des anciennes cultures, presque étouffé déjà par les espèces plus communes. Nous suivions Gérard sans parler, oppressés par la beauté du lieu, de la saison, de l'heure, et parce que nous sentions aussi tout ce que cette excessive opulence pouvait cacher d'abandon et de deuil. Nous parvînmes devant le perron du château, dont les premières marches étaient noyées dans l'herbe, celles d'en haut disjointes et brisées; mais, devant les portes-fenêtres du salon, les volets résistants nous arrêtèrent.

From *Isabelle*, by André Gide

EXERCISE 11.12

Translate the following sentences into French.

1. I missed the last subway.

2. This soup is missing salt.

3. I miss my friend Paula.

4. She misses me.

5. They are missing three documents.

6. He missed his ballet class.

7. We failed to meet our duty.

8. I used to miss the cold, but then I got used to it.

9. You are short on flour to make the cake. (*tu*)

10. I don't think I will miss my colleagues.

LE COIN DES CRÉATEURS

Je me souviens

Georges Perec's *I remember* consists of 480 statements, all beginning with *Je me souviens*. The book, a collective memoir, represents a secret key to his novels. It was published in 1978 shortly after *La vie mode d'emploi* (*Life, a User's Manual*) won the prix Médicis.

À l'instar de Perec, écrivez dix phrases, qui commencent par *Je me souviens*.

Je me souviens de ma bicyclette bleu ciel.
Je me souviens du goût de la tarte au citron de Mamie.
Je me souviens du jour où tu as pris le train pour Menton.

À votre tour!

NOTE CULTURELLE

BAC AND BEYOND—THE EDUCATION SYSTEM IN FRANCE

Passe ton bac d'abord is the title of a popular 1978 French film directed by Maurice Pialat that was released in the United States as *Graduate First*. While the English title gets the idea across, it also avoids having to explain exactly what a *bac* is to non-French audiences. The word *bac* is short for *baccalauréat*. It is similar to a U.S. high school diploma, but not an exact equivalent due to the differences between the French and American school systems. In France, mandatory education is divided into four stages: preschool (*prématernelle*), which includes day care, and preschool (*maternelle*), primary school (*école primaire*), middle school (*collège*—careful, the word is a false friend in English!), and high school (*lycée*).

Day care and preschool: In France, mandatory education begins at age six. However, parents are able to enroll children in day care as early as two years old, and in preschool from ages three to five. Once they reach the age of six, all children must be enrolled in a primary school.

Children attend primary school from six to eleven years of age. There are five grades, similar to a U.S. elementary school. Once a child completes primary school, the next step is middle school.

Middle school represents the first stage of French secondary education. It consists of four years of study for students ages eleven through fifteen, similar to U.S. middle school. There are four grade levels, with 3rd being the fourth year and 6th the last. During the last year, all students must take the exam for a *brevet*, which is the middle school diploma or school-leaving certificate. It is not unusual in French schools for students to repeat (*redoubler*) a year, thus completing middle school at age 16, the age at which schooling stops being compulsory. However, after receiving their *brevet*, most students choose to continue on to high school.

High school is the second stage of French secondary education. Students attend high school from fifteen to eighteen years of age. Those who are academically strong, typically attend a general or technical high school, while those who are not have the option of attending a professional high school. There are three grade levels: second, first, and terminal, corresponding to grades 10–12 in the United States. In general and technical high schools, the last year or terminal level is when students begin to focus on taking the *baccalauréat* or *bac* exam. This exam can be very stressful, and the pressure to pass is very high since a *bac* is required for admission to French publicly funded universities. However, a student who fails the exam does have the possibility of retaking it the following year. In professional high schools, students are offered three types of school completion credentials: the *baccalauréat professionnel* (*bac pro*), the CAP (*certificat d'aptitude professionnel*—Professional Aptitude Certificate), and the BEP (*Brevet d'enseignement professionnel*—General Certificate of Secondary Education). To be successful, students must pass an exam in addition to completing a set number of hours of on-the-job experience.

There are three types of higher education institutions in France: universities, *grandes écoles*, and specialized schools. The *bac* is a requirement for admission to all three.

Universities are public institutions that offer academic, technical, and professional degrees to any student who has obtained a *baccalauréat*. Degrees are awarded in many fields and at three different levels of achievement, called *cycles: licence, master, doctorat* (LMD), similar to the bachelor's, master's and doctoral degrees in U.S. universities.

France's *grandes écoles* are selective public and private institutions. Similar to universities, they offer a more specialized three-year course of study in subjects such as business, public administration, or engineering. Post-*bac* students are admitted to the *grandes écoles* based on their scores on a competitive exam (*concours*). Many often take a two-year preparatory course (*cours préparatoires* or *prépas*) to improve their chances. Students graduate from a *grande école* with a master's degree (master).

Specialized schools are public or private institutions that train students for professional careers in specific fields, such as art, architecture, social work, or tourism. They offer the licence and master.

The quality of French higher education is widely recognized throughout the world. Today, with more than 323,000 international students, France is the fourth most popular destination for international students. France is part of the European Higher Education Area (EHEA). The EHEA system helps ensure that higher-education systems across Europe are compatible—and that students, researchers, and academics in Europe can collaborate and study or work abroad more easily.

France has 75 universities, more than 220 schools of engineering, 150 schools of business and management, 120 public post-secondary schools of art, 20 schools of architecture, and 3,000 other specialized institutes and schools in specific sectors, such as social work, health professions, tourism, sports, fashion, and design, definitely a diverse menu of educational opportunities.

Thinking About the World in the Conditional Mood

MUST KNOW

 Using the conditional tense can help soften requests.

 We use **le conditionnel journalistique** for reporting unconfirmed facts.

 Having regrets? Use the **past conditional**.

 Avoir droit + à takes a noun, while **avoir le droit + de** is followed by a verb.

 All in-laws are **beau** or **belle**!

s Gérard Lenorman famously sang, **"Si j'étais président de la République, j'écrirais mes discours en vers et en musique."** If you could be president for a day, what would you do? The conditional mood allows us to express hypothetical statements and things we would like to change about the past.

The *Conditionnel Présent*

The **conditionnel présent** (*present conditional*) is a mood referring to hypothetical events that are not guaranteed to occur, and are often dependent on certain conditions. In many instances, it is used in **si** clauses, but it has many uses we'll explore in this chapter. It is formed by adding the endings of the imperfect to the future stem of a verb.

chanter   *to sing*

je chanterais	*I would sing*	nous chanterions	*we would sing*
tu chanterais	*you would sing*	vous chanteriez	*you would sing*
il/elle/on chanterait	*he/she/one would sing*	ils/elles chanteraient	*they would sing*

As we saw in Chapter 10, some verbs have an irregular stem in the future:

faire   *to do*

je ferais	*I would do*	nous ferions	*we would do*
tu ferais	*you would do*	vous feriez	*you would do*
il/elle/on ferait	*he/she/one would do*	ils/elles feraient	*they would do*

aller   *to go*

j'irais   *I would go*   nous irions   *we would go*

tu irais   *you would go*   vous iriez   *you would go*

il/elle/on irait   *he/she/one would go*   ils/elles iraient   *they would go*

■ The **conditionnel présent** is used to express a wish or a suggestion.

Je voudrais une tasse de thé.	*I would like a cup of tea.*
Aurélien aimerait trouver un stage.	*Aurélien would like to find an internship.*
À ta place, j'accepterais son offre.	*If I were you, I would accept his/her offer.*
Il pourrait te donner de bons conseils.	*He could give you some good advice.*

■ The **conditionnel présent** is used to make a statement or a request more polite.

J'aimerais que vous soyez à l'heure.	*I would like you to be on time.*
Est-ce que tu pourrais me présenter à Maya?	*Could you introduce me to Maya?*
Voudriez-vous visiter notre école de cuisine?	*Would you like to visit our cooking school?*
Pourriez-vous m'aider à trouver un emploi?	*Could you help me find a job?*

■ The **conditionnel présent** is used when a condition is implied. In most cases, when the main clause is in the **conditionnel présent**, the **si** clause is in the **imparfait**. (If you need to, review the **imparfait** in Chapter 11.)

J'irais au cinéma ce soir si j'avais le temps.	*I would go to the movie theater tonight if I had time.*
Nous ferions une fondue si nous avions du fromage.	*We would make a fondue if we had cheese.*
Nous dînerions dans le jardin s'il faisait chaud.	*We would eat in the garden if the weather was warmer.*
J'achèterais une guitare si je savais jouer.	*I would buy a guitar if I knew how to play.*

■ When **au cas où** (*in case*) implies a hypothetical fact, the conditional is used.

Prends l'adresse du consulat au cas où tu perdrais ton passeport.	*Take the address of the consulate in case you lose your passport.*
Prends ton parapluie au cas où il pleuvrait.	*Take your umbrella in case it rains.*

■ The **conditionnel présent** is also used in idiomatic expressions such as:

Ça te dirait d'aller au cinéma avec nous?	*Would you like to go to the movies with us?*
Ça vous dirait d'aller à la piscine cet après-midi?	*Do you feel like going to the pool this afternoon?*
Toujours tes mêmes remarques! On dirait Papa!	*Always your same remarks! You sound like Dad!*
On dirait que tu le fais exprès!	*It's like you are doing it on purpose!*
On dirait qu'il va pleuvoir.	*It looks like rain.*
Tu ferais mieux de laver la voiture avant l'arrivée de Tante Jocelyne.	*You'd better wash the car before Aunt Jocelyne arrives.*
Nous ferions mieux de nous concentrer sur une nouvelle approche.	*We'd better focus on a new approach.*

Il vaudrait mieux dire la vérité.	*It would be better to tell the truth.*
Il vaudrait mieux que tu finances tes études.	*It would be better if you paid for your studies.*

- The conditional mode is also used to express unconfirmed or alleged information. In this case it is called the **conditionnel journalistique**, most useful when reading the press or listening to the news. It is translated in English by "reportedly" or "allegedly."

Le président signerait le traité d'ici vendredi.	*The president will reportedly sign the treaty by Friday.*
Thierry Marx ouvrirait une autre école de cuisine au printemps prochain.	*Thierry Marx is reportedly opening another cooking school next spring.*
Massimo Bottura chercherait un emplacement pour un *refettorio* dans le Bronx.	*Massimo Bottura is reportedly looking for a space for a* refettorio *in the Bronx.*
La belle-sœur du prince serait impliquée dans une affaire de fraude fiscale.	*The prince's sister-in-law is allegedly involved in tax fraud.*

More examples of the **conditionnel journalistique** will be featured in the **conditionnel passé** section.

The *Conditionnel Passé*

The **conditionnel passé** (*past conditional*) expresses what would have happened if another event had taken place or if certain conditions had not been present. It is formed with the present conditional of **être** or **avoir** and the past participle of the main verb. The rules of agreement common to all compound tenses still apply.

visiter   *to visit*

j'aurais visité	*I would have visited*	nous aurions visité	*we would have visited*
tu aurais visité	*you would have visited*	vous auriez visité	*you would have visited*
il/elle aurait visité	*he/she would have visited*	ils/elles auraient visité	*they would have visited*

aller   *to go*

je serais allé (e)	*I would have gone*	nous serions allé(e)s	*we would have gone*
tu serais allé(e)	*you would have gone*	vous seriez allé(e)(s)	*you would have gone*
il/elle serait allé(e)	*he/she would have gone*	ils/elles seraient allé(e)s	*they would have gone*

■ The **conditionnel passé** can express regret or reproach.

L'oncle de Léa aurait tant voulu assister à son mariage.	*Léa's uncle would have like so much to attend her wedding.*
Maman aurait été si heureuse.	*Mom would have been so happy.*
Papa aurait aimé que tu étudies le droit.	*Dad would have liked you to study law.*
Cela aurait été plus difficile.	*It would have been more difficult.*
Nous y serions tous allés.	*We would have all gone there.*
Alex, tu aurais dû arriver à 6 heures de matin!	*Alex, you should have arrived at 6 this morning!*
Tu aurais été si déçu.	*You would have been so disappointed.*

■ The **conditionnel passé** is often found with a **si** clause in the **plus-que-parfait**. (For a review of the **plus-que-parfait**, see Chapter 11.)

Maya aurait aimé vivre aux Pays-Bas si elle avait trouvé un emploi.	*Maya would have liked to live in the Netherlands if she had found a job.*
Il se serait inscrit au cours s'il avait eu assez d'argent.	*He would have signed up for the course if he had (had) enough money.*
Je t'aurais appelé si j'avais su que tu étais en ville.	*I would have called you if I had known you were in town.*
Nous serions allés au pique-nique s'il n'avait pas plu.	*We would have gone to the picnic if it had not rained.*

■ The **conditionnel passé** is also used like the **conditionnel présent** as **conditionnel journalistique** to make a statement not confirmed by authorities. In most cases with "allegedly" or "reportedly," the conditional will be used.

L'ouragan aurait fait des victimes aux Bahamas	*The hurricane reportedly killed people in the Bahamas.*
L'apprenti aurait volé une recette au chef étoilé.	*The apprentice allegedly stole a recipe from the starred chef.*
Le chef aurait créé la meilleure recette de ratatouille.	*The chef reportedly created the best ratatouille recipe.*
Le chef aurait engagé un détective privé.	*The chef reportedly hired a private detective.*

The Verb *Devoir* in the Conditional

We have encountered "could" and "would" in the examples at the beginning of the chapter. Let's first refresh our memory before looking at "should" a little closer.

When "could" refers to a hypothesis, a suggestion, the **conditionnel présent** of **pouvoir** is used.

Pourrais-tu me prêter ton dictionnaire?	*Could you lend me your dictionary?*
Pourriez-vous m'envoyer votre C.V.?	*Could you send me your résumé?*

When "would" refers to a polite request, the **conditionnel** is used. Note the following examples:

Je voudrais vous poser une question.	*I would like to ask you a question.*
Voudriez-vous rencontrer Madame Azoulay?	*Would you like to meet Mrs. Azoulay?*

As we studied in Chapter 11, when "would" refers to a repeated action in the past, the **imparfait** is used.

Quand Aurélien était au jardin d'enfants, il dessinait tous les jours.	*When Aurélien was in kindergarten, he would draw every day.*
Nous allions au jardin du Luxembourg tous les dimanches.	*We would go to the Luxembourg Gardens every Sunday.*

When "should" means "ought to," the **conditionnel présent** or the **conditionnel passé** of the verb **devoir** is used. Like in English, it is followed by the infinitive.

First, let's conjugate **devoir** in the present and past conditional.

conditionnel présent		**conditionnel passé**	
je devrais	*I should*	j'aurais dû	*I should have*
tu devrais	*you should*	tu aurais dû	*you should have*
il/elle/on devrait	*he/she/one should*	il/elle/on aurait dû	*he/she/one should have*

nous devrions	*we should*	nous aurions dû	*we should have*
vous devriez	*you should*	vous auriez dû	*you should have*
ils/elles devraient	*they should*	ils/elles auraient dû	*they should have*

Tu devrais lire le nouveau roman d'Olivier Adam.	*You should read Olivier Adam's new novel.*
On devrait avoir le droit de changer la recette du chef!	*We should have the right to change the chef's recipe!*
Vous auriez dû jouer un adagio de Vivaldi.	*You should have played a Vivaldi adagio.*
J'aurais dû installer un nouveau logiciel.	*I should have installed new software.*

 DIALOGUE *Qu'est-ce que tu veux faire dans la vie?* **What do you want to do with your life?**

Maya is talking to her younger brother Aurélien about his plans for the future. While Maya is more pragmatic, Aurélien dreams of a world where everything would be perfectly to his liking.

MAYA: Julie m'a dit que, maintenant, tu aimerais être chef cuisinier!	*Julie told me that, now, you want to be a chef!*
AURÉLIEN: Ouais, peut-être...	*Yeah, maybe...*
MAYA: Depuis quand est-ce que tu t'intéresses à la cuisine? Je ne t'ai jamais vu faire cuire un œuf!	*Since when have you been interested in cooking? I have never seen you cook an egg!*

AURÉLIEN: J'aimerais devenir un chef comme Thierry Marx.

I'd like to become a chef like Thierry Marx.

MAYA: Tu aurais pu choisir plus facile! Il a eu un parcours si compliqué avant de décrocher ses étoiles au guide Michelin!

You could have picked an easier model! He had such a difficult career path before getting his Michelin stars!

 IRL Michelin stars are a rating system used by the blue Michelin guide to grade restaurants on their quality. One star indicates "a very good restaurant," two stars are "excellent cooking that is worth a detour" (**ça vaut le détour**), and three stars mean "exceptional cuisine that is worth a special journey."

AURÉLIEN: Les étoiles, je m'en fiche. Ce qui m'intéresse, c'est sa formation gratuite de douze semaines. Mais on n'a pas le droit de manquer une session ou d'être en retard.

I don't care about stars. I am interested in the twelve-week free training. But you are not allowed to miss one session or to be late.

MAYA: Dans ton cas...

In your case...

AURÉLIEN: Arrête! Ce n'est pas parce que tu es ma sœur aînée que...

Stop it! It is not because you are my big sister that...

MAYA: Je sais, mais il faut être réaliste. Cette formation gratuite est destinée à des gens qui n'ont pas la même chance que toi.

I know, but one must be realistic. This free training is intended to help people who are not as lucky as you.

 IRL Thierry Marx, a two-Michelin-starred chef, is the owner of many restaurants and cooking schools all over the world. He is also a philanthropist who offers a free culinary training course to unemployed people who need to find hope and a way back to a career. Practice your French by listening to his YouTube demonstrations.

AURÉLIEN: Tu sais Maya, j'aimerais bien monter des refettori, ces restaurants communautaires comme celui de Massimo Bottura dans la crypte de la Madeleine.

You know, Maya, I would like to start some refettori, the communal restaurants like Massimo Bottura's, in the crypt of the Madeleine Church.

 **IRL**   Massimo Bottura, founder of Food for Soul, has opened **refettori** all over the world. The main objective is to fight against food waste through social inclusion. The Refettori Paris is located in the crypt of La Madeleine Church, where recipes are created on the spot by renowned chefs with ingredients donated by supermarkets, restaurants, and hotels.

MAYA: Avant de te lancer dans la « gastronomie sociale », tu devrais commencer par limiter ton gaspillage à la maison....

Before engaging in "social gastronomy," you should start by cutting down on waste at home....

AURÉLIEN: Ça suffit!

Enough!

MAYA: Calme-toi, Aurélien! Je blague. Tu sais bien que j'aime te taquiner.

Calm down, Aurélien! I am just kidding! You know very well I like to tease you.

AURÉLIEN: Oui, mais c'est pas drôle. Je dois penser à l'avenir.

Yes, but it's not funny. I have to think about the future.

MAYA: Tu as encore le temps... Cela te dirait d'être bénévole à La Madeleine?

You still have time... Would you like to be a volunteer at the Madeleine?

AURÉLIEN: J'ai regardé le formulaire de candidature sur leur site. Ils veulent des bénévoles qui s'impliquent à long terme.

I looked at the application form on their website. They want volunteers who commit long-term.

MAYA: Passe ton bac d'abord!

Graduate first!

AURÉLIEN: On dirait Maman!

You sound like Mom!

MAYA: Aurélien, tu changes d'avis tous les jours! L'autre jour, tu me parlais d'Aloïse Sauvage et tu voulais être chanteur!

Aurélien, you change your mind every day! The other day you were talking about Aloïse Sauvage and you wanted to become a singer!

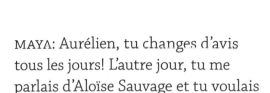

*The verb **changer** can be used with or without a preposition, taking on different meanings. **Elle a changé les paroles de sa chanson** implies she modified her song's lyrics. It is the same song but with modifications. **Il a changé son testament** means that he changed the content of his will. In contrast, **il a changé de chemise** implies he changed his shirt (one shirt for another shirt). **Elle a changé d'emploi** means she left her job for another one. **Changer** can also mean replacing an object in the house: **je viens de changer l'ampoule** means I just replaced the lightbulb. Careful with the nuances.*

 IRL Aloïse Sauvage is a singer, songwriter, musician, dancer, acrobat, and actress. She is one of the most fascinating artists of the 21st century and very much in touch with the Z generation that believes in collective action and commitment. Enjoy samples of her songs and lyrics online. There is nothing like hip-hop and slam to spice up your French study routine. And you'll get the rhythm!

AURÉLIEN: Ça, c'est mon rêve!

That's my dream!

MAYA: Aloïse, elle a bossé, elle aussi!

Aloïse worked so hard too!

AURÉLIEN: Elle a fait une prépa aux arts du cirque à Lille, ensuite elle est entrée à l'Académie Fratellini.

She went to prep school for circus arts in Lille, then she was accepted at the Fratellini Academy.

 IRL The **classes prépas**, or CPGE (**classes préparatoires aux grandes écoles**), consist of two years of intense studies after the **bac** to prepare for a **concours**, the national competitive exam for admission to a **grande école**. Some of the more important schools are: Sciences Po, l'École nationale d'administration (ENA), l'École normale supérieure, l'École des hautes études commerciales (HEC), Polytechnique, Saint-Cyr, l'École Navale.

MAYA: Tu joues de la guitare, mais tu ferais bien de te mettre au saxophone et à la batterie!

You are playing the guitar, but you'd better start playing the saxophone and drums!

AURÉLIEN: (rires) Ça ne plairait pas aux parents… J'aime beaucoup ses chansons, son rythme, sa façon d'assembler les mots. Elle est géniale!

(laughter) Our parents would not be too happy… I love her songs, her rhythm, the way she mixes the words. She is awesome!

BTW

Let's meet some family members: **le père** (father), **la mère** (mother), **la sœur** (sister), **le frère** (brother), **le gendre** (son-in-law), **la belle-fille** (daughter-in-law), **le grand-père** (grandfather), **la grand-mère** (grandmother), **le petit-fils** (grandson), **la petite-fille** (granddaughter), **la tante** (aunt), **l'oncle** (uncle), **le cousin**, **la cousine** (cousin), **la nièce** (niece), **le neveu** (nephew), **le beau-frère** (brother-in-law), **la belle-sœur** (sister-in-law), **le beau-père** (father-in-law and stepfather), **la belle-mère** (mother-in-law and stepmother), **la marraine** (godmother), **le parrain** (godfather).

MAYA: Je me souviens… quand tu étais petit, tu étais toujours en train de gribouiller des notes dans tes carnets. Aloïse, où est-ce qu'elle puise son inspiration pour écrire?

I remember… when you were little, you were always scribbling notes in your small notebooks. Where does Aloïse draw her inspiration?

AURÉLIEN: Elle lit beaucoup: des romans, des nouvelles, des BD, de la science-fiction.

She reads a lot: novels, short stories, comic books, fiction.

MAYA: Comme toi.

Like you.

AURÉLIEN: Ah, si seulement je pouvais écrire comme Aloïse!

Ah, if only I could write like Aloïse!

MAYA: Lance-toi! Je te vois mieux écrivain qu'acrobate. L'école du cirque, c'est pas pour toi.

Dive in! I can better see you as a writer than an acrobat. The circus school, it's not for you.

AURÉLIEN: Je sais, mais on peut toujours rêver.

I know but one can always dream.

MAYA: Cela te dirait de voir Aloïse en concert cet automne?

How would you like to see Aloïse in concert this fall?

AURÉLIEN: Tu blagues?

Are you kidding?

MAYA: Non, je ne blague pas. Ça sera ton cadeau d'anniversaire.

No, I am not kidding. It will be your birthday present.

AURÉLIEN: (singing one of Aloïse Sauvage's songs)
Et la neige recouvre mes pas
Je t'appelle...

And the snow covers my steps
I call you...

EXERCISES

EXERCISE 12.1

Conjugate the following verbs in the **conditionnel présent.**

1. dire (je) _____

2. voyager (elle) _____

3. aller (nous) _____

4. prendre (je) _____

5. savoir (elles) _____

6. avoir (tu) _____

7. répondre (ils) _____

8. devoir (nous) _____

9. commander (il) _____

10. accepter (vous) _____

EXERCISE 12.2

Conjugate the following verbs in the **conditionnel présent** *and the* **imparfait.**

1. Est-ce que tu (dîner) _____ avec nous si tu (être) _____ disponible?

2. Je (chanter) _____ une chanson si tu me le (demander) _____.

3. Nous (voyager) _____ davantage si nous (avoir) _____ plus de temps.

4. Il (s'inscrirc) _____ à un cours de cuisine s'il (vouloir) _____ devenir cuisinier.

5. Mamie (être) _____ contente si tu (venir) _____ la voir.

6. Nous (aller) _____ en Normandie si nous (pouvoir) _____ peindre en plein air.

7. Aurélien (se lancer) _____ dans la gastronomie sociale s'il (avoir) _____ un sponsor.

8. Je (emporter) _____ deux valises si je (faire) _____ une croisière.

9. Elle (numériser) _____ les photos si elle (être) _____ à Menton.

10. Vous (organiser) _____ votre vie autrement si vous le (pouvoir) _____.

EXERCISE 12.3

*Translate the following sentences using **vous** when necessary.*

1. We would go to France if we had the time.

2. She would buy a bicycle if she lived in Normandy.

3. Could you tell me at what time the class starts?

4. I would cook tonight if you brought some cheese.

5. He would be happy if the chef offered him an internship.

6. They would visit the school if you could show it to them.

7. We would go to the beach if there were fewer people.

8. You'd better study tonight!

9. We'd better listen to Maya's advice.

10. He would play the guitar if his sister bought him one.

11. I would launch an app if you helped me.

12. I would take care of it in case there is a problem.

13. Do you feel like going to the Picasso Museum?

14. It would be better not to reveal his secret.

15. We would take a walk if it was not raining.

EXERCISE 12.4

Match the items in the two columns. Choose the most logical answers.

1. Maya serait contente	a. seulement s'il était gratuit.
2. Elle décrocherait un emploi	b. si son frère se concentrait sur ses études.
3. Le chef garderait le stagiaire	c. si Mathéo m'apportait des épices.
4. Julien accepterait le stage	d. si son C.V. mettait en valeur ses compétences.
5. Je ferais la cuisine	e. s'il était ponctuel et plus motivé.

EXERCISE 12.5

*Conjugate the following verbs in the **conditionnel passé** and the **plus-que-parfait**.*

1. Elle (acheter) _____ des lunettes Vuarnet si elle en (trouver) _____.

2. Ils (lancer) _____ une app s'ils (réunir) _____ assez d'argent.

3. Vous (regarder) _____ le film si vous (arriver) _____ plus tôt.

4. Ils (décrocher) _____ leur bac avec mention s'ils (étudier) _____ plus sérieusement.

5. Tu (travailler) _____ dans l'hôtellerie si tu (pouvoir) _____.

6. La cheffe (faire) _____ une bouillabaisse si nous (être) _____ au moins quatre.

7. Je (changer) _____ l'ampoule si j'en (trouver) _____ une.

8. Elle (s'inscrire) _____ au cours de danse si son emploi du temps (être) _____ moins chargé.

9. Vous (arriver) _____ à l'heure s'il (ne pas y avoir) _____ un accident sur l'autoroute.

10. Je (acheter) _____ un nouveau sac à dos si je le (perdre) _____ dans le RER.

EXERCISE 12.6

*Translate the following sentences using the **tu** form.*

1. He would have sold his restaurant if he had lost one star.

2. You would have made a film on the chef if he had given you permission.

3. She would have gone on vacation if she had saved enough money.

4. They would have bought a house in Brittany if their brother had been able to help them.

5. I would have signed up for the Japanese course if you had signed up with me.

6. Julie would have gone to the concert with them if she had finished her project in time.

7. He would have sent the form if he had been sure to be accepted.

8. I would have sent you some flowers if I had known it was your birthday.

9. She would have bought your car if you had asked a reasonable price.

10. I would not have made so many mistakes if I had reviewed the conditional.

EXERCISE 12.7

*Conjuguate the verbs in the past conditional to convey the idea that an event might have occurred, using thus the **conditionnel** journalistique.*

1. La cheffe (créer) _____ une recette pour faire le soufflé basque au fromage de brebis.

2. Julia (envoyer) _____ le formulaire d'inscription à l'école de danse.

3. La chanteuse (improviser) _____ une nouvelle chanson à l'Espace culturel André Malraux.

4. L'agent (proposer) _____ un contrat de 500 000 euros au scénariste.

5. Les diplomates (revenir) _____ de mission en hélicoptère vers deux heures du matin.

6. La directrice de communication (démissionner) _____ suite à un désaccord.

7. Il (enregistrer) _____ son nouveau disque dans un studio à Berlin.

8. Le cyclone (détruire) _____ des centaines d'habitations.

9. Le président (signer) _____ un traité avec l'Allemagne.

10. La police (retrouver) _____ les lingots d'or volés dans le coffre-fort de la banque.

EXERCISE 12.8

Translate the following sentences using the **conditionnel journalistique,** *present or past. Proceed carefully!*

1. The French Minister of Education reportedly promised big changes.

2. The private detective reportedly found the palace's cat stolen by a neighbor.

3. The photographer reportedly retouched the picture of Lily-Rose, Chanel's model.

4. The thief allegedly sold my bike to a policeman.

5. The cyclone reportedly killed five people.

6. The scientist will reportedly announce the results of his research this weekend.

7. Aloïse Sauvage reportedly recorded her new song in a swimming pool.

8. Juliette and Vincent will reportedly get married in Iceland, far away from the journalists.

9. The young cook reportedly changed the chef's recipe!

10. Princess Victoria of Sweden will reportedly visit the first lady of France.

EXERCISE 12.9

Translate the following sentences into English.

1. Nous aimerions vous inviter à déjeuner.

2. Vous devriez organiser un voyage en Bourgogne.

3. Elle se serait inscrite au cours de yoga si elle avait eu du temps libre.

4. Tu devrais te dépêcher. On va être en retard.

5. Je serais allée à Amsterdam si tu avais pu m'y rejoindre.

6. Qu'est-ce que tu ferais si tu gagnais un million d'euros au loto?

7. Il aurait fait une paëlla aux crevettes si elles avaient eu faim.

8. Le président aurait refait le décor de son bureau.

9. J'aurais aimé avoir un appartement dans le 15e arrondissement.

10. Il devrait inviter tous les employés à la réception.

EXERCISE 12.10

Translate the following sentences using the **vous** *form when necessary.*

1. We should open a restaurant in the 18th arrondissement.

2. She will reportedly sing for the French president's birthday.

3. You should learn how to play the piano.

4. An admirer allegedly entered the queen's palace.

5. I would like to meet the volunteers at the Madeleine Church.

6. I would attend his conference if I could get a ticket.

7. Could you make a spinach quiche?

8. I should have read one of Flaubert's novels.

9. Don't you think they should have called us?

10. They should try not to waste food.

LE COIN DES CRÉATEURS

Écrire cinq petits paragraphes en expliquant ce que vous feriez face à une situation inattendue. La proposition si est à l'imparfait; la proposition principale est au conditionnel.

Si je rencontrais Massimo Bottura, je lui demanderais de m'engager.
Si j'étais un objet, je serais un secrétaire Empire en acajou.

À votre tour!

Si je gagnais à la loterie...
Si je trouvais un chaton dans la rue...
Si mes parents...
Si ma sœur...
Si j'étais un oiseau...
Si je décrochais un stage...
Si...

NOTE CULTURELLE

LE CENTRE NATIONAL DES ARTS DU CIRQUE –
THE NATIONAL CENTER FOR CIRCUS ARTS

If you plan to run off and join the circus, be sure to get your degree first!

Since the previous century, when "running off to join the circus" was often a reality, the idea has become a euphemism for leaving one's present life to seek adventure, excitement, and, perhaps, a bit of danger. Today's circus performers are no longer runaways! They are genuine artists, and like musicians, actors, dancers, and other performing artists, they devote a great deal of time to study and training. This was formerly done mostly through apprenticeship, but it is now possible to perfect one's craft academically, and France has been in the forefront of enabling aspiring circus artists to do so.

The French National Center for Circus Arts (Centre National des Arts du Cirque, CNAC) is an institution of higher education and research that was created in 1985 by the French Ministry of Culture as a way of "making a positive contribution to the renewal of circus arts and contemporary creation." It was given three primary missions: 1) to provide higher education in the circus arts, 2) to offer lifelong learning opportunities, and 3) to serve as a research and resource center. The CNAC very quickly incorporated its teaching project into the *"nouveau cirque"* ("new circus") movement, and the training it provides is of an uncompromisingly high standard with regard to technical learning and command of the vocabulary specific to each circus discipline.

The CNAC is located in the city of Châlons-en-Champagne, chosen, in part, for its beautiful concrete circus building, designed by architect Louis Gillet and built in 1898–1899. Since its inception, it has given students interested in circus arts and performance the opportunity to earn a university-level degree. In 2014, it combined its courses with the National School of Circus Arts (ENACR) and the University of Picardie Jules Verne (UPJV). Students do an optional preparatory year and their first year of study at the ENACR and their second and third years at CNAC. They also have a parallel registration at the UPJV. Admission is by application and requires a video, 7 minutes maximum, of the applicant performing with his/her apparatus. The course of study combines specialist training mainly with group classes in dance, drama, and general knowledge, as well as artistic research workshops. Some specific courses include acrobatic dance, aerial and floor acrobatics, clowning, tightrope, trampoline, trapeze, and unicycle. Upon successfully completing the program, students are awarded the Higher National Vocational Diploma for Circus Artists (DNSP-AC). There is a very high placement rate for graduates, who go on to perform in circuses throughout France, Europe, and the rest of the world.

For those who have already graduated and are working professionally, the CNAC also offers lifelong learning. Skills already acquired, not only by performers but also by circus technicians and administrators, can be maintained and new ones developed. Continuing education is available for teachers, along with the opportunity to earn the French State Diploma for Circus Teachers. Artistic and cultural education courses are also offered for those working outside the circus environment, such as designing and organizing cultural outreach circus projects.

The circus is international, so foreign students can apply, but some knowledge of French is required since it is the official language of instruction.

13 The Subjunctive Mood and Relative Pronouns

MUST KNOW

 Wishing for something? Use **pourvu que.**

 Use the subjunctive when **croire** and **penser** appear in the negative or interrogative form.

 With **Avoir beau**, you can avoid using the subjunctive.

 For **Je sais qui elle est**, don't use an elision.

he subjunctive is not a tense, but a mood. And as you'll learn in this chapter, there are three conditions that warrant the subjunctive: emotions, desires, and doubts.

The *Subjonctif Présent*

Whether you know it or not, you have previously studied moods: the indicative mood (**le passé composé**, **l'imparfait**, **le futur**, etc.), the imperative mood, and the conditional mood. Another mood, the subjunctive refers to someone's opinion or deals with a hypothetical action.

For regular verbs, the present of the subjunctive is formed by adding the subjunctive endings (-**e**, -**es**, -**e**, -**ions**, -**iez**, -**ent**) to the stem. And the stem for **je**, **tu**, **il**, **elle**, **on**, **ils**, and **elles** is formed by dropping the -**ent** ending from the third-person plural of the present tense. Note that the sound of the verb for these pronouns will remain the same, and that for irregular verbs the **nous** and **vous** forms of the verb are identical to those of the imperfect.

Regular Verbs in the *Subjonctif Présent*

Let's look at the the verb **écouter** (*to listen*):

- The third-person plural: **ils écoutent**

- The stem: **écout-**

j'écoute	*I listen*	nous écoutions	*we listen*
tu écoutes	*you listen*	vous écoutiez	*you listen*
il/elle/on écoute	*he/she/one listens*	ils/elles écoutent	*they listen*

Now let's conjugate the verb **lire** (*to read*) in the present subjunctive:

- The third-person plural: **ils lisent**

- The stem: **lis-**

je lise	*I read*	nous lisions	*we read*
tu lises	*you read*	vous lisiez	*you read*
il/elle/on lise	*he/she/one reads*	ils/elles lisent	*they read*

And finally, let's conjugate **attendre** (*to wait*) in the **subjonctif présent**:

- The third-person plural: **ils attendent**

- The stem: **attend-**

j'attende	*I wait*	nous attendions	*we wait*
tu attendes	*you wait*	vous attendiez	*you wait*
il/elle/on attende	*he/she/one waits*	ils/elles attendent	*they wait*

Irregular Verbs in the *Subjonctif Présent*

Être and **avoir** have irregular stems and endings for the subjunctive.

être   *to be*

je sois	*I am*	nous soyons	*we are*
tu sois	*you are*	vous soyez	*you are*
il/elle/on soit	*he/she/one is*	ils/elles soient	*they are*

avoir   *to have*

j'aie	*I have*	nous ayons	*we have*
tu aies	*you have*	vous ayez	*you have*
il/elle/on ait	*he/she/one has*	ils/elles aient	*they have*

There are three verbs that have an irregular subjunctive stem but regular endings:

faire   *to do*

je fasse	*I do*	nous fassions	*we do*
tu fasses	*you do*	vous fassiez	*you do*
il/elle/on fasse	*he/she/one does*	ils/elles fassent	*they do*

pouvoir   *can*

je puisse	*I can*	nous puissions	*we can*
tu puisses	*you can*	vous puissiez	*you can*
il/elle/on puisse	*he/she/one can*	ils/elles puissent	*they can*

savoir   *to know*

je sache	*I know*	nous sachions	*we know*
tu saches	*you know*	vous sachiez	*you know*
il/elle/on sache	*he/she/one knows*	ils sachent	*they know*

The verbs **aller** and **vouloir** have irregular stems and regular endings.

aller   *to go*

j'aille	*I go*	nous allions	*we go*
tu ailles	*you go*	vous alliez	*you go*
il/elle/on aille	*he/she/one goes*	ils/elles aillent	*they go*

vouloir   *to want*

je veuille	*I want*	nous voulions	*we want*
tu veuilles	*you want*	vous vouliez	*you want*
il/elle/on veuille	*he/she/one wants*	ils/elles veuillent	*they want*

Uses of the Subjunctive

There are three main concepts that use the subjunctive: emotions, wishes, and doubts. Most importantly, the subjunctive is used when the subject of the main clause and the subject of the dependent clause are different.

Compare the following sets of sentences:

Je veux passer ce concours international.	*I want to take this international test.*
Je veux qu'elle passe ce concours international.	*I want her to take this international test.*

Il est content d'étudier à Sciences Po.	*He is happy to study at Sciences Po.*
Il est content que vous étudiiez à Sciences Po.	*He is happy that you study at Sciences Po.*

- The subjunctive is used with **emotions**

Nous sommes contents que tu veuilles devenir pilote.	*We are happy that you want to become a pilot.*
Elle est triste que tu ailles dans un autre service.	*She is sad you are going to another department.*
Je suis ravie que vous fassiez un voyage en Islande.	*I am thrilled that you are taking a trip to Iceland.*

- The subjunctive is used with **wishes**

Je voudrais qu'il s'inscrive à un cours d'anthropologie.	*I would like him to sign up for an anthropology class.*
Nous souhaitons que vous réussissiez à votre examen.	*We hope you'll pass your exam.*
Elle aimerait que je sois à l'heure.	*She would like me to be on time.*

- The subjunctive is used with **doubts**

Je doute qu'il puisse trouver un logement facilement.	*I doubt that he can easily find a place to stay.*
Nous ne pensons pas que l'examen soit trop difficile.	*We don't think that the exam is too hard.*
Croyez-vous qu'il ait assez de temps pour finir sa thèse?	*Do you think that he has enough time to finish his thesis?*

When the verbs **penser** (*to think*) and **croire** (*to believe*) are used in the affirmative, they are followed by the indicative mood. On the other hand, when they are used in the negative or interrogative, the subjunctive can be used to emphasize uncertainty.

| Je ne crois pas que Monsieur Hulot est innocent. | *I don't believe that Monsieur Hulot is innocent.* |

This sentence implies that the speaker is sure that Monsieur Hulot is guilty.

| Je ne crois pas que Monsieur Hulot soit innocent. | *I don't believe that Monsieur Hulot is innocent.* |

But here, because the subjunctive is used, the speaker is somewhat doubtful about Monsieur Hulot's innocence.

BTW

The difference in meaning between the sentences can also be attributed to the intonation of the voice and to the speaker's gestures.

Conjunctions Using the Subjunctive

In Chapter 10, we saw that many conjunctions like **quand** and **pendant que** are followed by the indicative mood. As you can infer from the title of this section, there are other conjunctions that are followed by the subjunctive mood. Let's take a look at a few of them.

afin que	*so that, in order to*
pour que	*so that, in order to*
de peur que	*for fear that*
de crainte que	*for fear that*
avant que	*before*
jusqu'à ce que	*until*
bien que	*although*
quoique	*although*
sans que	*without*
à moins que	*unless*

pourvu que	provided that
à condition que	on the condition that
en attendant que	waiting for

Quoiqu'il pleuve, nous allons nous promener.

Although it's raining, we are going for a walk.

Je sauvegarde mes fichiers de peur qu'il les perde.

I am saving my files for fear that he loses them.

Elle a organisé la fête d'anniversaire sans que nous le sachions.

She organized the birthday party without our knowing.

Nous préparons la présentation avant que le PDG n'arrive.

We are preparing our presentation before the CEO arrives.

BTW

*You might have noticed that the **ne** stands by itself before **arrive**. It is not a negation. It is called the **ne explétif**, a grammar construction used in formal and written French. It is often used after verbs that express fear or doubt, in addition to conjunctions such as **avant que**, **à moins que**, **de peur que**, and **de crainte que**: Je crains qu'elle ne soit en retard./Il viendra à moins qu'il ne soit occupé.*

The Conjunction *Pourvu que*

Pourvu que means *provided that*.

Nous irons à Lorient en train pourvu qu'il n'y ait pas de grèves.

We'll go to Lorient by train provided that there aren't any strikes.

When used in a single clause, **pourvu que** takes on a different meaning: *let's hope*. This usage of **pourvu que** expresses hopes and desires—and when you use it, people will delight in your mastery of the subjunctive.

Pourvu que Maria puisse venir ce soir!

Let's hope Maria can come tonight!

Pourvu que la banque soit encore ouverte!

Let's hope the bank is still open!

Pourvu qu'il décroche son diplôme!

Let's hope he gets his degree!

IRL **Pourvu que** comes in handy in conversation. It is also the title of a play **Pourvu qu'il soit heureux** (*Let's Hope He'll Be Happy*), by Laurent Ruquier, that you can read, or see on French stages. Ruquier is a TV and radio host, producer, and comedian. You'll hear **pourvu que** in songs like « **Pourvu** » (*Let's Hope*) by Gauvain Sers.

The Subjunctive with Impersonal Expressions

Some impersonal expressions are used with the indicative mood, while others are followed by the subjunctive. Here are some impersonal expressions followed by the indicative:

il est certain	*it is certain*
il est sûr	*it is sure*
il est évident	*it is obvious*
il est vrai	*it is true*
il est exact	*it is true*
il est probable	*it is probable*
il me semble	*it seems to me*

Il me semble qu'il y a une erreur.   *It seems to me that there's a mistake.*
Il est probable qu'il viendra ce soir.   *He will probably come tonight.*

Here are some impersonal expressions followed by the subjunctive:

il faut	*one must*
il est possible	*it is possible*
il est essentiel	*it is essential*
il est indispensable	*it is imperative*
Il semble	*it seems*
il se peut	*it may*
il est important	*it is important*
il vaut mieux	*it is better*
il est préférable	*it is preferable*
il est souhaitable	*it is desirable*

il est naturel	it is natural
il est normal	it is normal
il est rare	it is rare
il est utile	it is useful
il est étrange	it is strange
il est bizarre	it is odd
il est étonnant	it is amazing
il est surprenant	it is surprising
il est triste	it is sad
il est dommage	it is a shame
il est regrettable	it is unfortunate
cela vaut la peine	it is worth it

Il est possible que tu obtiennes ce poste.   *It is possible you get this job.*

Il est indispensable que vous apportiez tous les dossiers.   *It is imperative you bring all the files.*

Il est normal que tu sois surpris par cette décision.   *It is normal for you to be surprised by this decision.*

Il est essentiel que vous vérifiiez l'orthographe.   *It is essential that you check the spelling.*

Let's compare the following sentences, one in the indicative, the other in the subjunctive:

Il est certain qu'il pleuvra ce soir.   *It will certainly rain tonight.*
Il est possible qu'il pleuve ce soir.   *It might rain tonight.*

The Subjunctive and the Superlative

The subjunctive is also used after a superlative, or an adjective that conveys a superlative idea such as **premier** (*first*), **dernier** (*last*), **seul** (*only*), and **unique** (*unique*).

C'est la seule chose qui soit importante.	*It's the only thing that matters.*
C'est la personne la plus généreuse qui soit.	*He/she is the most generous person ever.*
C'est le meilleur restaurant que je connaisse à Paris.	*It's the best restaurant that I know in Paris.*

The Subjunctive and Uncertain Existence or Outcome

The relative pronouns **qui** and **que** can sometimes be followed by the subjunctive. If there is doubt about the existence of someone or something, or about the possible realization of something, the subjunctive may precede the relative pronoun.

Je cherche quelqu'un qui **sache** parler le samoan.	*I'm looking for someone who can speak Samoan.*
Connaîtriez-vous quelqu'un qui **puisse** concevoir un nouveau logiciel pour mon entreprise?	*Do you know someone who can design new software for my company?*

BTW

Another use of the subjunctive is to concede to multiple possibilities or to express an exhortation: **Qu'il pleuve ou qu'il vente, Julien randonne dans le Jura** (Rain or shine, Julien will hike in the Jura); **Que son âme repose en paix** (May his soul rest in peace).

The Past Subjunctive

The past subjunctive follows the same principles as the present subjunctive; however, the action of the independent clause is anterior to the action of the main clause. To form the past subjunctive, use the present subjunctive of **être** or **avoir** with the past participle.

voir   *to see*

j'aie vu	*I saw*	nous ayons vu	*we saw*
tu aies vu	*you saw*	vous ayez vu	*you saw*
il/elle/on ait vu	*he/she/one saw*	ils/elles aient vu	*they saw*

aller   *to go*

je sois allé(e)	*I went*	nous soyons allé(e)(s)	*we went*
tu sois allé(e)	*you went*	vous soyez allé(e)(s)	*you went*
il/elle/on soit allé(e)	*he/she/one went*	ils/elles soient allé(e)(s)	*they went*

Nous sommes heureux que vous ayez pu vous joindre à nous.	*We are so happy that you were able to join us.*
J'ai peur qu'il se soit perdu.	*I'm worried he got lost.*
Nous sommes soulagés qu'il ait dit la vérité.	*We are relieved that he told the truth.*
Je ne crois pas qu'elle ait payé son loyer à temps.	*I don't think she paid her rent in time.*

Whatever, Whoever, Wherever

The present of the subjunctive is used with the indefinite expressions *whatever*, *wherever*, and *whoever*. When *whatever* is followed by a verb, the neutral **quoi que** is used.

Quoi que Marc fasse, il réussit.	*Whatever Marc does, he succeeds.*
Quoi que vous en pensiez, c'est le meilleur avion qu'Airbus ait jamais construit.	*Whatever you think, this is the best plane Airbus has ever built.*

BTW

*Do not confuse **quoi que** (whatever) with **quoique** (although):* **Quoi qu'il dise, je ne suis pas d'accord** (Whatever he says, I do not agree); **Quoiqu'il dise la vérité, personne ne le croit** (Although he is telling the truth, no one believes him).

When *whatever* is followed by a noun, **quel que** is used. **Quel que** agrees in gender and number with the subject.

Quel que soit le stage à Airbus, je l'accepterai.

Whatever the internship at Airbus might be, I'll accept it.

Quelle que soit la situation, vous devriez rester calme.

Whatever the situation, you should stay calm.

To express wherever, use **où que** plus the subjunctive:

Où que tu sois, tiens-moi au courant du résultat du match de tennis.

Wherever you are, keep me informed about the result of the tennis game.

Où que tu ailles, emporte une lampe de poche.

Wherever you go, take a flashlight.

 IRL Listen to Amaury Vassili's moving tribute to Mike Brant, and follow the lyrics online to « **Où que tu sois** », a song Mike Brant had never released. And listen to « **Où que tu ailles** », by La Grande Sophie. It is always easier to remember to use the subjunctive when you can sing along!

The subjunctive is also used to express *whoever*. For example:

Qui que vous soyez, notre station thermale est parfaite pour vous!

Whoever you are, our thermal spa is perfect for you!

Qui qu'elle soit, elle doit respecter notre code d'éthique.

Whoever she is, she must respect our code of ethics.

Avoir beau

The expression **avoir beau** can be translated as *although* or *however much*. You cannot understand a conversation or a film and you cannot read a newspaper or a 19th- or 21st-century novel without mastering **avoir beau**. Although its origin goes back to the Middle Ages, it is used every day in oral or written French. It may express a reservation about an idea, a contradiction, a concession, or a difficulty.

Il a beau dormir, il est toujours fatigué.	*However much he sleeps, he is always tired.*
Ils ont beau réfléchir, ils ne comprennent pas le problème.	*Although they have been reflecting on it, they cannot understand the problem.*

BTW

Note that we connect the two clauses with a comma, without using **mais**. It is clear and concise and allows us to avoid the subjunctive, as **avoir beau** is followed by the infinitive form.

Avoir beau can be used in the past and the future:

Ils ont beau avoir vécu à Albertville, ils n'ont jamais appris à skier.	*Although they lived in Albertville, they never learned how to ski.*
Madame Tran **a eu beau** lire de nombreux CV, elle n'a pas réussi à trouver le candidat idéal.	*Although Mrs. Tran read many résumés, she was not able to find the ideal candidate.*
Jonas **avait beau** avoir du temps libre, il ne jouait jamais au foot avec nous.	*Although Jonas had some free time, he would never play football with us.*
Il **aura beau** essayer, il ne parviendra jamais à convaincre son frère jumeau d'habiter dans une grande ville.	*However much he tries, he'll never manage to convince his twin brother to live in a big city.*
Elle **aurait beau** t'aimer, elle ne te suivrait pas au bout du monde.	*However much she loved you, she would not follow you to the end of the world.*

 IRL You will hear **avoir beau** in songs like « **J'ai beau t'aimer** », by Frédéric Monteil, or « **Chercher ailleurs** », by Kaysha.

Les Pronoms Relatifs

In order to link ideas back to people and things already mentioned, the **pronoms relatifs**—relative pronouns—are used. Relative pronouns relate two sentences, making one dependent on the other. Choosing the correct relative pronoun depends on the pronoun's function in the sentence (subject, direct object, or object of a preposition).

Qui

Let's start with the relative pronoun **qui** used as a subject. **Qui** may refer to people or things and may mean *who, whom, which, what,* or *that.*

Le candidat **qui** attend Madame Tran s'appelle Jean.	*The candidate who is waiting for Mrs. Tran is Jean.*
Jean a pris un plan de Toulouse **qui** était sur la table.	*Jean took a map of Toulouse that was on the table.*

The **i** of **qui** is never dropped before a vowel sound.

Madame Grandet? Sais-tu **qui elle** est?	*Madame Grandet? Do you know who she is?*
Jonas ne m'a pas dit avec **qui il** venait ce soir.	*Jonas did not tell me with whom he was coming tonight.*

The verb following **qui** agrees with the noun or pronoun that **qui** replaces.

C'est moi qui **ai** trouvé le studio, rue Homère.	*It's me who found the studio, rue Homère.*
C'est toi qui **as** mentionné cette organisation.	*It's you who mentioned this organization.*
C'est vous qui **avez** engagé Erwan.	*It's you who hired Erwan.*

Que

When the clause introduced by a relative pronoun already has a subject, the relative pronoun is the object of the verb of the clause it introduces. In this case, the relative pronoun **que** (*whom*, *which*, *that*) is used. **Que** may also refer to people and things.

Erwan est le candidat **que** la direction veut engager.	*Erwan is the candidate the management wants to hire.*
C'est le poste **que** chaque candidat veut obtenir.	*This is the position each candidate wants to get.*

The **e** of **que** is dropped before a vowel.

Les ingénieurs **qu'elle** engage sont trilingues.	*The engineers she hires speak three languages.*
La hausse de salaire **qu'ils** proposent est de 5%.	*The raise they are offering is 5%.*

In the past tense, if the direct object is placed before the verb, the past participle agrees in gender and number with the object.

La veste **que** tu m'as prêté**e** pour l'entretien me va bien.	*The jacket you lent me for the interview fits me well.*
Je vous remercie de la lettre de recommandation **que** vous m'avez écrit**e**.	*I thank you for the recommendation letter you wrote to me.*

Relative Pronouns Followed by Prepositions

When verbs are followed by prepositions, the relative pronouns **qui**, **quoi**, **lequel**, **laquelle**, **lesquels**, and **lesquelles** are used. The preposition is placed before the relative pronoun. **Qui** is used to refer to people only, whereas **lequel**, **laquelle**, **lesquels**, and **lesquelles** refer mostly to things. **Lequel**, **laquelle**, **lesquels**, and **lesquelles** may also be used for people; this usage, however, is less common.

À quoi penses-tu?	*What are you thinking about?*
Voici le service de streaming musical **auquel** je suis abonné.	*Here's the streaming service to which I subscribe.*

C'est la date **à laquelle** la réunion a eu lieu.	*This is the date the meeting took place.*
Pourriez-vous nous dire **pour qui** vous avez créé cette app?	*Could you tell me for whom you created this app?*
L'organisation **pour laquelle** il travaillait est à Bruxelles.	*The organization for which he was working is in Bruxelles.*
C'est l'étudiant **avec qui** je partage un appartement.	*He is the student with whom I share an apartment.*
Le logiciel **avec lequel** il travaille est performant.	*The software with which he works is performing.*
Sur qui peux-tu compter? Je peux compter sur Jonas.	*Whom can you rely on? I can rely on Jonas.*
C'est une théorie **sur laquelle** on peut s'appuyer.	*It's a theory one can rely upon.*
Il y avait quinze candidats pour le poste **parmi lesquels** trois diplômés de HEC.	*There were fifteen candidates, among whom were three HEC graduates.*

BTW

*Note an exception: with the preposition **parmi** (among), **qui** cannot be used.*

Dont

The relative pronoun **dont** acts as an object and can refer to people and things. It is used mostly to refer to objects of verbs or adjectives that are followed by the preposition **de**. You may want to review the verbs and their prepositions in Chapter 6.

Carl a parlé **des** réformes.	*Carl talked about the reforms.*
Voici les réformes **dont** Carl a parlé.	*Here are the reforms Carl talked about.*
Nous avons besoin **de** nouvelles chaises.	*We need new chairs.*
Ce sont les nouvelles chaises **dont** nous avons besoin.	*These are the new chairs we need.*

Elle se souvient **du** CV de Chloé.	*She remembers Chloé's résumé.*
C'est le CV **dont** elle se souvient.	*It's the résumé she remembers.*
Je me sers **d'**un iPad.	*I use an iPad.*
L'iPad **dont** je me sers n'est pas ici.	*The iPad I use is not here.*

Où

The relative pronoun **où** often replaces **dans lequel**, **sur lequel**, or **par lequel**.

Grasse est la ville **où** l'on fabrique les meilleurs parfums.	*Grasse is a town where the best perfumes are made.*
C'est la maison **où** a vécu Balzac de 1840 à 1847.	*It's the house where Balzac lived from 1840 to 1847.*

   Où is also used after expressions of time: **l'instant où**, **le moment où**, **le jour où**, **la semaine où**, **l'année où**, etc.

Ils se souviennent du jour **où** ils ont lancé leur application.	*They remember the day they launched their app.*
Dès l'instant **où** je l'ai vu, je savais que vieillirions ensemble.	*From the moment I saw him, I knew we would grow old together.*

Ce que, Ce qui, Ce dont, and Ce à quoi

When there is no specific word or antecedent for the relative pronoun to refer to, the antecedent **ce** is added. **Ce qui**, **ce que**, **ce dont**, and **ce à quoi**, all meaning *what*, refer to ideas, not to persons, and do not have gender or number. Choosing the correct indefinite relative pronoun again depends on the pronoun's function in the sentence (subject, direct object, or object of a preposition). Often, the indefinite relative pronouns, **ce qui**, **ce que**, **ce à quoi**, and **ce dont**, are placed at the beginning of a sentence to stress a point. It compensates for the English intonation that is much more marked. When a verb requires a preposition, it is repeated in the second clause.

Je me demande **ce qui** se passe.	*I am wondering what's happening.*
Ce qui est bizarre, c'est le comportement de Paul!	*Paul's behavior is strange!*

Je ne comprends pas **ce qu**'il veut.	*I don't understand what he wants.*
Ce que je vous dis est confidentiel.	*What I am telling you is confidential.*

Ce dont is used when verbs take the preposition **de**.

J'aimerais savoir **ce dont** vous avez besoin d'ici lundi.	*I'd like to know what you need by Monday.*

Note that **de** is repeated in the second clause:

Ce dont ils se plaignent, c'est **du** manque de temps libre.	*What they are complaining about is the lack of free time.*

Ce à quoi is used with verbs that take the preposition **à**. Note that **à** is repeated in the second clause:

Ce à quoi il s'oppose, c'est **à** la réforme des retraites!	*What he opposes is the pension reform!*

Note that **ce** is often omitted in questions or statements like:

Erwan ignore **à quoi** s'attendre.	*Erwan does not know what to expect.*
À **quoi** penses-tu?	*What are you thinking about?*
Je ne sais pas **à quoi** elle pense.	*I don't know what she is thinking about.*

DIALOGUE *Décrocher un boulot chez Airbus et vivre à Toulouse*
Getting a job with Airbus and settling in Toulouse

Erwan Le Goff is being interviewed for a job at Airbus aerospace corporation in Toulouse by the HR director, Madame Maïka Darrieussecq. After landing the job, he tells his friend Jonas how he and many students in France have found an affordable housing solution.

IRL Some French surnames are based a person's trade, like a shepherd (**Monsieur Berger**), a baker (**Madame Boulanger**); some come from the Bible, like **Martin, Thomas, and Matthieu**. It is often possible to tell which region someone's family comes from just by the family name. A surname starting with **"Qu-," "Ker-,"** or **"Le"** is most likely from Breton origin. **Erwan Le Goff?** You cannot find a more Breton first and last name! When a last name starts with **"Etch-," "Hiri-,"** or **"Darrieu-,"** like **Etcheverry, Hirigoyen,** or **Darrieumerlou,** it definitely has a Basque or a Gascon origin—like Madame **Darrieussecq!** If you want to get acquainted with first names of all origins used in France, read *L'Officiel des prénoms,* by Stéphanie Rapoport.

MME DARRIEUSSECQ: Je vois dans votre lettre de motivation que l'aviation vous passionne depuis votre enfance. Comment l'expliquez-vous?

I see in your cover letter that you have been passionate about aviation since childhood. How do you explain this?

ERWAN LE GOFF: Ma mère est née en Argentine. Avant de rencontrer mon père, elle était vétérinaire pour les éleveurs de moutons.

My mother was born in Argentina. Before meeting my father, she was a veterinarian working for sheep farmers.

BTW

*When talking about your birthplace or birth date, French uses the **passé composé** of naître: **Elle est née à Carnac** (She was born in Carnac). When talking about a person who has passed away, both the **passé composé** and the **plus-que-parfait** can be used: **Baudelaire est né** or **était né à Paris en 1821** (Baudelaire was born in Paris in 1821). Remember to use the **passé composé** when referring to yourself: **Je suis né à Ajaccio en 2005** (I was born in Ajaccio in 2005).*

MME DARRIEUSSECQ: Quel est le rapport?

What does it have to with it?

ERWAN LE GOFF: Le pays est si vaste, elle devait souvent se déplacer dans un petit avion privé pour soigner les animaux. Ça lui manque beaucoup.

The country is so big, she often had to fly a small private plane to reach the animals she was taking care of. She misses it a lot.

MME DARRIEUSSECQ: Quelle aventure! Elle est toujours vétérinaire?

What an adventure! Is she still a veterinarian?

ERWAN LE GOFF: Oui, mais pour les chats et les chiens dans les Yvelynes. Ce n'est pas pareil.

Yes, but for cats and dogs in the Yvelynes department. It is not the same.

IRL In Chapter 4, we disovered the regions of France. **L'Île de France** is one of the regions that is made up of eight departments: **Paris** (75), **l'Essonne** (91), **les Hauts-de-Seine** (92) , **la Seine-Saint-Denis** (93), **la Seine-et-Marne** (77), **le Val-de-Marne** (94), **le Val-d'Oise** (95), and **les Yvelines** (78). Each department has a unique number that is used for license plates and zip codes. Take note if you want to send a postcard.

MME DARRIEUSSECQ: C'est donc votre mère qui vous a transmis sa passion?

So is it your mother who generated the enthusiasm that you have?

ERWAN LE GOFF: Absolument. Nous discutons ensemble de l'évolution des nouvelles technologies. Ma mère voudrait que je sois pilote, mais je préférerais être ingénieur aéronautique.

Absolutely. We often discuss the evolution of new technologies. She would like me to become a pilot, but I would prefer to be an aeronautical engineer.

MME DARRIEUSSECQ: Connaissez-vous les appareils Airbus?

Are you familiar with Airbus aircraft?

ERWAN LE GOFF: J'ai eu la chance de voler en tant que passager sur un A380, et je suis de près le A321XRL qui est moins coûteux et moins polluant. Mon objectif principal est de participer au développement des nouveaux produits Airbus.

I was lucky to be a passenger on an A380 and I am closely following the A321XRL, which is less costly and less polluting. My main goal is to participate in the development of new Airbus products.

BTW

Je suis *is the first person of the verb* **être** *and also the verb* **suivre: Je suis pilote** *(I am a pilot);* **Je suis la carrière de ce pilote** *(I am following this pilot's career).*

MME DARRIEUSSECQ: À votre avis, quels sont les éléments essentiels à ce développement?

In your opinion, what are the key elements for this development?

ERWAN LE GOFF: Le numérique, l'intelligence artificielle et aussi la recherche de nouveaux matériaux de construction.

Digital technology, artificial intelligence, and also the search for new construction materials.

MME DARRIEUSSECQ: Quelles sont les valeurs d'Airbus qui vous attirent le plus?

What Airbus values are you the most attracted to?

ERWAN LE GOFF: L'intégrité, la transparence, l'engagement, et l'esprit d'équipe.

Integrity, transparency, commitment, and team spirit.

MME DARRIEUSSECQ: Bon! Quelles sont vos compétences linguistiques?

Good! What are your language skills?

ERWAN LE GOFF: Je suis bilingue en anglais et en espagnol. J'ai des notions d'italien et d'allemand. Actuellement, je suis des cours de mandarin, niveau intermédiaire.

I am bilingual in English and Spanish. I have basic knowledge of Italian and German. I am presently taking a Mandarin course at the intermediate level.

MME DARRIEUSSECQ: Les langues sont-elles aussi la passion de votre mère?

Is your mother also passionnate about languages?

ERWAN LE GOFF: Ce n'est pas faux. Mais je suis aussi un aficionado d'opéra. Je regarde les retransmissions en direct du Metropolitan Opera en HD.

That is true. But I am also an opera aficionado. I watch the Metropolitan Opera live broadcasts in HD.

BTW

Note that in French, a positive idea is sometimes expressed in the negative form. When Erwan says **Ce n'est pas faux**, *he means it is quite right.* **Ce film n'est pas mal**, *depending on the tone of voice, will probably mean that the film is quite good.* **Je vous assure, le vent du nord n'est pas chaud!** *definitely means that the east wind is awfully cold.*

MME DARRIEUSSECQ: Impressionnant! Comme vous le savez, nous valorisons les candidats qui savent travailler en équipe, mais il est essentiel qu'ils aient une culture générale étendue. À partir de quelle date seriez-vous disponible?

Impressive. As you know, we value candidates who know how to work in teams, but it is essential they be knowledgeable about a wide range of subjects. When would you be available?

ERWAN LE GOFF: Dès maintenant.

Right now.

MME DARRIEUSSECQ: Très bien. Pourriez-vous me faire parvenir par mail trois références professionnelles?

Very well. Could you email me three professional references?

ERWAN LE GOFF: Je vous les envoie cet après-midi.

I'll send them to you this afternoon.

MME DARRIEUSSECQ: Merci. Je reviens vers vous sous peu pour vous faire part de notre décision.

Thank you. I'll get back to you shortly to let you know our decision.

ERWAN LE GOFF: Merci.

Thank you.

MME DARRIEUSSECQ: Enchantée d'avoir fait votre connaissance. Au revoir.

Nice meeting you. Good-bye.

BTW

When you meet someone, you say: **Je suis ravi(e)** *or* **enchanté(e) de faire votre connaissance.** *When you leave:* **Je suis ravi(e) d'avoir fait votre connaissance,** *using the past infinitive of the verb* **faire.**

ERWAN LE GOFF: Merci, Madame. Au revoir.

Thank you, Madame. Bye.

Une semaine plus tard...

A week later...

Erwan a décroché un emploi chez Airbus. Il parle de son nouveau logement à son ami Jonas.

Erwan got a job with Airbus. He is talking about his new home to his friend Jonas.

JONAS: Félicitations! Alors tu loges sur le campus?

Congratulations! So are you staying on campus?

ERWAN: Non, il n'y avait rien de disponible.

No, there was nothing available.

JONAS: Tu vas louer un appartement au centre-ville?

Are you going to rent an apartment downtown?

ERWAN: Non, c'est trop cher. J'ai trouvé une organisation qui met en contact les étudiants ou les stagiaires avec des seniors. C'est ce qu'on appelle la cohabitation intergénérationnelle.

No, it's too expensive. I found an organization that puts students or interns in contact with seniors. It's what's called intergenerational co-living.

JONAS: Comment ça marche exactement?

How does it work exactly?

ERWAN: Je loge gratuitement chez Madame Grandet. C'est une dame très gentille qui était assistante sociale. Elle a pris sa retraite l'an dernier.

I am staying free of charge at Madame Grandet's. She is a very nice lady who used to be a social worker. She retired last year.

JONAS: Tu as ta propre chambre?

Do you have your own room?

ERWAN: J'ai une chambre spacieuse et lumineuse, une salle de bain, et un grenier qui a été aménagé en bureau.

I have a bright and spacious room, a bathroom, and an attic converted into a study.

JONAS: Ouah! C'est classe! Tu as plus d'espace que moi. Et qu'est-ce que tu dois faire?

Wow! Pretty cool! You have more space than I have. And what are you supposed to do?

ERWAN: Je fais quelques courses pour elle, je passe l'aspirateur, je change une ampoule, etc.

I run some errands for her, I vacuum, I change a lightbulb, etc.

JONAS: Pas mal...

Not bad...

ERWAN: Ce dont elle a vraiment besoin, c'est d'une présence, quelqu'un à qui parler le soir.

What she really needs is for someone to be there that she can talk to in the evening.

JONAS: Ce n'est pas embêtant parfois?

Isn't that annoying sometimes?

ERWAN: Pas du tout. Madame Grandet est contente que je puisse dîner avec elle de temps en temps. En fait, elle n'est pas mauvaise cuisinière....	*Not at all. Madame Grandet is happy I can have dinner with her from time to time. In fact, she is quite a good cook....*
JONAS: Et elle te nourrit! Toi, tu as du bol! C'est super que tu puisses faire des économies.	*And she feeds you! You are lucky! It's great you can save money.*

BTW

Avoir du bol *(to be lucky)*, **avoir du pot**, *and* **avoir de la veine** *are informal synonyms of* **avoir de la chance**, *the expression we learned in Chapter 1.*

ERWAN: J'en ai besoin pour mon billet de train quand je retourne à Lorient.	*I need it for my train ticket when I go back to Lorient.*
JONAS: Quoi que tu fasses, tu réussis! Je suis vraiment impressionné.	*Whatever you do, you succeed! I am really impressed.*
ERWAN: Pourvu que tout se passe bien demain chez Airbus! C'est mon premier jour.	*Let's hope everything will go well tomorrow at Airbus! It's my first day.*
JONAS: Bonne chance et à bientôt.	*Good luck and see you soon.*
ERWAN: Ciao.	*Bye.*

 IRL Lorient is a beautiful town and seaport in the Morbihan department of Brittany. It is renowned for its Interceltic Festival. Every summer, musicians from Brittany, Scotland, Wales, Cornwall, the Isle of Man, Ireland, and northern Spain (Galicia and Asturias) celebrate the Celtic spirit with Breton bagpipes, Irish fiddles, and Galician pipes. The festival highlights music, dance, crafts, and traditions of the Celtic nations.

EXERCISES

EXERCISE 13.1

Conjugate the following verbs in the present subjunctive.

1. Tu (prendre) _____.

2. Nous (savoir) _____.

3. Vous (mettre) _____.

4. Ils (être) _____.

5. Elle (croire) _____.

6. Je (avoir) _____.

7. On (aller) _____.

8. Tu (apprendre) _____.

9. Elle (dire) _____.

10. Elles (vouloir) _____.

EXERCISE 13.2

*Conjugate the following verbs in the **subjonctif présent**.*

1. Elle est triste que tu (ne pas aller) _____ dans son université.

2. Je crains que ce (être) _____ difficile d'être accepté dans cet institut.

3. J'aimerais mieux qu'il (n'y a pas) _____ trop de travail à faire ce week-end.

4. Nous doutons qu'il (vouloir) _____ s'inscrire au Lycée Naval en Bretagne.

5. Il est content que tu (pouvoir) _____ faire de la voile pendant le week-end.

6. Vous doutez qu'elle (connaître) _____ cette école d'agronomie.

7. Elles ne croient pas que cela (correspondre) _____ à leurs besoins.

8. Je voudrais que tu (faire) _____ des photos du studio.

9. Ne croyez-vous pas que ce (être) _____ un bon choix?

10. Je ne pense pas que cela (pouvoir) _____ marcher.

EXERCISE 13.3

Conjugate each verb in the present tense of either the indicative or the subjunctive.

1. Je sais que cette formation (être) _____ très intense.

2. Nous ne sommes pas sûrs que cet appartement (avoir) _____ assez de pièces.

3. Elle a l'impression que vous (ne pas connaître) _____ ce sujet.

4. Est-ce qu'il a peur que tu (ne pas pouvoir) _____ venir ce soir?

5. Je doute que Sophie (vouloir) _____ habiter sur le campus.

6. On ne pense pas que le directeur de communication (savoir) _____ gérer cette affaire.

7. Aimeriez-vous que nous (aller) _____ à la Cité de l'espace avec vous?

8. Il croit qu'on (ne pas comprendre) _____ la situation.

9. J'exige que vous (arriver) _____ à l'heure tous les matins.

10. Elle est étonnée que nous (ne pas vouloir) _____ assister à la cérémonie.

EXERCISE 13.4

*Translate the following sentences using the **vous** form when applicable. When asking a question, use inversion.*

1. She is happy you are on her team.

2. Do you think he can drop me off at the station?

3. They are afraid that she won't have enough time.

4. I would like them to sign up for music class.

5. The teacher demands that we hand over our homework before Monday.

6. I'm not sure that the weather will be nice tomorrow.

7. Would you like to host some foreign students?

8. I regret that there aren't enough computers in this office.

9. We doubt that he is trying his best.

10. I am surprised that they want to collaborate with us.

EXERCISE 13.5

*Conjugate the following verbs in the **subjonctif présent**.*

1. Il étudie le mandarin quoique ce (être) _____ difficile.

2. Elles posent leur candidature en avance de peur qu'il (n'y a pas) _____ de places.

3. Les employés préparent un test sans que le directeur (être) _____ au courant.

4. Nous te soutiendrons à condition que tu (obtenir) _____ de bons résultats.

5. En attendant que je (recevoir) _____ une réponse de Madame Darrieussecq, mon frère essaie de me distraire.

6. La directrice des ressources humaines fait le grand ménage avant que nous (arriver) _____ .

7. Ses parents travaillent dur pour qu'ils (pouvoir) _____ faire des études supérieures.

8. Bien qu'il (avoir) _____ de bonnes notes, il n'a pas réussi le concours d'entrée.

9. Nous avons déplacé les meubles afin qu'ils (repeindre) _____ le studio.

10. Elle révisera sa copie jusqu'à ce que le directeur du marketing (être) _____ satisfait.

EXERCISE 13.6

*Conjugate the following verbs in the **subjonctif présent**.*

1. Il étrange que ce cours d'économie (ne pas être) _____ offert en anglais.

2. Il vaut mieux que vous (réunir) _____ tous vos documents à l'avance.

3. Il est dommage que nous (ne pas pouvoir) _____ aller à Albi ce week-end.

4. Il est possible qu'elle nous (remettre) _____ les clés du studio lundi.

5. Il est normal que vous (faire) _____ la queue à la cafétéria.

6. Il faut que les frais de scolarité (être) _____ réglés avant le premier septembre.

7. Il se peut que nous (avoir) _____ le temps d'aller faire des courses.

8. Il est naturel que vous (s'inquiéter) _____ de l'avenir de vos enfants.

9. Il est préférable que vous (suivre) _____ ces deux cours à la fois.

10. Il est rare que les élèves (passer) _____ le bac à l'âge de 15 ans.

EXERCISE 13.7

*Translate the following sentences using the **vous** form when applicable.*

1. Hugo prepared some sandwiches, fearing that we might be hungry.

2. Although he is tired, he is going to study until midnight.

3. It is normal for roommates to fight from time to time.

4. Let's hope they make couscous tonight.

5. They are studying Mandarin before their friends from Shanghai arrive.

6. It's the most beautiful museum I know.

7. I bought the tickets in advance so that we don't wait in line.

8. Let's hope we find an apartment with a nice view.

9. I am looking for a university that can host handicapped students.

10. While waiting for the problems to be resolved, we thank you for your patience.

EXERCISE 13.8

Conjugate the following verbs in the past subjunctive.

1. Je suis contente qu'elle (choisir) _____ cette profession.

2. Il doute que tu (réussir) _____ à ton examen.

3. Nous ne croyons pas qu'il (suivre) _____ nos conseils.

4. Tu ne pourras pas assister à la conférence à moins que ton professeur ne te (inscrire) _____ sur la liste.

5. Il est dommage que vous (s'inscrire) _____ trop tard.

6. Il a passé son bac avec mention bien qu'il (s'amuser) _____ toute l'année.

7. Pensez-vous qu'il (vraiment) (finir) _____ sa thèse?

8. Il vaut mieux que tu (ne pas perdre) _____ ton dossier.

9. On est content que tu (trouver) _____ un appartement.

10. Il est possible qu'ils (se tromper) _____ d'adresse.

EXERCISE 13.9

*Translate the following sentences using the **vous** form and the inversion if necessary.*

1. I am surprised you refused their offer.

2. They are sorry you were not able to open a bakery in their neighborhood.

3. Do you think artificial intelligence has already transformed our lives?

4. We regret you did not send a cover letter.

5. It is possible François lost his wallet.

6. It is a shame you did not get an apartment on campus.

7. Do you really think his mother had bought a private plane?

8. I doubt they read this novel by André Gide.

9. I don't think he sent his résumé to the right address.

10. We are happy he finally told the truth.

EXERCISE 13.10

*Translate the following sentences using the **tu** form when necessary.*

1. Whatever your decision, I'll accept it.

2. Wherever you go, Erwan will help you.

3. Whatever the price of the rent, we want to live downtown.

4. Whatever you do, don't forget your friend Jonas.

5. Wherever the farm is located, Madame Le Goff will take care of the sheep.

6. Whatever your language skills, they'll hire you.

7. Whatever may happen, be careful.

8. Whatever the students' age, Madame Grandet rents them a room.

9. Whatever you think, I don't care.

10. Whatever your dreams may be, follow them.

EXERCISE 13.11

*Replace the conjunction **quoique** by the **avoir beau** construction. Careful when choosing the tense.*

Quoiqu'il soit riche, il est radin. → **Il a beau être riche, il est radin.**

1. Quoiqu'il vive au Brésil depuis trois ans, il ne parle pas portugais.

2. Quoiqu'elle ait vécu à Nice pendant des années, elle n'a jamais appris à nager.

3. Quoiqu'elle cherche, elle ne trouve pas sa carte d'identité.

4. Quoiqu'il ait toujours fui son identité, ses racines lui collaient à la peau.

5. Quoiqu'il passe des annonces, il ne trouve pas de logement.

6. Quoiqu'elle ait gagné le prix Goncourt, elle n'a pas la grosse tête.

7. Quoique tu aies dit la vérité, ils n'ont rien voulu entendre.

8. Quoique Madame Grandet ait pris sa retraite, elle est toujours occupée.

9. Quoiqu'il ait étudié le wolof, il ne le parle pas couramment.

10. Quoiqu'ils vivent à la campagne, ils n'ont pas d'animaux de compagnie.

EXERCISE 13.12

Complete with the appropriate **pronom relatif.**

1. Le studio _____ il veut louer est spacieux.

2. Le quartier_____ nous plaît est le quartier Côte-Pavée.

3. C'est un écrivain _____ je connais bien. Je vous le recommande vivement.

4. Pour _____ préférez-vous travailler? Pour M. Jeannot ou Mme Hidalgo?

5. Les ustensiles _____ le chef a besoin sont dans ce placard.

6. L'entreprise pour _____ il travaille va fermer ses portes.

7. Le stylo avec _____ Madame Darrieussecq signe le contrat est un stylo-plume Montblanc.

8. La photo _____ ai besoin se trouve dans les archives d'Alger.

9. Chez _____ dînez-vous demain soir?

10. Le directeur de communication _____ j'ai rencontré s'appelle Monsieur Ferrand.

11. C'est la maison _____ Victor Hugo a écrit *Les Misérables* quand il était en exil à Guernesey.

12. Êtes-vous sûr de savoir _____ il est?

13. J'ignore pour _____ Madame Grandet a voté aux élections européennes.

14. Les histoires _____ je me souviens remontent aux années 2000.

15. Dès le jour _____ nous avons commencé, je savais que ça marcherait.

EXERCISE 13.13

Match the items in the two columns. Choose very carefully the most logical answers!

1. Je me demande   a. qui prouve son innocence.

2. C'est le document   b. où Erwan est né.

3. Je me souviens de l'année   c. qui a été aménagée en bureau.

4. Il y a une pièce   d. que l'avocat nous a fournis.

5. Voici les dossiers   e. pour qui Alex a voté.

EXERCISE 13.14

Complete with the appropriate indefinite pronoun.

1. _____ je pense, c'est à mon entretien chez Hermès.

2. _____ Nicolas s'attend, c'est à une augmentation de salaire.

3. Je ne comprends pas _____ ils veulent dire.

4. _____ je m'intéresse, c'est à votre expérience à la Madeleine avec Massimo Bottura.

5. _____ elle a envie, c'est de faire Sciences Po.

6. Pourrais-tu me dire _____ se passe?

7. _____ lui plaît, c'est le grenier aménagé chez Madame Grandet.

8. _____ il a peur, c'est de la fermeture de l'entreprise.

9. Pour faciliter notre enquête sur le vol, nous voudrions savoir tout _____ vous vous souvenez.

10. C'est _____ on appelle la cohabitation intergénérationnelle!

EXERCISE 13.15

*Translate the following sentences using the **vous** form when necessary.*

1. I like the studio Jonas found in Toulouse.

2. Madame Bessis? I don't know who she is.

3. The manual she is talking about is written in English.

4. What I need is a dictionary.

5. What she is interested in is the new Airbus.

6. What are you talking about?

7. —What are you thinking about? —I am thinking about Lorient's festival.

8. What I remember is her Montblanc fountain pen on her desk.

9. What we want is more free time.

10. It's the piece of furniture she wants to take to Menton.

Flashcard App

LE COIN DES CRÉATEURS

ÉCRIRE L'ÉBAUCHE D'UNE LETTRE DE MOTIVATION

Vous répondez à une annonce dans le journal qui recrute un vendeur/une vendeuse ou un serveur/une serveuse ou autre emploi pour les mois de juillet et août. Vous devez convaincre le responsable qui cherche le ou la candidat(e) idéal(e). Faire une liste de:

- vos qualités humaines

- vos compétences

- vos expériences

- vos passions

- votre raison de vouloir travailler pour eux

- vos disponibilités

Quelques pistes pour vous aider: je suis sociable et souriante; je connais bien vos produits; je suis très organisée; je parle trois langues; j'ai fait un stage l'an passé. Rédigez au moins dix arguments en puisant dans le vocabulaire des chapitres précédents.

À votre tour!

NOTE CULTURELLE

MADE IN FRANCE: THE FRENCH ECONOMY

When we think of "Made in France," a variety of consumable products come to mind: baguettes and brioches, pastries and macarons, champagne and cognac, Camembert and Roquefort. Or we may think of other consumer goods: couture and prêt-à-porter fashion, fine jewelry and watches or other luxury goods. While they all represent a considerable source of income for France, the country's economy is actually much more diverse. It is the seventh largest in the world and the third largest of the Eurozone countries based on gross domestic product (GDP). Services rather than goods are the main contributor to the country's economy, with over 70 percent of GDP stemming from this sector. So what are some of the key players in the French economy? The country's top companies are:

- Total – oil extraction and natural gas mining, transport, distribution, and marketing

- AXA – insurance

- BNP Paribas – banking

- Engie, aka GDF Suez – electricity generation, natural gas, and renewable energy

- Carrefour – hypermarket superstores and supermarkets

- Crédit Agricole – banking

- Société Générale – banking

- Éléctricité de France – electrical energy distribution

- Groupe PSA (Peugeot Société Anonyme) – automotive

- Groupe BPCE – banking

France's closest trading partner is Germany, which accounts for more than 17 percent of France's exports. Its primary exports are machinery and transportation equipment, aircraft and spacecraft, vehicles, electronic equipment, and pharmaceuticals. What French companies account for the most exports? The top exporting companies are:

- Total – oil and gas

- Renault – automotive

- Sanofi – pharmaceuticals

- Christian Dior – clothing and accessories

- Peugeot – automotive

- Danone – processed food and beverages

- Saint-Gobain – construction materials

- Schneider Electric – electrical equipment

- L'Oréal Group – household, personal care

- Hermès International – clothing and accessories

France is also one of the world's largest exporters of farm and agricultural products. And then there is tourism, a key export since France is the most visited country in the world. It is truly a major economic player on the world stage. So exactly where does it stand? The world's largest economies are:

- United States

- China

- Japan

- Germany

- United Kingdom

- India

- France

- Italy

- Brazil

- Canada

Describing Things and Talking About Events

MUST KNOW

⚡ Some adjectives can precede or follow a noun, taking on different meanings.

⚡ Don't use a liaison with **les hors-d'oeuvre** (or make **oeuvre** plural), and don't forget the hyphen!

⚡ Compound adjectives always remain singular and masculine.

⚡ **Meilleur** is an adjective, while **mieux** is an adverb.

ongratulations on making it to the last chapter! You have come quite a long way as a language learner. Now, you are ready to brighten up your world with vibrant adjectives. This final dialogue celebrates the flourishment of graphic novels, science fiction, digital technologies, and artificial intelligence, human achievements that promise thrilling adventures for the years to come. Join us for this final stop on our **must know** journey together.

Qualitative Adjectives

Adjectives agree in gender and number with the noun they modify. One common rule is to add an **e** to the feminine form.

Gaël est français.	*Gaël is French.*
Emily est américain**e**.	*Emily is American.*
Le bateau est grand.	*The boat is big.*
La péniche est petit**e**.	*The barge is small.*

If an adjective ends with an **e** in the masculine form, the feminine form remains the same.

Le système est efficace.	*The system is efficient.*
La méthode est efficace.	*The method is efficient.*
Le processus est simple.	*The process is simple.*
La recette est simple.	*The recipe is simple.*

BTW

Most adjectives are placed after the noun. However, some adjectives can sometimes be moved in front of the noun to stress an idea. Compare **c'est un jeune femme charmante** *(she is a charming young woman) with* **c'est une charmante jeune femme.** *In the second example,* **charmante** *is stressed.*

Be aware that the feminine of an adjective can take on several forms according to their endings. Here are a few examples:

Gaël est heur**eux**.

Gaël is happy.

Félicie est heur**euse**.

Félicie is happy.

Loïc est ambit**ieux**.

Loïc is ambitious.

Cécile est ambit**ieuse**.

Cécile is ambitious.

Henri est impuls**if**.

Henri is impulsive.

Béatrice est impuls**ive**.

Béatrice is impulsive.

Rémi est na**ïf**.

Rémi is naive.

Mona est na**ïve**.

Mona is naive.

Luiz est brésil**ien**.

Luiz is Brazilian.

Marisa est brésil**ienne**.

Marisa is Brazilian.

Tsai Chen est vietnam**ien**.

Tsai Chen is Vietnamese.

Mai Hien est vietnam**ienne**.

Mai Hien is Vietnamese.

un étudiant étrang**er**

a foreign student

une stagiaire étrang**ère**

a foreign intern

le prem**ier** candidat

the first candidate

la prem**ière** gagnante

the first winner

Ce pain **frais** est délicieux.

This fresh bread is delicious.

On ne peut pas vivre d'amour et d'eau **fraîche**.

One cannot live on love alone.

Qui est ton un acteur **favori**?

Who is your favorite actor?

Quelle est ton équipe **favorite**?

What's your favorite team?

Son entraîneur est un homme **gentil**.

His/her trainer is a nice gentleman.

La coach de vie de Joé est une personne très **gentille**.

Joé's life coach is a very nice person.

Ce lit est trop **mou** pour mon dos.

This bed is too soft for my back.

La neige est trop **molle** aujourd'hui.

Snow is too soft today.

Ce projet est **fou**.	*This project is crazy.*
Cette pression est **folle**.	*This pressure is crazy.*

Il est **nul** en maths.	*He is bad at math.*
Cette blague est **nulle**.	*It is a terrible joke.*

Le sucre **roux** est-il meilleur pour la santé?	*Is brown cane sugar better for your health?*
La perruque de Batwoman est **rousse**.	*Batwoman's wig is red.*

Many adjectives are irregular and are often placed before the noun. You just need to memorize them.

C'est un **bon** film.	*It's a good film.*
C'était une **bonne** décision.	*It was a good decision.*

Chouki est le **jeune** chien que Maud a adopté.	*Chouki is the young dog Maud has adopted.*
La *jeune* musicienne est un tableau de Michel Garnier.	*The Young Musician is a painting by Michel Garnier.*

C'est un **long** poème d'Aimé Césaire.	*It is a long poem by Aimé Césaire.*
C'est une **longue** histoire au sujet de tes aïeux.	*It is a long story about your ancestors.*

C'est un **faux** problème.	*It's a false problem.*
Il vit à Paris sous une **fausse** identité.	*He lives in Paris under a false identity.*

Ne dis pas de **gros** mots en public!	*Do not use swear words in public!*
C'est une **grosse** erreur!	*It's a huge mistake!*

In front of a vowel or a mute **h**, **beau** becomes **bel** and **vieux** becomes **vieil**.

Le costume d'Alice est **beau**.	*Alice's costume is beautiful.*
Sa perruque est **belle**.	*Her wig is beautiful.*
C'est un **bel** édifice.	*It's a beautiful building.*
C'est un **vieux** marché.	*It's an old market.*
C'est une **vieille** armoire.	*It's an old armoire.*
C'est un **vieil** homme.	*He is an old man.*
Votre **nouveau** projet est fascinant.	*Your new project is fascinating.*
Ils vendent les **nouvelles** baskets autolaçantes.	*They are selling the new self-lacing sneakers.*
Mon **nouvel** ordinateur est performant.	*My new computer is performing.*

Some adjectives change meaning when they precede or follow the nouns. For a literal meaning, the adjective is placed after the noun. In a figurative sense, it precedes the noun.

un trou **profond**	*a deep hole*
une **profonde** tristesse	*a great sadness*
son **ancienne** adresse	*his former address*
un meuble **ancien**	*an antique piece of furniture*
une chemise **propre**	*a clean shirt*
sa **propre** fortune	*his/her own fortune*
des chaussettes **sales**	*dirty socks*
un **sale** coup	*a dirty trick*
notre **cher** ami	*our dear friend*
un terrain **très** cher	*an expensive piece of land*
la **pauvre** petite fille	*the poor little girl*
des pays **pauvres**	*poor countries*
un **grand** homme	*an important man*
un homme **grand**	*a tall man*

l'an **dernier**	*last year*
la **dernière** année	*the last year*

Most adjectives describing colors agree in gender and number with the noun they modify, and they are placed after the noun.

masculine	feminine	
beige	beige	*beige*
blanc	blanche	*white*
bleu	bleue	*blue*
gris	grise	*gray*
jaune	jaune	*yellow*
noir	noire	*black*
rose	rose	*pink*
rouge	rouge	*red*
vert	verte	*green*
violet	violette	*violet*

Sa combinaison **violette** lui va bien. *Her purple jumpsuit suits her well.*
Il porte toujours une chemise **blanche**. *He always wears a white shirt.*
Vous avez de jolies chaussures **noires**! *You have beautiful black shoes!*
Ils ont randonné dans la vallée **Verte**. *They hiked in the vallée Verte.*

Adjectives that are also nouns of fruit, plants, or minerals remain in the singular masculine form. There is no agreement. Here are some examples you can easily identify:

abricot	*apricot*
acajou	*mahogany*
ambre	*amber*
argent	*silver*
azur	*azure*
cerise	*cherry*

champagne	*champagne*
châtain	*auburn*
citron	*lemon*
corail	*coral*
émeraude	*emerald*
fraise	*strawberry*
framboise	*raspberry*
indigo	*indigo*
ivoire	*ivory*
jade	*jade*
lavande	*lavender*
lilas	*lilac*
maïs	*maize*
marron	*brown*
menthe	*mint*
miel	*honey*
moutarde	*mustard*
noisette	*hazel*
olive	*olive*
pistache	*pistachio*
sable	*sand*
safran	*saffron*
turquoise	*turquoise*

Les bottes **marron** d'Alice ne sont pas en daim.

Alice's brown boots are not made of suede.

Rihanna, l'égérie de Chanel, a les yeux **noisette**.

Rihanna, Chanel's muse, has hazelnut eyes.

Ils tricotent des cardigans **moutarde**. *They are knitting mustard cardigans.*
Ces chaussettes **turquoise** sont en laine *These turquoise socks are made of*
épaisse. *thick wool.*

Another exception: **les adjectifs composés**. When two adjectives
are combined to provide more specificity, both adjectives remain in the
masculine singular form.

bleu ciel	*sky blue*
bleu clair	*light blue*
bleu foncé	*dark blue*
bleu marine	*navy blue*
bleu nuit	*midnight blue*
châtain clair	*light brown*
gris acier	*steel gray*
gris perle	*pearl gray*
jaune citron	*lemon yellow*
jaune maïs	*corn yellow*
jaune paille	*straw yellow*
rouge tomate	*tomato red*
vert amande	*almond green*
vert bouteille	*bottle green*
vert olive	*green olive*
vert pale	*pale green*

Alice a choisi de la soie **bleu ciel**. *Alice chose some sky-blue silk.*
Ella a trouvé des chaussures **vert amande**. *She found almond-green shoes.*
Tyler a commandé deux pulls **gris acier**. *Tyler ordered two steel-gray sweaters.*
L'actrice portait une robe **jaune citron**. *The actress was wearing a lemon-*
yellow dress.

Comparisons

In French, comparisons of adjectives take three forms, **plus... que** (*more... than*), **moins... que** (*less...than*), and **aussi... que** (*as...as*).

Mathéo est **plus** qualifié **que** Paul.	*Mathéo is more skilled than Paul.*
Votre maison est **plus** grande **que** la leur.	*Your house is bigger than theirs.*
Ce canal est **moins** long **que** cette rivière.	*This canal is less long than this river.*
Sa cravate est **moins** élégante **que** ton nœud papillon.	*His tie his less elegant than your bow tie.*
Simon est **aussi** doué **que** Marc.	*Simon is as gifted as Marc.*
Son deuxième entretien à la radio est **aussi** nul **que** le premier.	*His/her second radio interview is as horrible as the first one.*

To compare quantities, **plus de... que**, **moins de... que**, and **autant de... que** are used.

Maëlys a **plus de** travail **qu'**Alice.	*Maëlys has more work than Alice.*
Manges-tu **plus de** légumes **qu'**elle?	*Do you eat more vegetables than she does?*
Tu as **moins de** vacances **qu'**Odile.	*You have less vacation time than Odile.*
Dépensent-ils **moins d'**argent **que** lui?	*Do they spend less money than he does?*
Il a **autant de** problèmes **que** toi.	*He has as many problems as you do.*
Ils ne possèdent pas **autant de** terrain **qu'**eux.	*They do not own as much land as they do.*

Note that the stressed pronoun **toi** is used, whereas the subject pronoun is used in English. **Il a moins de problèmes que moi, que toi, que lui, qu'elle, que nous, que vous, qu'eux, qu'elles.**

Some comparatives have irregular forms.

Ses deux premiers romans étaient bons, mais son troisième est **meilleur**.	*His first two novels were good, but his third is better.*
Ce plat est bon, mais il est **meilleur** avec du romarin.	*This dish is good, but it is better with some rosemary.*
Nora est une **meilleure** joueuse de tennis **que** toi.	*Nora is a better tennis player than you.*
Cette soupe est **plus** mauvaise **que** je le pensais.	*This soup is worse than I thought.*

When refering to situations or abstract concepts, **pire que** is used:

La situation économique est **pire que** jamais.	*The economic situation is worse than ever.*

To express the ideas of *the most, the least, the best, the worst*, etc., one uses the superlative. To form the superlative, simpy add the definite article to the comparative form. Note that **de** follows the superlative, while *in* is used in English.

C'est **le plus grand** festival littéraire.	*It's the largest literary festival.*
C'est le bistrot **le moins cher** du marché au puces.	*It's the least expensive bistro in the flea market.*
C'est **le meilleur** film **que** j'aie vu.	*It's the best film I saw.*
C'est **le pire** tableau **qu'**il ait jamais vendu.	*It's his worst painting he ever sold.*

Verbs Ending in –*eindre* and –*aindre*

Some verbs ending in **-eindre** or **-aindre** follow a specific conjugation.
   Let's conjugate the verb **atteindre** (*to reach*):

j'atteins	*I reach*	nous atteignons	*we reach*
tu atteins	*you reach*	vous atteignez	*you reach*
il/elle/on atteint	*he/she/one reaches*	ils/elles atteignent	*they reach*

Nous comptons atteindre notre objectif d'ici novembre.	*We are expecting to reach our goal by November.*
Éteins la lumière dans le couloir!	*Turn off the light in the hallway!*

   Se plaindre (*to complain*) follows a similar pattern.

je me plains	*I complain*	nous nous plaignons	*we complain*
tu te plains	*you complain*	vous vous plaignez	*you complain*
il/elle/on se plaint	*he/she/one complains*	ils/elles se plaignent	*they complain*

   Other verbs with this conjugation include:

peindre	*to paint*
éteindre	*to turn off*
teindre	*to dye*
atteindre	*to reach*
restreindre	*to restrain*
feindre	*to feign*
craindre	*to fear*
plaindre	*to pity*
se plaindre	*to complain*
contraindre	*to constrain*

De quoi te plains-tu?	*What are you complaining about?*
Elle craint ne pas pouvoir retourner à l'Atelier des Lumières ce mois-ci.	*She fears she might not be able to return to the Atelier des Lumières this month.*

 IRL L'Atelier des Lumières is a digital art exhibition in the 11th arrondissement offering an immersion in the paintings of great artists. Download their free app, www.atelier-lumieres.com, set it on French language, and explore the artistic world in French! **Du bonheur à l'état pur.**

 DIALOGUE *Rendez-vous à Comic Con Paris!*
Let's meet at Comic Con Paris!

Alice is trying on her Batwoman costume for the Comic Con Paris, a European pop culture festival that has become a reference. Thousands of fans, geeks, and professionals meet at the **Grande halle de la Villette** in the 19th arrondissement.

 **IRL** The **Parc de la Villette** is one of the largest parks in Paris, home of cultural centers like **la Cité des Sciences et de l'Industrie; la Géode** IMAX theater; **la Cité de la musique; le Zénith**, a rock and pop concert arena with more than 6,000 seats; **la Philarmonie**, a new symphony hall designed by Jean Nouvel and inaugurated in 2015; and la **Grande halle de la Villette**, a venue for concerts, music and film festivals, trade fairs, and events like Comic Con. If you are not in a rush, take a two-and-a-half-hour barge cruise on the Seine and Canal Saint-Martin, from the **musée d'Orsay** to **la Villette**.

ALICE: Ça me va? Qu'est-ce que vous en pensez?	*Does it look good on me? What do you think about it?*
MAËLYS: Ouah! Batwoman dans toute sa splendeur! Oui, ça te va bien, mais...	*Wow! Batwoman in all her glory! It suits you very well, but...*

LOÏC: Qu'est-ce qui ne va pas? Alice a une combinaison violette, une ceinture jaune canari, un masque noir, des gants noirs, des bottes dorées...

What's wrong? Alice has a purple jumpsuit, a canary-yellow belt, a black mask, black gloves, golden boots...

ALICE: Je vous assure, c'est un boulot fou!

I swear to you, it was a huge amount of work!

MAËLYS: C'est génial, mais la cape n'a pas d'ailes!

It's awesome, but the cape has no wings.

LOÏC: Et alors?

So what?

MAËLYS: Batwoman a besoin d'une cape ailée pour voler plus vite!

Batwoman needs a winged cape to fly faster!

ALICE: Ah, tu as raison. J'ai assez de tissu pour ajouter des volants.

You're right. I have enough fabric to add some ruffles.

BTW

If, like Alice, you decide to make a costume, here are some terms that may come in handy:

une chemise à carreaux	a checked shirt
à rayures	striped
une veste croisée	double-breasted jacket
un costume cintré	slim-fit suit
un pantalon à pinces	pleated pants
une robe à fleurs	floral dress
à pois	polka-dot
à volants	flounced
à plis	pleated
une jupe courte/longue	short/long skirt
un tutu	tutu

LOÏC: Alice, tu as fait ça fait toute seule?

Alice, did you do all this by yourself?

ALICE: Presque tout. 80% du costume doit être fait main. J'ai acheté les bottes, mais j'ai fait les protège-poignets noirs et les couvre-bottes marron foncé.

Almost everything. 80% of the costume must be handmade. I bought the boots, but I made the black wristbands and the dark brown boot covers.

LOÏC: En quoi sont les bottes?

What are the boots made of?

ALICE: En similicuir. J'ai trouvé tous les tissus au marché Saint-Pierre dans le 18ᵉ.

In synthetic leather. I found all the fabric at the marché Saint-Pierre in the 18th arrondissement.

 IRL The **marché Saint-Pierre**, a five-story building in Montmartre, near the Sacré-Cœur basilica, is one of the largest fabric shops in the world. It offers a wide selection of classic fabric and exclusive prints for fashion or home design. Whether you are a fashion designer or a textile enthusiast, make a detour and visit the 18th arrondissement fabric district.

BTW

When buying fabric, you'll have a wide range of choices:

le cuir	leather	le satin	satin
le daim	suede	le velours	velvet
le coton	cotton	la dentelle	lace
le lin	linen	la flanelle	flannel
la laine	wool	la polaire	fleece
le cachemire	cashmere	le nylon	nylon
la soie	silk	le lycra	lycra

MAËLYS: Où as-tu déniché la boucle en forme de chauve-souris?

Where did you find this bat-shaped buckle?

ALICE: Sur eBay. Et le collier au marché aux puces de Saint-Ouen. Il me reste plus qu'à teindre la perruque que j'ai faite.

On eBay. And the necklace at the Saint-Ouen flea market. I still have to dye the wig I made.

LOÏC: Tu ne peux pas te teindre les cheveux?

Can't you dye your hair?

ALICE: Dans l'épisode 3 du film, Batwoman a de longs cheveux roux. Mes cheveux sont trop courts.

In Episode 3 of the film, Batwoman has long red hair. My hair is too short.

BTW

Alice needs to dye her hair, do her makeup, and make sure she has all her accessories in order. Here is more vocabulary related to parts of the body, whether you're having an everyday conversation or you're transforming into a superhero!

le visage	face	**le bras**	arm
l'œil	eye	**le coude**	elbow
les yeux	eyes	**le poignet**	wrist
le sourcil	eyebrow	**la main**	hand
le cil	eyelash	**le doigt**	finger
le nez	nose	**l'ongle**	nail
la bouche	mouth	**la jambe**	leg
les lèvres	lips	**le genou**	knee
l'oreille	ear	**la cheville**	ankle
le dos	back	**le pied**	foot

 IRL The flea market of **Saint-Ouen**, located at **Porte de Clignancourt**, has become one of the most popular destinations for tourists in the **Ile-de-France** area, with millions of visitors a year exploring **les Puces**, as it is called. You'll find high-end antiques, secondhand furniture, knickknacks, antique books, vintage clothing, and quaint restaurants. Do not hesitate to **marchander** (*to bargain*), as it is part of the tradition.

LOÏC: Il faut vraiment avoir envie de participer à ce championnat de Cosplay!

You have to really want to take part in this Cosplay championship!

ALICE: C'est une expérience extraordinaire.

It is an extraordinary experience.

LOÏC: J'en suis sûr.

I am sure it is.

ALICE: Les juges prennent en compte la qualité du costume, le choix des matériaux et des couleurs et surtout le respect de l'image de référence. La concurrence est féroce.

Judges take into account the quality of the costume, the choice of materials, and above all, how faithful the costume is to the original character. It is a tough competition.

LOÏC: C'est trop de pression pour moi. Et pour gagner quoi?

Too much pressure for me. And for what?

ALICE: On peut gagner environ 4500 euros.

You can win up to 4,500 euros.

LOÏC: Pas mal... Alors Mayëlis, pourquoi est-ce que tu ne t'inscris pas?

Not bad... So Maëlys, why aren't you signing up?

MAËLYS: Je ne saurais pas quel personnage incarner.

I wouldn't know what character to portray.

ALICE: Tu te souviens du roman graphique, *La Rose écarlate* de Patricia Lyfoung, que je t'avais prêté?

Do you remember Patricia's Lyfoung's graphic novel, La Rose éclarlate I had lent you?

MAËLYS: Comment aurais-je pu l'oublier? J'adore ses costumes mais je ne sais pas coudre et je ne veux pas rivaliser avec toi.

How could I have forgotten? I love her costumes, but I can't sew and I don't want to compete with you.

ALICE: Ça m'est complètement égal.

It's really OK.

BTW

Cela (ça) m'est égal *can mean "it's OK," "it does not matter," "it is all the same to me," or "I don't care." It depends on the context and the tone of voice.* Je m'en fiche *is less formal.*

MAËLYS: Je ne veux pas participer mais j'aimerais assister au championnat. Je suis curieuse de savoir qui sera couronné meilleur(e) cosplayeur ou cosplayeuse de France cette année.

I don't want to participate, but I'd like to attend the championship. I am curious to find out who will be crowned the best cosplayer in France this year.

ALICE: En fait, il n'y a pas que le championnat. C'est fascinant de regarder les costumes inspirés des jeux vidéo, des films et des séries.

Actually, it's not only the championship. It is fascinating to look at the costumes inspired by films and series.

LOÏC: Est-ce que les acteurs des films sont invités?

Are the actors invited?

ALICE: Évidemment, les acteurs et les réalisateurs des films, et aussi les artistes du monde de la BD, des mangas, et les stars du cosplay.

Of course, actors, filmmakers, and also artists from the comic book and manga world, and the cosplay stars.

MAËLYS: C'est génial! La Villette se transforme en un univers de science-fiction, de fantaisie où l'on peut envisager un monde remodelé par le numérique et l'intelligence artificielle.

That's awesome! La Villette becomes a science-fiction and fantasy universe where one can envision a world reshaped by digital technology and artificial intelligence.

LOÏC: Utopie ou dystopie?

Utopia or dystopia?

ALICE: Qui sait?

Who knows?

LOÏC: Je dois avouer que c'est intrigant.

I have to admit it's intriguing.

ALICE: C'est le lieu idéal pour rencontrer des créateurs, participer à des ateliers et assister à une séance de dédicace.

It's the ideal place to meet creators, to take part in workshops, and to attend signing sessions.

MAËLYS: Le citoyen lambda côtoie les super-héros. Et Alice sera notre super-héroïne!

The average citizen rubs elbows with superheroes. And Alice will be our superheroine!

BTW

*The word "hero" in French is **le héros** in the singular, masculine form and **les héros** in the plural, without a liaison, as it is an **h aspiré**. On the contrary, in the feminine form, **l'héroïne** needs an elision. **Les héroïnes** involves a liaison pronounced with a **z** sound. We have already encountered other words with an **h aspiré**:*

la hausse	increase	**le haut**	top
la Hollande	Holland	**les hors-d'oeuvre**	appetizers
le haricot	bean	**le hibou**	owl
le homard	lobster		

EXERCISES

EXERCISE 14.1

Complete the following sentences with the adjective in the appropriate form.

1. La péniche est trop (petit) _____ pour notre groupe.

2. Ta ceinture est vraiment très _____ (beau).

3. Cette salle de cinéma est la plus (vieux) _____ de la ville.

4. Émilie est très (actif) _____ dans le syndicat étudiant.

5. J'aimerais un verre d'eau (frais) _____, s'il vous plaît.

6. Julien a besoin de peinture (blanc) _____ pour repeindre sa salle de bain.

7. Madame Morel est (fier) _____ de ses enfants.

8. Nous avons ressenti une (vif) _____ émotion en entendant la nouvelle.

9. L'offre qu'ils nous ont faite n'est pas (sérieux) _____.

10. Margot est aussi (ambitieux) _____ que (généreux) _____.

EXERCISE 14.2

Complete the following sentences using the nationality in the feminine form.

1. Le gagnant est indien. La gagnante est _____.

2. Le gagnant est suédois. La gagnante est _____.

3. Le gagnant est marocain. La gagnante est _____.

4. Le gagnant est français. La gagnante est _____.

5. Le gagnant est indonésien. La gagnante est _____.

6. Le gagnant est sénégalais. La gagnante est _____.

7. Le gagnant est américain. La gagnante est _____.

8. Le gagnant est argentin. La gagnante est _____.

9. Le gagnant est canadien. La gagnante est _____.

10. Le gagnant est écossais. La gagnante est _____.

EXERCISE 14.3

Turn the sentence into the feminine form.

L'avocat est français. → **L'avocate est française.**

1. L'ingénieur est intuitif.

2. Le boulanger est heureux.

3. Le pharmacien est occupé.

4. Le conseiller est européen.

5. Le traducteur est consciencieux.

6. Le vendeur est élégant.

7. L'illustrateur est fou de joie.

8. Le jardinier est franc et direct.

9. L'ouvrier est nouveau dans l'équipe.

10. Le danseur est talentueux.

EXERCISE 14.4

Translate the following sentences using **vous** *and the* **est-ce que** *form when necessary.*

1. It's the last time I lend my comic books to my youngest brother!

2. Alice brought a pair of clean sneakers to walk in the parc de la Villette.

3. Loïc's former girlfriend works in Finland.

4. Our dear friends Luc and Laurent will meet us in Normandy in May.

5. Céleste sold her antique books before going to Menton.

6. Are you going to launch your own company?

7. They sent me a picture of the deepest lake in the world.

8. Marguerite Duras became a woman of great prestige in the French literary world.

9. Why did you buy such an expensive mask just for one night?

10. His poor mother would like him to get married soon.

EXERCISE 14.5

Translate the adjectives in parentheses.

1. Sa veste (*navy blue*) _____ est un cadeau de Florence.

2. La Renault Twingo (*pistachio green*) _____ se vend très bien.

3. La peinture (*mint green*) _____ du salon est apaisante.

4. Il portait une casquette (*corn yellow*) _____.

5. Les rideaux (*indigo*) _____ de la chambre sont très épais.

6. Les capes (*orange*) _____ seront utilisées pour le film.

7. Nos chaussettes (*white*) _____ sont sales.

8. Je crois qu'il a les yeux (*light brown*).

9. Sa combinaison (*sky blue*) _____ est en viscose.

10. L'écharpe (*mustard*) _____ du candidat est trop longue.

EXERCISE 14.6

Write full sentences with the elements provided.

Nola/Théo/méticuleux /+ → Nola est plus méticuleuse que Théo.

1. Nolan/Florent/ambitieux/-

2. Cécile/Victorine/impulsif/=

3. Josépha/Maria/sportif/+

4. Mila/Corinne/gentil/+

5. Christian/son benjamin/motivé/=

EXERCISE 14.7

*Translate the following sentences using **tu** and the **est-ce que** form when necessary.*

1. Did you wear your pale green jumpsuit?

2. This is the best hot chocolate in our town.

3. Did Alice make more costumes than Angèle?

4. Do you have as much homework as I do?

5. I doubt you have less chance to win than Estelle.

6. You have as much chance to win as she does.

7. Why did you use more silk and less linen to make your costume?

8. It is the best science-fiction novel we have ever read in our French class.

9. Judges take into account the quality of the work and they also want to see the best mix of colors.

10. You should have brought back some lace from Burano and some glass necklaces from Murano.

EXERCISE 14.8

Conjugate the following verbs in the appropriate tense depending on the meaning.

1. Elle (peindre) _____ des tournesols après avoir visité l'Atelier des Lumières.

2. Les marathoniens (atteindre) _____ des records de vitesse impressionnants.

3. Hier, elle (se teindre) _____ les cheveux en gris argenté.

4. Je vous (plaindre) _____. Votre situation est si difficile!

5. Méfiez-vous, ils (feindre) _____ la tristesse.

6. La ville d'Essaouira, (ceindre) _____ de remparts, est protégée contre les assauts de l'océan.

7. Les apprentis du Tintoret (peindre) _____ les plafonds d'un palais à Venise.

8. Elle (être atteint) _____ d'une maladie chronique.

9. Les circonstances économiques les (contraindre) _____ à délocaliser leur entreprise en Asie du Sud-Est.

10. Elles (se plaindre) _____ de ne pas comprendre les acronymes français comme mdr dans les emails.

If you want to read and write text messages, the **SMS** or **texto**, you need to learn the basic abbreviations: **mdr** means **mort de rire**, dying of laughter, the equivalent of *LOL*.

Other common abbreviations are:

pdp	pas de problème
cc,cv, twa?	coucou, ça va, toi?
dsl	désolé
stp	s'il te plaît
svp	s'il vous plaît
A+	À plus
mr6	merci
bjr	bonjour
bsr	bonsoir
slt	salut
a2m1	à demain
bcp	beaucoup
pk	pourquoi
chu	je suis
ras	rien à signaler
jam	j'en ai marre
cpg	c'est pas grave
jtbf	je t'embrasse bien fort
jtm	je t'aime

Flashcard App

LE COIN DES CRÉATEURS

French writers like Roland Barthes, Alain Robbe-Grillet, and François Bon have used inventories to reflect on society. You will easily find online the famous *J'aime, je n'aime pas,* by Roland Barthes. Following the example below, make your own **inventaire** with nouns, adjectives, verbs, and adverbs.

Le thème de l'eau:
J'aime les lacs, la mer, les cascades...
J'aime tout ce qui est bleu, éphémère, fluide...
J'aime nager, flotter, naviguer...
J'aime plonger agilement, profondément, fluidement...

Choisir un thème: le feu, la lumière, les animaux, les minéraux, la cuisine, etc.

Dresser un inventaire avec cinq ou dix noms, adjectifs, verbes, et adverbes.

À votre tour!

NOTE CULTURELLE

COMIC BOOKS, COSTUMES, AND CONVENTIONS

For U.S. comic book fans, the Francophone version known as the *bande dessinée* or BD (which can be translated as comic book, comic strip, or comics) is much closer to what we call a graphic novel. As in the United States, BDs were originally intended as fun entertainment, appearing in newspapers and magazines and often targeting younger readers. However, in France and Belgium, as the writing and artwork developed and became more sophisticated, so did their length and the intended audience. Unlike American comic books, which were usually limited to a maximum of 32 pages, they were often published as separate hardcover books or "albums." Their readership also expanded, and today it is just as common to see adults in the BD section of bookstores as it is to see younger fans, stretched out on the floor reading the latest work by their favorite artists and authors. Classic francophone BD characters like Tintin, Titeuf, and Lucky Luke are known throughout the world. Traditionally considered to be more of interest to male readers, newer authors and artists are also working to broaden the gender appeal of the BD. There is Penelope Bagieu, whose webcomic *My Quite Fascinating Life* recounts tales from her own life and experiences through her fictional self, Zoe. A pioneer in the BD blog format, the title of her nonfiction album, *Brazen: Rebel Ladies Who Rocked the World*, tells it all. There is also Maud, the fictional heroine in Patricia Lyfoung's series *The Scarlet Rose*. This empowered young woman relies on her wits and fighting ability, both of which are formidable, in equal measure. While a dashing prince would be nice, she is quite capable of handling even the most difficult situations.

Dressing up as one's favorite BD character is as popular in France as it is elsewhere in the world. Cosplay (the word is the same in French), however, is more than just dress-up. It has developed into an artistic practice in its own right, one with its roots in popular culture, a phenomenon that now includes regional and international competitions. At these events, competitors have the option of participating solo, or in duos or trios in which all are required to wear costumes representing characters from the same source. Winners of national and regional competitions ultimately qualify for the annual world championships (WCS). These are serious events, and participants spend considerable time preparing for them. In 2019, participants from 24 countries and regions, all clad in elaborate handmade costumes, gathered in Nagoya, Japan, to compete. Contestants were judged by the quality of their costumes, the art direction, and their overall performance onstage. Team France proved itself to be a strong competitor, taking third place behind Australia and the USA in 2019.

For French BD fans not interested in competing, or even in cosplay, there are still conventions and festivals. Comic Con™ Paris is held annually and attracts fans of comics, cosplay, films, and TV series from the world of superheroes, science fiction, heroic fantasy, and the fantastic. Lasting three days, it is the largest such event in France and is akin to other Comic Con™ events held throughout the world.

More specifically France holds the Angoulême International Comics Festival, the third largest such festival in the world (after Lucca, Italy, and Tokyo, Japan) with more than two hundred thousand attendees each year. First held in 1974, the festival is a major showcase for exhibitors and presents awards for the best work of the year by established and newly discovered artists and authors, as well as a career prize given to a major figure in the world of BD. The festival has made Angoulême, in southwestern France, the comics capital of France.

Answer Key

1

Meeting People

EXERCISE 1.1

1. sont   2. es   3. êtes   4. est   5. sommes   6. est
7. suis   8. sont   9. suis   10. sont

EXERCISE 1.2

1. C'est un infirmier compétent.   2. C'est une dentiste compétente.
3. C'est un secrétaire de direction compétent.   4. Ce sont des coiffeurs compétents.   5. Ce sont des serveuses compétentes.   6. C'est une directrice de communication compétente.   7. C'est un serveur compétent.
8. C'est une coach de vie compétente.   9. C'est un entraîneur sportif compétent.   10. C'est une animatrice multimédia compétente.

EXERCISE 1.3

1. a   2. a   3. a   4. ont   5. a   6. avez   7. a   8. avez
9. avons   10. J'ai

EXERCISE 1.4

1. Nous   2. Je   3. Nous   4. Ils/Elles   5. Il/Elle/On
6. Tu   7. Ils/Elles   8. Vous   9. Nous   10. Ils/Elles

EXERCISE 1.5

1. She has a dictionary.   **2.** You are cold.   **3.** We are American.
4. You have a bicycle.   **5.** I am cold.   **6.** I am French.   **7.** They
are hungry.   **8.** You have time to visit the Orsay Museum.
9. He is Spanish.   **10.** We have a Persian cat.

EXERCISE 1.6

1. as   **2.** êtes   **3.** a   **4.** ont   **5.** J'ai   **6.** sommes
7. a   **8.** J'ai   **9.** a   **10.** êtes

EXERCISE 1.7

1. Vous avez un appartement à La Rochelle.   **2.** Nous sommes d'accord
avec Loïc.   **3.** Ils/Elles sont en vacances à Nice.   **4.** Mon ami Adrien
est très amusant.   **5.** J'ai quinze ans.   **6.** Anas a très faim. Il mange un
croissant.   **7.** Vous avez une voiture noire.   **8.** Nous avons de la chance
d'être à Paris.   **9.** Elle est américaine et il est espagnol.   **10.** J'ai mal à
la tête.

EXERCISE 1.8

1. une   **2.** vingt   **3.** deux   **4.** trente-trois   **5.** trois
6. une   **7.** onze   **8.** quatre; cinq   **9.** Quinze; trente-six
10. vingt-huit

Languages and Nationalities

EXERCISE 2.1

1. ma   **2.** sa   **3.** notre   **4.** Sa   **5.** Nos   **6.** son
7. Ta   **8.** ma   **9.** leur   **10.** Sa

EXERCISE 2.2

1. pensez 2. J'arrive 3. donnons 4. entres 5. cherche
6. portent 7. parlez 8. pose 9. J'aime 10. ferme

EXERCISE 2.3

1. nageons 2. mélangeons 3. corrigeons 4. changeons
5. partageons 6. rangeons 7. protégeons 8. échangeons
9. voyageons 10. téléchargeons

EXERCISE 2.4

1. commençons 2. remplaçons 3. finançons 4. effaçons
5. prononçons 6. avançons 7. dénonçons 8. plaçons
9. lançons 10. recommençons

EXERCISE 2.5

1. enlève 2. J'achète 3. emmenez 4. levons 5. congèlent
6. achetez 7. J'emmène 8. soulèvent 9. gèle 10. enlevons

EXERCISE 2.6

1. appelle 2. appelons 3. jetez 4. rejette 5. projette
6. projetons 7. épelles 8. épelons 9. jette 10. feuillette

EXERCISE 2.7

1. gère 2. déménage 3. j'achète 4. j'espère 5. nous
commençons 6. J'appelle 7. mangeons 8. j'emmène
9. effaçons 10. répète

EXERCISE 2.8

1. espagnol 2. danois 3. arabe/français 4. anglais/
swahili 5. mandarin 6. japonais 7. allemand
8. indonésien 9. turc 10. italien

EXERCISE 2.9

1. Parlez-vous mandarin?   2. Achètes-tu les croissants chez Poilâne?
3. Habite-t-elle dans un studio à Lille?   4. Mange-t-on dans le jardin ce soir?   5. Pose-t-il une question en anglais?   6. Apportes-tu les baguettes pour le pique-nique?   7. Prononce-t-elle le mot correctement
8. Chantent-elles la chanson d'Angèle   9. Dînent-ils avec Agathe demain?   10. Commencez-vous un nouveau projet?

EXERCISE 2.10

1. Est-ce qu'elle préfère jouer au golf?   2. Est-ce que vous cherchez une maison dans ce quartier?   3. Est-ce que nous invitons Julien?
4. Est-ce que tu étudies le japonais?   5. Est-ce qu'ils aiment étudier les langues étrangères?   6. Est-ce que nous voyageons à l'Île Maurice cet été?   7. Est-ce que tu m'appelles ce soir?   8. Est-ce qu'elle emmène Justin à l'opéra?   9. Est-ce que vous déménagez bientôt?
10. Est-ce que tu gardes les enfants ce week-end?

EXERCISE 2.11

1. Je ne chante pas une chanson de Renaud.   2. Elle ne s'appelle pas Christine.   3. Vous ne passez pas vos vacances au Danemark.
4. Ils ne déménagent pas dimanche.   5. Tu n'achètes pas le journal au kiosque.   6. Nous n'habitons pas dans un appartement.
7. Il n'apporte pas le dessert.   8. Vous ne regardez pas le match de tennis.   9. Je n'arrive pas en retard à la cérémonie.   10. Nous ne travaillons pas dans le centre-ville.

EXERCISE 2.12

1. Posez-vous les questions en anglais?   2. Je n'habite pas dans un studio. Alex et moi, nous partageons un appartement au centre-ville.   3. Nous voyageons en Argentine avec notre ami, Micaelo.   4. Elle emmène son amie Amélia au théâtre.
5. Où achetez-vous les journaux chinois?   6. Aime-t-elle parler français?

Oui, elle parle le français couramment.   **7.** Apportez-vous le dessert?
8. Babette et Clara travaillent pour une entreprise italienne.   **9.** Nous commençons un nouveau chapitre.   **10.** Nous ne prononçons pas ce mot correctement!

The Verb *Aller* and Speaking About Time

EXERCISE 3.1

1. vais   **2.** va   **3.** allons   **4.** vais   **5.** va   **6.** allons
7. va; va   **8.** vas   **9.** Allez   **10.** allez

EXERCISE 3.2

1. Allez-vous à Monoprix cet après-midi?   **2.** Vas-tu au pique-nique d'Alice sur l'Île aux Cygnes?   **3.** Va-t-il au Théâtre du Rond-Point?
4. Vont-elles à l'Institut de Touraine pour apprendre le français?
5. Va-t-il chez sa grand-mère samedi?   **6.** Allons-nous faire une promenade sur un bateau-mouche?   **7.** Va-t-elle au conservatoire de musique de Marseille?   **8.** Allez-vous en Louisiane cet été?   **9.** Vas-tu à Milan en avion?   **10.** Allez-vous au bureau ce matin?

EXERCISE 3.3

1. Je vais inviter mes voisins à prendre un verre.   **2.** Il va téléphoner à son coiffeur dans le Marais.   **3.** Elles vont étudier la musique baroque au conservatoire.   **4.** Elle va travailler en Asie.   **5.** Vous allez jouer au tennis avec Maude.   **6.** Tu vas prendre des photos pendant les vacances.   **7.** Guillaume va déjeuner avec sa patronne.   **8.** Je vais rester chez moi ce week-end.   **9.** Frédéric et Line vont préparer leurs valises.   **10.** Nous allons chanter une chanson pour son anniversaire.

EXERCISE 3.4

1. Nous n'allons pas visiter le château de Chambord aujourd'hui.   2. Je ne vais pas étudier le français dans une école à Perpignan.   3. Il ne va pas prendre une semaine de vacances en avril.   4. Elle ne va pas avoir le temps d'aller au supermarché ce soir.   5. Vous n'allez pas être en retard pour votre rendez-vous.   6. Ils ne vont pas être à l'aise en classe économique.   7. Elles ne vont pas parler anglais avec Justin.   8. Tu ne vas pas apporter le livre d'économie en classe.   9. Je ne vais pas mélanger le citron et le miel dans la tasse.   10. Ils ne vont pas financer l'organisation.

EXERCISE 3.5

1. Je vais acheter une carte Navigo pour le métro.   2. Ils vont jouer dans le parc André Citroën.   3. Julien va avoir faim après le tennis.   4. Nous allons commencer une nouvelle leçon aujourd'hui.   5. Je ne vais pas travailler ce week-end.   6. On va déjeuner à midi.   7. Ils vont organiser une réception pour soixante personnes.   8. Est-ce que vous allez poser des questions difficiles?   9. Pauline va avoir quinze ans demain.   10. Florent va téléphoner à sa mère après le dîner.

EXERCISE 3.6

1. b   2. a   3. e   4. d   5. c

EXERCISE 3.7

1. Marion va acheter une carte Navigo lundi.   2. En mars, Alexis va étudier le français à l'Université de Rennes.   3. En automne, les parents de Noémie vont aux Îles Canaries.   4. Est-ce que ton anniversaire est en septembre?   5. Je joue au tennis avec Matthias le mercredi après-midi.   6. Thomas et Léa vont rencontrer Justin mardi.   7. Est-ce que la réception est samedi ou dimanche?   8. Nous allons à la Fête de la Musique en juin.   9. L'hiver est très long en Sibérie.   10. Je vais voyager en Louisiane au printemps.

EXERCISE 3.8

1. aujourd'hui; demain   2. cet après-midi; demain après-midi
3. demain; le lendemain   4. cette semaine; la semaine prochaine
5. souvent; de temps en temps   6. dans une semaine; dans un mois
7. parfois/quelquefois; toujours   8. tous les jours/chaque jour; tous les
jours   9. souvent; jamais   10. parfois; rarement

EXERCISE 3.9

1. Nous allons en France la semaine prochaine.   2. Gérard va en
Australie dans un mois.   3. Aujourd'hui, c'est l'anniversaire de
Muriel.   4. Nous allons rencontrer François pour la première fois à Paris
la semaine prochaine.   5. —Allez-vous appeler les amis d'Alice demain?
—Non, dans deux ou trois jours.   6. Elle passe son examen la semaine
prochaine. La semaine suivante, elle va voyager en Inde.   7. Demain,
je vais porter mon costume bleu.   8. La veille de l'anniversaire de
Daniel, c'était mon anniversaire.   9. Allez-vous partir demain? Non, je
pars après-demain.   10. Il arrive à Strasbourg jeudi et il va à Prague le
lendemain.

EXERCISE 3.10

1. seize heures trente   2. dix-sept heures quarante-cinq   3. vingt
heures dix   4. vingt et une heures quarante   5. vingt-trois heures
cinquante

EXERCISE 3.11

1. J'entends   2. descend   3. rends   4. vend   5. attendez
6. prétend   7. répand   8. perdons   9. tend   10. répondons

EXERCISE 3.12

1. d   2. e   3. b   4. c   5. a

EXERCISE 3.13

1. comprenons **2.** entreprennent **3.** apprenez **4.** prends
5. surprend **6.** comprennent **7.** surprennent **8.** comprend
9. J'apprends **10.** entreprend

EXERCISE 3.14

1. On attend la visite de Janine. **2.** Est-ce que vous vendez des
magazines français? **3.** Pourquoi est-ce que tu apprends le japonais?
4. Ils/Elles prennent rarement le métro pour aller au centre-ville. **5.** Je
rends le livre à la bibliothèque demain matin! Je le promets! **6.** Nous
répondons au professeur en français. **7.** Je ne comprends pas pourquoi
ils sont toujours en retard. **8.** Pierre ne perd jamais rien dans le train.
9. Elle prétend être mon amie. **10.** Nous descendons les Champs-Élysées.

Nouns and Their Genders

EXERCISE 4.1

1. Nous n'avons pas de maison en France. **2.** Elle n'aime pas le silence
à la campagne. **3.** Il n'a pas de villa sur la Côte d'Azur. **4.** Nous
n'achetons pas de croissants. **5.** Je n'ai pas de compte en banque
en France. **6.** Vous ne connaissez pas la route pour aller à
Cahors. **7.** Nous n'avons pas de chien. **8.** Je n'ai pas d'amis à
Paris. **9.** Il ne lit pas le journal chaque matin. **10.** Je n'achète pas de
journaux en vacances.

EXERCISE 4.2

1. la **2.** la **3.** le **4.** la **5.** le **6.** le **7.** le **8.** la
9. la **10.** le **11.** le **12.** le **13.** le **14.** le **15.** la
16. la **17.** la **18.** le **19.** le **20.** la

EXERCISE 4.3

1. un   2. une   3. un   4. une   5. une   6. un
7. une   8. une   9. un   10. un   11. une   12. un
13. un   14. une   15. un   16. une   17. un   18. un
19. une   20. un

EXERCISE 4.4

1. e; à   2. d; au   3. b; en   4. a; en   5. c; aux

EXERCISE 4.5

1. le; au   2. le; au   3. la; en   4. le; au   5. l'; en
6. la; en   7. le; au   8. la; en   9. le; au   10. l'; en

EXERCISE 4.6

1. Jeanne va en Amazonie en février.   2. Carole va à Florence en mai.
3. Marc et Claude vont au Rwanda au printemps.   4. Victor et moi, nous allons au Pérou en septembre.   5. Henri va en Roumanie en été.
6. Sylvain va au Chili en automne.   7. Nathalie va en Namibie en janvier.
8. Odile va en Tunisie en hiver.   9. Michel va au Laos en mars.
10. Carl va aux Pays-Bas en juin.

EXERCISE 4.7

1. en   2. en   3. au   4. en   5. au   6. en
7. en   8. en   9. en   10. en

EXERCISE 4.8

1. Chaque année, nous randonnons au Canada   2. Est-ce qu'il habite au Brésil ou en Argentine?   3. Elle est originaire d'Italie./Elle est d'origine italienne.   4. Est-ce que vous allez visiter le Musée Picasso?
5. Le lycée de Marc est en Normandie.

EXERCISE 4.9

Le Pont Mirabeau

Sous le pont Mirabeau coule la Seine
Et nos amours
Faut-il qu'il m'en souvienne
La joie venait toujours après la peine

Vienne la nuit sonne l'heure
Les jours s'en vont je demeure

Les mains dans **les** mains restons face à face
Tandis que sous
Le pont de nos bras passe
Des éternels regards l'onde si lasse

Vienne **la** nuit sonne l'heure
Les jours s'en vont je demeure

L'amour s'en va comme cette eau courante
L'amour s'en va
Comme **la** vie est lente
Et comme **l'**Espérance est violente

Vienne **la** nuit sonne l'heure
Les jours s'en vont je demeure

Passent **les** jours et passent **les** semaines
Ni temps passé
Ni **les** amours reviennent
Sous **le** pont Mirabeau coule **la** Seine

Vienne **la** nuit sonne **l'**heure
Les jours s'en vont je demeure

—Guillaume Apollinaire

5

Asking Questions and Talking About the Immediate Past

EXERCISE 5.1

1. Combien coûte un yaourt glacé?   2. Où est la patinoire de Nantes?
3. Que faites-vous samedi?   4. Comment allez-vous?   5. Pourquoi
voulez-vous patiner dans le noir?   6. À quelle heure arrive-t-elle à
Nantes?   7. À quelle heure vont-ils au cinéma?   8. Qui joue de la
guitare?   9. Pourquoi écoutez-vous Benoît?   10. Combien coûtent
les accessoires?

EXERCISE 5.2

1. choisit   2. J'agis   3. bâtissent   4. finissons
5. agrandit   6. grandissent   7. choisissez   8. applaudissons
9. réfléchis   10. réussissent

EXERCISE 5.3

1. b   2. d   3. e   4. a   5. c

EXERCISE 5.4

1. sortons   2. sers   3. sent   4. dormons   5. partez
6. mentent   7. cours   8. fuient   9. servent   10. pars.

EXERCISE 5.5

1. e   2. d   3. a   4. c   5. b

EXERCISE 5.6

1. découvre   2. offres   3. souffrent   4. ouvre
5. accueillent   6. bous   7. recueille   8. découvre
9. cueillez   10. couvrent

EXERCISE 5.7

1. d   **2.** a   **3.** c   **4.** e   **5.** b

EXERCISE 5.8

1. cueillons   **2.** J'ouvre   **3.** sortez   **4.** démolissent
5. grossissons   **6.** vieillit   **7.** finissent   **8.** mentent
9. servez   **10.** cours

EXERCISE 5.9

1. tenons   **2.** reviens   **3.** viennent   **4.** tient   **5.** tiennent
6. proviennent   **7.** tiens   **8.** tient   **9.** viens   **10.** tient

EXERCISE 5.10

1. Ils viennent de commencer un nouveau livre.   **2.** Je viens de faire un jogging dans le bois de Boulogne.   **3.** Elle vient de prononcer un discours. **4.** Je viens d'écouter le nouvel album de Mika.   **5.** Vous venez de révéler la vérité.   **6.** Nous venons de remplacer les meubles de son bureau. **7.** Il vient de placer un vase de fleurs sur la table.   **8.** Ils viennent de découvrir un morceau de météorite.   **9.** Nous venons d'acheter un sofa bleu nuit.   **10.** Elle vient de chanter une chanson.

EXERCISE 5.11

1. Il fait chaud. Je viens d'ouvrir la fenêtre.   **2.** Nous venons de cueillir des framboises.   **3.** Vous venez de téléphoner à Benoît.   **4.** Je viens de lire un article dans *Le Monde*.   **5.** Ils viennent de choisir un restaurant pour le mariage.   **6.** Cécile vient d'acheter une carte Navigo.   **7.** Elle vient de finir de remplir le formulaire.   **8.** Je viens de finir mon essai. **9.** Il vient de nous servir une délicieuse pizza.   **10.** Ils viennent de célébrer l'anniversaire de Quentin.

EXERCISE 5.12

1. Je ne vais pas au cinéma ce week-end.   2. Elle ne parle pas espagnol.
3. Il ne dort pas huit heures par nuit.   4. Vous ne jouez pas de la guitare.
5. Ils ne vont pas à la patinoire.   6. Tu ne cherches pas la rue des
Carmes.   7. Nous n'écoutons pas le nouvel album.   8. Elle n'aime pas
le froid.   9. Nous ne nageons pas dans la mer.   10. Nous ne restons
pas à la maison le samedi soir.

EXERCISE 5.13

1. Il ne connaît personne à Paris.   2. Ils ne font rien pour aider Jean-
Claude.   3. Je ne mange jamais de frites.   4. Tu ne joues plus au ping-
pong avec tes copains.   5. Ils ne vendent ni glace ni yaourt glacé.

EXERCISE 5.14

1. ce   2. ces   3. cette   4. Ce   5. cet   6. cet
7. cet   8. cet   9. ces   10. ces

EXERCISE 5.15

1. quatre-vingt-huit   2. soixante-seize   3. cent   4. cent un
5. deux cent quarante-six   6. quatre-vingts   7. mille   8. quatre-
vingt-onze   9. quatre-vingt-dix-neuf   10. deux mille dix

The Verb *Faire* and Using Prepositions

EXERCISE 6.1

1. Il y a une patinoire dans notre ville.   2. Y a-t-il du savon dans la
cuisine?   3. Il y a de l'eau sur la table.   4. Il n'y a pas de billets pour ce
soir.   5. Il y a des légumes dans le frigo.

EXERCISE 6.2

1. L'ouragan Katrina.   2. Un tremblement de terre.   3. Un tsunami et un séisme.   4. Un grand incendie.   5. L'éruption volcanique de la montagne Pelée.

EXERCISE 6.3

1. faisons   2. fait   3. Faites   4. font   5. font   6. fais
7. fais   8. fait   9. font   10. fais

EXERCISE 6.4

1. e   2. c   3. d   4. a   5. b

EXERCISE 6.5

1. Ils font une randonnée dans les Alpes.   2. Je fais du vélo en Martinique.   3. Il fait semblant de ne pas me voir.   4. Elle fait partie d'une association écologique.   5. Le réchauffement climatique me fait peur.   6. Quel temps fait-il ce matin?   7. Il fait froid et il y a de la brume.   8. Ils font des économies pour aller en France l'année prochaine.
9. Vous faites de l'exercice tous les jours.   10. Le nouvel album d'Aloïse Sauvage fait un tabac.

EXERCISE 6.6

1. Il fait réparer la moto par le mécanicien.   2. Je fais repeindre mon appartement par mon frère.   3. Nous faisons faire un gâteau par le pâtissier.   4. Vous faites préparer le dossier par votre collègue.
5. Est-ce que tu fais laver ta voiture par ton neveu?   6. Ils font envoyer les paquets par leur stagiaire.   7. Elle fait taper le rapport par son assistant.   8. Thomas fait faire le ménage par un étudiant.   9. Je fais faire mes robes par un couturier.   10. Carole se fait couper les cheveux par le coiffeur.

EXERCISE 6.7

1. à   2. de   3. à   4. de   5. à   6. à   7. de
8. à   9. à; à   10. de

EXERCISE 6.8

1. J'ai besoin d'arroser le jardin.   2. Noha m'aide à nettoyer la cuisine.
3. Il se souvient de la date de l'ouragan.   4. Ils ont peur d'une autre marée noire.   5. Je m'intéresse à cette série.   6. Avez-vous envie de randonner en Bretagne?   7. Nous nous attendons à un changement majeur dans notre entreprise.   8. J'oublie souvent d'acheter un yaourt glacé pour Benoît.   9. Elle m'encourage à faire des progrès en français.   10. Il réussit toujours à arroser son jardin en une heure.

EXERCISE 6.9

1. à; du   2. au; au   3. de   4. À; à   5. du   6. à
7. De   8. de   9. par; par   10. de; du

EXERCISE 6.10

1. Je n'aime pas faire du vélo quand il pleut.   2. Je sais préparer des plats indiens.   3. Il faut signer cette pétition.   4. Comptez-vous investir au Rwanda?   5. Je n'ose pas vous promettre la lune.   6. Ils peuvent aller à Bruxelles par le train.   7. Nous espérons faire leur connaissance bientôt.   8. Je dois apprendre à faire du savon solide.   9. Elle prétend être une princesse.   10. La génération Z va faire bouger les gens.

Pronominal Verbs

EXERCISE 7.1

1. Nous nous lavons   2. Il se coupe   3. Je me baigne
4. Tu te peignes   5. Vous vous couchez   6. Nous nous baladons
7. Elles se préparent   8. Je me maquille   9. On s'amuse
10. Ils se brossent

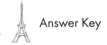

EXERCISE 7.2

1. Jérémie ne se promène pas dans le parc avec son chien. 2. Caroline ne se coupe pas les cheveux elle-même. 3. Je ne me détends pas en regardant des films d'horreur. 4. Nous ne nous asseyons pas dans l'herbe. 5. Ils ne s'amusent pas à Euro Disney. 6. Vous ne vous baladez pas au bord de la mer. 7. Il ne s'habille pas formellement pour la réunion. 8. Tu ne te réveilles pas à cinq heures le matin. 9. Amanda ne se baigne pas dans l'océan Atlantique. 10. Je ne m'entraîne pas pour le match à Roland-Garros.

EXERCISE 7.3

1. Se brosse-t-elle les dents après le petit déjeuner? 2. Te reposes-tu avant l'examen? 3. Vous brossez-vous les cheveux avec un peigne? 4. Se couche-t-il toujours à minuit? 5. Vous amusez-vous dans les arcades de jeux? 6. Nous chargeons-nous encore de tous les détails? 7. Se douche-t-il avant de se coucher? 8. Te maquilles-tu pour jouer Aïda? 9. Vous occupez-vous de ce communiqué de presse? 10. Se prépare-t-elle pour l'entretien?

EXERCISE 7.4

1. se voient 2. nous disputons 3. s'aiment 4. se disent 5. vous détestez 6. se quittent 7. se croisent 8. nous rencontrons 9. se connaissent 10. s'embrassent

EXERCISE 7.5

1. d 2. b 3. a 4. c 5. e

EXERCISE 7.6

1. c 2. d 3. b 4. a 5. e

EXERCISE 7.7

1. Je ne me moque jamais de mes amis. 2. Margaux s'habille pour une cérémonie. 3. Se baigner dans une fontaine publique; ça ne se fait pas. 4. Qui s'occupe des enfants aujourd'hui? 5. Nous nous promenons/ nous nous baladons sur les Champs-Élysées. 6. Ils/Elles se téléphonent le dimanche. 7. Se marient-ils en juin? 8. Quentin se fie à son intuition. 9. Comment ça se dit en japonais? 10. Te rends-tu compte de l'importance de cette décision?

EXERCISE 7.8

1. C'est moi qui m'occupe du verger. 2. Ce sont eux qui portent des vêtements en fibres végétales. 3. C'est toi qui dessines les feuilles de l'abricotier. 4. C'est lui qui anime l'atelier sur l'origine des plantes. 5. C'est vous qui expliquez la germination des graines. 6. C'est elle qui nous apprend à reconnaître les arbres. 7. C'est toi qui vas nous informer sur la protection des espèces végétales. 8. C'est elle qui a gagné le concours de « À Fleur de Ville » de Tours. 9. C'est toi qui vas partager tes expériences avec nous. 10. Ce sont eux qui vont nous faire découvrir les plantes indispensables aux animaux et aux humains.

EXERCISE 7.9

1. —Qui est le jardinier qui travaille pour eux? —Je ne sais pas. 2. Lui, il n'a pas la main verte. 3. Marc est plus grand que moi. 4. Elle, elle est toujours en retard. 5. Milo n'aime pas partager ses outils avec nous. 6. Toi et ton ami(e), vous avez beaucoup de chance. 7. Je vais dessiner cet arbre pour toi. 8. —Tu aimes les roses rouges.— Moi aussi. 9. Iza cueille toujours des fleurs pour nous. 10. —Vous n'aimez pas les lentilles.—Moi non plus.

Talking About the Past

EXERCISE 8.1

1. a passé   2. avons nettoyé   3. a repassé   4. avez rangé
5. as débarrassé   6. a vidé   7. J'ai ciré   8. a demandé
9. avons arrosé   10. ont vérifié

EXERCISE 8.2

1. ont investi   2. avons attendu   3. a choisi   4. a ralenti
5. avez réussi   6. avons applaudi   7. J'ai perdu   8. as agrandi
9. J'ai senti   10. ont fait

EXERCISE 8.3

1. Est-ce que tu as fait la cuisine hier soir?   2. Il a repassé sa chemise
et ciré ses chaussures.   3. Nous avons fait la lessive dimanche matin.
4. Qui est-ce qui a vidé le lave-vaisselle?   5. Il a nettoyé le réfrigérateur.
6. J'ai trié mes vêtements d'été.   7. Nous n'avons pas fait la vaisselle
hier soir.   8. Tu n'as pas essuyé toutes les tables.   9. Est-ce que tu as
passé l'aspirateur dans la chambre?   10. Elle a mis la table et allumé les
bougies.

EXERCISE 8.4

1. a vu; a paniqué   2. avons suivi   3. as lu   4. a mis
5. a fallu   6. a reçu   7. avons vécu   8. avez acquis
9. a repeint   10. ai offert

EXERCISE 8.5

1. b   2. e   3. d   4. a   5. c

EXERCISE 8.6

1. êtes-vous née   **2.** est tombé   **3.** suis parti(e)   **4.** êtes rentrés
5. sont restées   **6.** est descendu   **7.** est devenue   **8.** est montée
9. est mort   **10.** sommes allé(e)s

EXERCISE 8.7

1. L'enfant timide a peu parlé.   **2.** Nous avons bien dormi.
3. Elle a souvent téléphoné à sa collègue Patrice.   **4.** Vous n'avez pas assez
mangé.   **5.** Ils ont trop dépensé dans le magasin d'électronique.   **6.** Il
a bien écrit le scénario.   **7.** Je me suis mal exprimé(e).
8. Il a toujours menti.   **9.** Nous avons mal vécu cette expérience.
10. Je suis souvent allé(e) au Bénin.

EXERCISE 8.8

1. Il est descendu du train et il a vu ses parents sur le quai.   **2.** J'ai
marché pendant une heure puis j'ai bu deux verres d'eau.   **3.** René, est-
ce que tu es sorti ce week-end?   **4.** Elle est allée au studio d'animation.
5. Nous avons pris le train de Paris à Lille.   **6.** Marie a reçu un nouvel
ordinateur.   **7.** Ils ont dépensé beaucoup d'argent pendant leurs vacances.
8. Sophie, à quelle heure est-ce que tu es rentrée hier soir?   **9.** J'ai déjà
fait la vaisselle!   **10.** Il a attendu une heure puis il est parti.

EXERCISE 8.9

1. s'est promenée   **2.** ne se sont pas écrit   **3.** s'est fait faire
4. se sont rencontrées   **5.** s'est assise   **6.** ne s'est pas souvenu
7. se sont embrassés   **8.** ne se sont pas habituées   **9.** se sont parlé
10. s'est offert

EXERCISE 8.10

1. a retourné   **2.** a passé   **3.** est montée   **4.** est retournée
5. sommes passés   **6.** as rentré   **7.** est sorti   **8.** est monté
9. J'ai descendu   **10.** a sorti

EXERCISE 8.11

1. e   **2.** c   **3.** a   **4.** b   **5.** d

EXERCISE 8.12

1. Nous sommes allés chez Henri vendredi soir.   **2.** Jonathan s'est souvenu de son rendez-vous avec M.Rufin.   **3.** Elle ne s'est pas habituée à son nouvel emploi à Paris.   **4.** As-tu rentré ton vélo/ta bicyclette? **5.** Ils ont fait construire une maison en Sicile.   **6.** Yves ne s'est pas reposé avant son examen.   **7.** Ils se sont téléphoné presque tous les jours. **8.** Benoît et Alexandra, où vous êtes-vous rencontrés?   **9.** Elle est passée par Lyon pour aller à Menton.   **10.** Pourquoi n'as-tu pas sorti le chien ce matin?

EXERCISE 8.13

1. c   **12.** a   **3.** d   **4.** e   **5.** b

EXERCISE 8.14

1. Depuis quand   **2.** Depuis combien de temps   **3.** Depuis quand **4.** Depuis quand   **5.** Depuis combien de temps   **6.** Depuis combien de temps   **7.** Depuis quand   **8.** Depuis combien de temps **9.** Depuis combien de temps   **10.** Depuis quand

EXERCISE 8.15

1. Cela fait deux heures qu'il pleut sans cesse.   **2.** Cela fait un mois que j'ai cette chaise ergonomique.   **3.** Cela fait plusieurs années qu'ils sont autonomes.   **4.** Cela fait une heure que la repasseuse repasse le linge. **5.** Cela fait des années qu'elle écrit ses mémoires.   **6.** Cela fait une heure et demie que Clara et Marie se parlent.   **7.** Cela fait des heures que nous conduisons sur l'A7.   **8.** Cela fait un certain temps qu'on boit du thé vert. **9.** Cela fait trois ans que vous suivez un cours en ligne.   **10.** Cela fait un an qu'il fait du judo.

EXERCISE 8.16

1. Nous connaissons Marie depuis longtemps. **2.** Il lit ce livre de science-fiction depuis deux heures. **3.** Vous cherchez un appartement depuis des mois. **4.** Elle dessine depuis une demi-heure. **5.** Ils portent des vêtements vintage depuis les années 1980. **6.** Nous randonnons dans la forêt depuis des heures. **7.** Il est amoureux de Sara depuis trois ans. **8.** Elle organise ces fêtes depuis des années. **9.** Il est le petit ami de Claire depuis un mois. **10.** Tu conduis malgré la tempête de neige depuis une heure.

EXERCISE 8.17

1. Depuis quelle année travaillez-vous pour cette entreprise? **2.** Ils habitent dans le 15e arrondissement depuis toujours. **3.** Je ne suis pas allé(e) à Paris depuis trois ans. **4.** Depuis combien de temps habitez-vous dans cet appartement? **5.** Nous n'avons pas vu nos parents depuis décembre. **6.** Depuis combien de temps connaissez-vous Roland? **7.** Je vous attends depuis une demi-heure! **8.** Depuis quand mangez-vous du quinoa? **9.** Elle joue Phèdre depuis deux mois. **10.** J'étudie le mandarin depuis deux ans.

To Know and How to Use Object Pronouns

EXERCISE 9.1

1. connais **2.** ne sais pas **3.** sait **4.** connaissez
5. sait **6.** ne connaît pas **7.** connaissons **8.** connais
9. savez **10.** savent

EXERCISE 9.2

1. connaît   **2.** savez   **3.** sait   **4.** connaît   **5.** connais
6. connaissent   **7.** sais   **8.** savons   **9.** Connaissez-vous
10. sais

EXERCISE 9.3

1. Est-ce que tu connais Arthur?   **2.** Claire et Gaspard savent parler japonais.   **3.** Simon sait toutes les chansons de Dalida par cœur.
4. Ils/Elles ne savent pas si ce village est en Provence.   **5.** Comment est-ce que tu connais la sœur de Liam?   **6.** Le nouveau film de Louis-Julien Petit connaît un grand succès.   **7.** Nous savons où se trouve le meilleur restaurant chinois dans le 13e arrondissement.   **8.** Je ne sais pas si Oscar sait nager.   **9.** Nous connaissons un logiciel qui peut traduire des documents en grec ancien.   **10.** Est-ce que vous connaissez le poème de Baudelaire qui s'appelle *L'invitation au voyage*?

EXERCISE 9.4

1. Les élèves la comprennent.   **2.** Le suivez-vous?   **3.** Nolan ne la porte pas.   **4.** Il le regarde à la télé.   **5.** Le professeur les apporte pour la présentation.   **6.** Le prenez-vous à la gare Montparnasse ou à la gare d'Austerlitz?   **7.** La famille Thominet ne l'invite pas à leur soirée.
8. Lola et Isabelle les racontent.   **9.** Nous ne les aimons pas.   **10.** Est-ce que tu l'appelles Angélique ou Angie?

EXERCISE 9.5

1. Je te crois.   **2.** Est-ce qu'on l'invite?   **3.** Il le prend avec du sucre.
4. Elle me remercie.   **5.** Elles ne nous comprennent pas.   **6.** Nous les respectons.   **7.** Il ne les connaît pas.   **8.** Est-ce que vous me voyez?
9. Ils/Elles m'appellent tous les jours.   **10.** Pourquoi est-ce que tu le fais?

EXERCISE 9.6

1. Il lui écrit.   2. Le guide leur montre les sculptures de Nikki de Saint Phalle.   3. Cette planche de surf lui appartient.   4. L'employée leur explique comment remplir les formulaires.   5. Sylvain lui raconte l'histoire de « Réparer les vivants ».   6. Pourquoi est-ce que tu lui donnes ton argent de poche?   7. Nous leur faisons souvent des cadeaux.   8. Xavier lui téléphone.   9. Hugo lui rend le roman de Maylis de Kerangal.   10. Je ne sais pas comment lui répondre. C'est trop compliqué!

EXERCISE 9.7

1. Clara s'en occupe.   2. Est-ce que tu en as envie?   3. Son copain s'y intéresse.   4. Nous y pensons.   5. Noémie ne s'en souvient pas.   6. Pierre y renonce.   7. Elles ne s'y habituent pas.   8. Y pensez-vous?   9. J'en ai peur.   10. Delphine y tient.

EXERCISE 9.8

1. Clément la lui a prêté**e**.   2. Je le lui ai emprunté.   3. Le lui avez-vous recommandé?   4. Sophia me l'a envoyé**e**.   5. Ils te l'ont promis**e**.   6. Vous les avez encore fait**es**.   7. Alexandra le leur a vendu.   8. Je le leur ai donné.   9. Pourquoi est-ce que Adam ne nous les a pas encore servi**s**?   10. On les a mis**es** dans le lave-vaisselle.

EXERCISE 9.9

1. Agathe sait cette chanson française par cœur.   2. En a-t-il peur?   3. Lise ne nous a pas remercié(e)s.   4. On s'en est débarrassé.   5. Je ne sais pas si tu te souviens de moi.   6. Romane pense à lui.   7. Les plongeurs n'en ont pas besoin.   8. Connaissez-vous les voisins d'Alicia?   9. Je ne m'y suis jamais habitué(e).   10. Sais-tu qui me les a envoyé(e)s?

10
Discussing the Future and Making Plans

EXERCISE 10.1

1. suivrai   2. chercherons   3. écouteront   4. resteras
5. ne perdra pas   6. choisira   7. sortirez   8. dînera
9. ne travaillerai pas   10. remplacera

EXERCICE 10.2

1. pleuvra   2. viendrai   3. s'apercevra   4. irons
5. seras   6. auront   7. Ferez   8. recevra   9. faudra
10. ne vaudra rien

EXERCICE 10.3

1. préviendrai; saurai   2. m'enverras; pourras   3. prendrons; aurons
4. reviendra; commencera   5. fera; dînerons
6. j'arriverai; téléphonerai   7. J'achèterai; se mariera   8. devra; travaillera   9. feras; seras   10. seront; joueront

EXERCICE 10.4

1. j'aurai appris   2. aura déménagé   3. auras appris   4. auront présenté   5. aurons visité   6. aurez lu   7. auras essuyé
8. sera arrivé   9. aura changé   10. auront écrit

EXERCICE 10.5

1. Elle vous téléphonera dès qu'elle sera prête.   2. J'espère qu'il ne pleuvra pas demain.   3. D'ici la fin de la semaine, ils auront résolu le problème.
4. Tant qu'il y aura des hommes, il y aura des guerres.   5. D'ici la fin du mois, le directeur aura signé le contrat de Xavier.   6. Est-ce que tu te

souviendras de l'anniversaire de ta sœur?   **7.** Je suis sûr que tu ne mourras pas de faim en France.   **8.** Dès que j'aurai fini de préparer le dîner, je mettrai la table.   **9.** Nous ne saurons jamais qui a pris le sac à dos de Mathieu.   **10.** Tant qu'on s'aimera, on sera heureux.

EXERCISE 10.6

1. peux   **2.** ne peux pas   **3.** voulons   **4.** veux   **5.** peuvent
6. ne veux pas   **7.** veut   **8.** pouvez   **9.** voulons   **10.** Puis

EXERCISE 10.7

1. dois   **2.** devez   **3.** dois   **4.** doit   **5.** ne doit pas
6. doivent   **7.** devons   **8.** devez   **9.** dois   **10.** ne doit pas

EXERCISE 10.8

1. Je ne peux pas me souvenir du mot de passe.   **2.** Nous voulons passer nos vacances au Mexique.   **3.** Elle nous doit une excuse.   **4.** Pouvez-vous me déposer au cinéma?   **5.** Ils veulent prendre leur temps pour réfléchir.   **6.** Vous devez toujours dire la vérité.   **7.** Il doit pleuvoir ce week-end.   **8.** Puis-je vous aider à choisir une robe pour le mariage? **9.** Devons-nous apprendre ces verbes par cœur?   **10.** Ils veulent faire la connaissance du nouveau professeur d'histoire.

EXERCISE 10.9

1. e   **2.** b   **3.** c   **4.** a   **5.** d

EXERCISE 10.10

1. Je vous téléphonerai/appellerai dans trois jours.   **2.** Il a mis son sac à dos sous le siège.   **3.** Voulez-vous vous asseoir à côté de nous? **4.** Devez-vous aller à la banque aujourd'hui?   **5.** Entre nous, je pense que Julien aime beaucoup ma cousine Claire.   **6.** Puis-je garer ma voiture devant votre maison?   **7.** Nous irons les accueillir à leur arrivée

à La Havane.   **8.** Elle peut écrire un discours en moins de 24 heures.
9. Vous êtes avec nous ou contre nous.   **10.** Il a dû partir sans eux.

11

In Search of Lost Time... *with French Past Tenses*

EXERCISE 11.1

1. faisait   **2.** marchaient   **3.** avaient   **4.** suivions   **5.** s'appelait
6. était   **7.** réfléchissiez   **8.** avait   **9.** partagions   **10.** s'habillait

EXERCISE 11.2

1. jouais   **2.** faisait   **3.** paraissait   **4.** allais   **5.** J'étais;
craignais   **6.** déménageait   **7.** remplaçait   **8.** avions
9. partageaient   **10.** peignait   **11.** buviez   **12.** se voyaient
13. voyageais   **14.** n'effaçait jamais   **15.** faisait   **16.** s'habillaient
17. savaient   **18.** changeait   **19.** choisissais   **20.** exigeait

EXERCISE 11.3

1. faisais; est tombé   **2.** marchaient; ont vu   **3.** venait; l'a appelée
4. lisais; a frappé   **5.** conduisait; a éclaté   **6.** venait; a trouvé
7. nous reposions; a sonné   **8.** parlait; a disparu   **9.** montraient; s'est
mise   **10.** regardais; j'ai reconnu

EXERCISE 11.4

1. Je pensais à toi quand tu es entré dans la pièce.   **2.** Est-ce que tu
portais un uniforme à l'école?   **3.** Ils regardaient un film quand le chat
a sauté sur la table.   **4.** Nous jouions au basketball quand nous étions au
lycée.   **5.** Aisha se promenait le long de la Seine quand elle a remarqué

un restaurant sur une péniche. **6.** Quand ma tante faisait la cuisine, elle utilisait beaucoup d'épices. **7.** Diego écrivait une lettre à sa grand-mère quand elle a appelé. **8.** Il n'y avait pas un nuage dans le ciel quand je suis arrivé(e) à la bibliothèque. **9.** Je faisais des recherches à la bibliothèque quand j'ai trouvé l'article dont j'avais besoin. **10.** Est-ce que tu as pris une photo de l'article quand tu l'as trouvé.

EXERCISE 11.5

1. ne savais pas; j'ai eu   **2.** j'ai pensé; j'étais   **3.** J'avais; me suis fiancé(e)   **4.** a soudain semblé   **5.** n'espérait pas; est apparue

EXERCISE 11.6

1. Je tondais la pelouse tandis que mon neveu lisait un roman policier.
2. Elle écoutait de la musique pendant qu'elle se promenait avec son chien.
3. Il voulait manger des pâtes alors que nous voulions partager une pizza.
4. Il riait aux éclats tandis que leur collègue pleurait à chaudes larmes. Pas gentil!   **5.** Elle se plaisait sur cette île isolée au Japon alors qu'elle ne parlait pas un mot de japonais.

EXERCISE 11.7

1. avait espéré   **2.** avions établi   **3.** m'étais promené(e)   **4.** avaient effectué   **5.** aviez mis   **6.** s'était souvenue   **7.** n'avait pas réussi **8.** J'avais interrogé   **9.** ne s'étaient jamais rencontrées   **10.** avait recueilli

EXERCISE 11.8

1. c   **2.** e   **3.** d   **4.** a   **5.** b

EXERCISE 11.9

1. Si on prenait une photo sur la plage?   **2.** Si on commandait une pizza?   **3.** Si seulement tu savais!   **4.** Si on numérisait toutes ces photos?   **5.** Si on choisissait un film?   **6.** Si seulement il était arrivé à l'heure!   **7.** Si on achetait une douzaine de roses?   **8.** Si seulement tu savais faire une tarte aux pommes!   **9.** Si on appelait Julie?   **10.** Si seulement tu avais gardé le chapeau de Papy!

EXERCISE 11.10

1. se souvint   **2.** ravivèrent   **3.** perdit; recouvrit   **4.** effacèrent   **5.** feuilleta; reconnut   **6.** j'éprouvai   **7.** évoqua   **8.** conservèrent   **9.** rendirent   **10.** vinrent

EXERCISE 11.11

Le passé simple: retrouvâmes; mena; céda; parvînmes; arrêtèrent

L'imparfait: s'éployait; défendait; pâturaient; cherchaient; distinguait; suivions; sentions; pouvait; étaient

EXERCISE 11.12

1. J'ai raté/manqué le dernier métro.   **2.** Cette soupe manque de sel.   **3.** Mon amie Paula me manque.   **4.** Je lui manque.   **5.** Il leur manque trois documents.   **6.** Son cours de ballet lui manque.   **7.** Nous avons manqué à notre devoir.   **8.** Le froid me manquait, mais je m'y suis habitué.   **9.** Il te manque de la farine pour faire le gâteau.   **10.** Je ne crois pas que mes collègues me manqueront.

Thinking About the World in the Conditional Mood

EXERCISE 12.1

1. dirais   **2.** voyagerait   **3.** irions   **4.** prendrais   **5.** sauraient   **6.** aurais   **7.** répondraient   **8.** devrions   **9.** commanderait   **10.** accepteriez

EXERCISE 12.2

1. dînerais; étais   2. chanterais; demandais   3. voyagerions; avions
4. s'inscrirait; voulait   5. serait; venais   6. irions; pouvions
7. lancerait; avait   8. J'emporterais; faisais   9. numériserait; était
10. organiseriez; pouviez

EXERCISE 12.3

1. Nous irions en France si nous avions le temps.   2. Elle achèterait une
bicyclette si elle habitait/vivait en Normandie.   3. Pourriez-vous me dire
à quelle heure commence le cours ?   4. Je ferais la cuisine ce soir si vous
apportiez du fromage.   5. Il serait heureux si le chef lui proposait un
stage.   6. Ils visiteraient l'école si vous pouviez la leur montrer.
7. Nous irions à la plage s'il y avait moins de monde.   8. Vous feriez
mieux d'étudier ce soir !   9. Nous ferions mieux d'écouter les conseils
de Maya.   10. Il jouerait de la guitare si sa sœur lui en achetait une.
11. Je lancerais une app si vous m'aidiez.   12. Je m'en occuperais au cas
où il y aurait un problème.   13. Ça vous dirait d'aller au musée Picasso ?
14. Il vaudrait mieux ne pas révéler son secret.   15. Nous ferions une
promenade s'il ne pleuvait pas.

EXERCISE 12.4

1. b   2. d   3. e   4. a   5. c

EXERCISE 12.5

1. aurait acheté; avait trouvé   2. auraient lancé; avaient réuni
3. auriez regardé; étiez arrivé(e)(s)   4. auraient décroché; avaient étudié
5. aurais travaillé; avais pu   6. aurait fait; avions été   7. J'aurais
changé; avais trouvé   8. se serait inscrite; avait été   9. seriez
arrivé(e)(s); n'y avait pas eu   10. J'aurais acheté; l'avais perdu

EXERCISE 12.6

1. Il aurait vendu son restaurant s'il avait perdu une étoile.
2. Tu aurais fait un film sur le chef s'il t'avait donné la permission.
3. Elle serait allée en vacances si elle avait économisé assez d'argent.
4. Ils auraient acheté une maison en Bretagne si leur frère avait pu les aider.
5. Je me serais inscrit(e) au cours de japonais si tu t'étais inscrit(e) avec moi.
6. Julie serait allée au concert avec eux si elle avait fini son projet à temps.
7. Il aurait envoyé le formulaire s'il avait été sûr d'être admis.
8. Je t'aurais envoyé des fleurs si j'avais su que c'était ton anniversaire.
9. Elle aurait acheté ta voiture si tu avais demandé un prix raisonnable.
10. Je n'aurais pas fait tant de fautes si j'avais révisé le conditionnel.

EXERCISE 12.7

1. aurait créé   2. aurait envoyé   3. aurait improvisé
4. aurait proposé   5. seraient revenus   6. aurait démissionné
7. aurait enregistré   8. aurait détruit   9. aurait signé
10. aurait retrouvé

EXERCISE 12.8

1. Le ministre de l'Éducation aurait promis de grands changements.
2. Le/la détective privé(e) aurait retrouvé le chat du palais volé par un voisin.   3. Le/la photographe aurait retouché la photo de Lily-Rose, la modèle de Chanel.   4. Le voleur aurait vendu ma bicyclette à un policier.
5. Le cyclone aurait tué cinq personnes.   6. Le scientifique annoncerait les résultats de ses recherches ce week-end.   7. Aloïse Sauvage aurait enregistré sa nouvelle chanson dans une piscine.   8. Juliette et Vincent se marieraient en Islande, loin des journalistes.   9. Le jeune cuisinier aurait changé la recette du chef!   10. La princesse Victoria de Suède rendrait visite à la première dame de France.

EXERCISE 12.9

1. We would like to invite you for lunch.   2. You should organize a trip in Burgundy.   3. She would have signed up for the yoga class if she had (had)

some free time.   **4.** You should hurry up. We are going to be late.   **5.** I would have gone to Amsterdam if you had been able to join me.   **6.** What would you do if you earned one million euros in the lotto?   **7.** He would have made a shrimp paella if they had been hungry.   **8.** The president reportedly redecorated his office.   **9.** I would have liked to have an apartment in the 15th arrondissement.   **10.** He should invite all the employees to the reception.

EXERCISE 12.10

1. Nous devrions ouvrir un restaurant dans le 18ᵉ arrondissement. **2.** Elle chanterait pour l'anniversaire du président français.   **3.** Vous devriez apprendre à jouer du piano.   **4.** Un admirateur serait entré dans le palais de la reine.   **5.** Je voudrais rencontrer/faire la connaissance des bénévoles à l'église de la Madeleine.   **6.** J'assisterais à la conférence si je pouvais obtenir un billet.   **7.** Pourriez-vous faire une quiche aux épinards?   **8.** J'aurais dû lire un des romans de Flaubert.   **9.** Ne pensez-vous pas qu'ils auraient dû nous appeler?   **10.** Ils devraient essayer de ne pas gaspiller la nourriture.

The Subjunctive Mood and Relative Pronouns

EXERCISE 13.1

1. prennes   **2.** sachions   **3.** mettiez   **4.** soient   **5.** croie
6. J'aie   **7.** aille   **8.** apprennes   **9.** dise   **10.** veuillent

EXERCISE 13.2

1. n'ailles pas   **2.** soit   **3.** n'y ait pas   **4.** veuille   **5.** puisses
6. connaisse   **7.** corresponde   **8.** fasses   **9.** soit   **10.** puisse

EXERCISE 13.3

1. est   2. ait   3. ne connaissez pas   4. ne puisses pas
5. veuille   6. sache   7. allions   8. ne comprend pas
9. arriviez   10. ne voulions pas

EXERCISE 13.4

1. Elle est contente que vous soyez dans son équipe.   2. Pensez-vous qu'il puisse me déposer à la gare?   3. Ils ont peur qu'elle n'ait pas assez de temps.   4. Je voudrais qu'ils s'inscrivent à un cours de musique.
5. Le professeur exige que nous remettions nos devoirs avant lundi.
6. Je ne suis pas sûr(e) qu'il fasse beau demain.   7. Aimeriez-vous/ voudriez-vous héberger des étudiants étrangers?   8. Je regrette qu'il n'y ait pas assez d'ordinateurs dans la salle de classe.   9. Nous doutons qu'il fasse de son mieux.   10. Je suis surpris(e) qu'ils veuillent collaborer avec nous.

EXERCISE 13.5

1. soit   2. n'y ait pas   3. soit   4. obtiennes   5. reçoive
6. arrivions   7. puisse   8. ait   9. repeignent   10. soit

EXERCISE 13.6

1. ne soit pas   2. réunissiez   3. ne puissiez pas   4. remette
5. fassiez   6. soient   7. ayons   8. vous inquitiez   9. suiviez
10. passent

EXERCISE 13.7

1. Hugo a préparé des sandwiches de peur que nous ayons faim.
2. Quoiqu'il/bien qu'il soit fatigué, il va étudier jusqu'à minuit.
3. Il est normal que les camarades de chambre se disputent de temps en temps.
4. Pourvu qu'ils fassent du couscous ce soir!
5. Ils étudient le mandarin avant que leurs amis de Shanghai (n')arrivent.
6. C'est le plus beau musée que je connaisse.

7. J'ai acheté les billets à l'avance pour que/afin que nous ne fassions pas la queue.

8. Pourvu que nous trouvions un appartement avec une belle vue!

9. Je cherche une université qui puisse héberger les étudiants handicapés.

10. En attendant que les problèmes soient résolus, nous vous remercions de votre patience.

EXERCISE 13.8

1. ait choisi   **2.** aies réussi   **3.** ait suivi   **4.** ait inscrit(e)
5. vous soyez inscrit(e)   **6.** se soit amusé   **7.** ait vraiment fini
8. n'aies pas perdu   **9.** aies trouvé   **10.** se soient trompés

EXERCISE 13.9

1. Je suis surpris(e) que vous ayez refusé leur offre.   **2.** Je suis désolé(e) que vous n'ayez pas pu ouvrir une boulangerie dans leur quartier.   **3.** Pensez-vous que l'intelligence artificielle ait déjà transformé notre vie ?   **4.** Nous regrettons que vous n'ayez pas envoyé une lettre de motivation.   **5.** Il est possible que François ait perdu son portefeuille.   **6.** Il est dommage que vous n'ayez pas obtenu un appartement sur le campus.   **7.** Pensez-vous vraiment que sa mère ait acheté un avion privé ?   **8.** Je doute qu'ils aient lu ce roman d'André Gide.   **9.** Je ne crois pas qu'il ait envoyé son CV à la bonne adresse.   **10.** Nous sommes contents qu'ils aient enfin dit la vérité.

EXERCISE 13.10

1. Quelle que soit ta décision, je l'accepterai.   **2.** Où que tu ailles, Erwan t'aidera.   **3.** Quel que soit le prix du loyer, nous voulons habiter dans le centre-ville.   **4.** Quoi que tu fasses, n'oublie pas ton ami Jonas.
5. Où que la ferme se situe, Madame Le Goff soignera les moutons.
6. Quelles que soient tes compétences linguistiques, ils t'engageront/t'emploieront.   **7.** Quoi qu'il arrive, fais attention.   **8.** Quel que soit l'âge des étudiants, Madame Grandet leur loue une chambre.   **9.** Quoi que tu penses, je m'en fiche.   **10.** Quels que soient tes rêves, poursuis-les.

EXERCISE 13.11

1. Il a beau vivre au Brésil depuis trois ans, il ne parle pas portugais.
2. Elle a beau avoir vécu à Nice pendant des années, elle n'a jamais appris à nager.
3. Elle a beau chercher, elle ne trouve pas sa carte d'identité.
4. Il avait beau fuir son identité, ses racines lui collaient à la peau.
5. Il a beau passer des annonces, il ne trouve pas de logement.
6. Elle a beau avoir gagné le prix Goncourt, elle n'a pas la grosse tête.
7. Tu as beau avoir dit la vérité, ils n'ont rien voulu entendre.
8. Madame Grandet a beau avoir pris sa retraite, elle est toujours occupée.
9. Il a beau avoir étudié le wolof, il ne le parle pas couramment.
10. Ils ont beau vivre à la campagne, ils n'ont pas d'animaux de compagnie.

EXERCISE 13.12

1. qu'il   2. qui   3. que   4. qui   5. dont   6. laquelle
7. lequel   8. dont   9. qui   10. que   11. où   12. où/qui
13. qui   14. dont où

EXERCISE 13.13

1. e   2. a   3. b   4. c   5. d

EXERCISE 13.14

1. Ce à quoi   2. Ce à quoi   3. ce qu'ils   4. Ce à quoi
5. Ce dont   6. ce qui   7. Ce qui   8. Ce dont   9. ce dont
10. ce qu'on

EXERCISE 13.15

1. J'aime le studio que Jonas a trouvé à Toulouse.   2. Madame Bessis ? Je ne sais pas qui elle est.   3. Le manuel dont elle parle est écrit en anglais.
4. Ce dont j'ai besoin, c'est d'un dictionnaire.   5. Ce à quoi elle s'intéresse, c'est au nouvel Airbus.   6. De quoi parlez-vous ?   7. —À quoi pensez-vous ? —Je pense au festival de Lorient.   8. Ce dont je me souviens, c'est de son stylo-plume Montblanc sur son bureau.   9. Ce que nous voulons,

c'est plus de temps libre.   **10.** C'est le meuble qu'elle veut emporter à Menton.

14
Describing Things and Talking About Events

EXERCISE 14.1

1. petite   **2.** belle   **3.** vieille   **4.** active   **5.** fraîche
6. blanche   **7.** fière   **8.** vive   **9.** sérieuse   **10.** ambitieuse; généreuse

EXERCISE 14.2

1. indienne   **2.** suédoise   **3.** marocaine   **4.** française
5. indonésienne   **6.** sénégalaise   **7.** américaine   **8.** argentine
9. canadienne   **10.** écossaise

EXERCISE 14.3

1. L'ingénieure est intuitive.   **2.** La boulangère est heureuse.
3. La pharmacienne est occupée.   **4.** La conseillère est européenne.
5. La traductrice est consciencieuse.   **6.** La vendeuse est élégante.
7. L'illustratrice est folle de joie.   **8.** La jardinière est franche et directe.
9. L'ouvrière est nouvelle dans l'équipe.   **10.** La danseuse est talentueuse.

EXERCISE 14.4

1. C'est la dernière fois que je prête mes BD à mon frère benjamin.
2. Alice a acheté une paire de baskets propres pour marcher dans le parc de la Villette.   **3.** L'ancienne petite amie de Loïc travaille en Finlande.
4. Nos chers amis Luc et Laurent nous retrouveront en Normandie en mai.
5. Céleste a vendu ses livres anciens avant d'aller à Menton.   **6.** Est-ce

que vous allez lancer votre propre entreprise ?   **7.** Ils m'ont envoyé une photo du lac le plus profond du monde.   **8.** Marguerite Duras est devenue la grande dame du monde littéraire français.   **9.** Pourquoi est-ce que vous avez acheté un masque si cher juste pour une soirée ?   **10.** Sa pauvre mère aimerait qu'il se marie bientôt.

EXERCISE 14.5

1. bleu marine   **2.** vert pistache   **3.** vert menthe   **4.** jaune maïs   **5.** indigo   **6.** orange   **7.** blanches   **8.** marron clair   **9.** bleu ciel   **10.** moutarde

EXERCISE 14.6

1. Nolan est moins ambitieux que Florent.   **2.** Cécile est aussi impulsive que Victorine.   **3.** Josépha est plus sportive que Maria.   **4.** Mila est plus gentille que Corinne.   **5.** Christian est aussi motivé que son benjamin.

EXERCISE 14.7

1. Est-ce que tu as porté ta combinaison vert pâle?   **2.** C'est le meilleur chocolat chaud de notre ville.   **3.** Est-ce qu'Alice a fait plus de costumes qu'Angèle?   **4.** Est-ce que tu as autant de devoirs que moi?   **5.** Je doute que tu aies moins de chances de gagner qu'Estelle.   **6.** Tu as autant de chances de gagner qu'elle.   **7.** Pourquoi est-ce que tu as utilisé plus de soie et moins de lin pour faire ton costume?   **8.** C'est le meilleur roman de science-fiction que nous ayons jamais lu dans notre cours de français.   **9.** Les juges tiennent compte de la qualité du travail et ils veulent aussi voir le meilleur mélange de couleurs.   **10.** Tu aurais dû rapporter de la dentelle de Burano et des colliers en verre de Murano.

EXERCISE 14.8

1. a peint   **2.** atteignent/ont atteint   **3.** s'est teint   **4.** plains   **5.** feignent   **6.** ceinte   **7.** peignaient   **8.** est/était atteinte   **9.** contraignent/ont contraints   **10.** se plaignent/se plaignaient